Together We Can

Uniting Families, Schools, and Communities to Help ALL Children Learn

KATHY H. BARCLAY
Western Illinois University

KENDALL/HUNT PUBLISHING COMPANY
4050 Westmark Drive   Dubuque, Iowa 52002

Cover photos provided by author.

Copyright © 2005 by Kendall/Hunt Publishing Company

ISBN 978-0-7575-1996-3

Printed in the United States of America
10   9   8   7   6   5   4   3

Contents

Acknowledgments

In a sense, every book is a community effort, and this one is certainly no exception. I am grateful to the many individuals who allowed me to share their ideas and creative efforts as examples for others. For the support and assistance of my colleagues, especially that of Diana Goff for her never ending optimism and encouragement, and to Sara Simonson for the wonderful cover photography, I am especially thankful. I owe much to Liz Boone, former principal of Oakwood School in Hannibal, Missouri, my first co-author, without whom this current book would not have been possible. My special thanks to Michelle Franzoni Hunt, my research assistant, for her valuable time and energy in preparing figures and researching information for the appendices.

My family is a large part of my writing. I thank my husband, Scott, and our youngest daughter, Erin, for their incredible patience throughout the writing of this book; I especially thank Erin for her talent and creativity in designing the book cover. I also thank my parents for being wonderful models of parental involvement in children's learning.

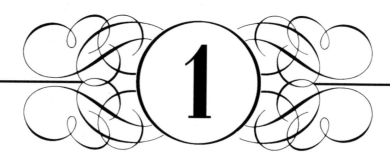

Moving Beyond Open Houses and Fund Raisers: What Research Tells Us About Parent and Community Involvement

Increasingly, classroom teachers and school administrators are called upon to do more than ever before. With changing demographics and societal pressures have come new legislation and new mandates, many of which are unfunded. Although not a new challenge for schools, establishing and maintaining effective partnerships with families and members of the community are certainly challenges that require a great deal of time and effort. Teachers, in particular, want proof that the time and energy expended will yield significant gains in students' achievement and behaviors. This chapter provides that proof-and sets the stage for later chapters that provide strategies for building strong and lasting partnerships.

INTRODUCTION

There is a widespread recognition that families, schools, and communities must work together in the process of educating today's youth. This recognition dovetails with the realization that young people must be educated to a higher standard than ever before, and that, generally speaking, most people will need to keep learning throughout their lives. The critical role that parents play in influencing their children's development, including basic feelings of security and self-esteem, attitudes, values, and academic success, is well-documented (Boethel 2003, 2004; Henderson & Mapp 2002). Joyce Epstein, professor of sociology at Johns Hopkins University and noted

1

researcher, stated: "No longer is parental involvement activated only when students are in trouble. Rather, well-planned and well-implemented family and community involvement activities contribute to student achievement and school success" (Epstein 2001, p. 5). This is not a new message. Over twenty years ago, in his discussion of the results of the 1981 Gallup Poll (Gallup 1981, p. 1), George Gallup stated:

> A careful examination of survey findings for the past ten-year period leads to this conclusion: Many of the problems of the schools can be solved only if parents become more involved than they presently are in the educational process. Parents must, in fact, be regarded as part of the teaching team. A joint effort by parents and teachers is essential to deal more successfully with problems of discipline, motivation, and the development of good work habits at home and in school.

In the years since Gallup's 1981 call for the creation of strong parent-teacher partnerships, we have witnessed the development of many new programs and materials aimed at providing parents with a wide range of information and ideas for helping their youngsters grow-physically, emotionally, socially, and academically. Major reform efforts, state and federal grant application guidelines, and intervention programs such as at-risk pre-kindergarten, special education, and Title I all list parental involvement as an important and necessary component tied to program funding, implementation, and evaluation. And in every demographic group, agreement exists with respect to parent involvement. In fact, 93 percent of respondents answered "great deal/fair amount" in response to this question on the 35th Annual Phi Delta Kappa/Gallup Poll of the Public's Attitudes Toward the Public Schools: "How much does lack of home or parental support contribute to learning failures in the public schools in your community?" (Rose & Gallup 2003, p. 51). Similarly, when asked in the 36th Annual Poll to identify factors that are very or somewhat important in closing the achievement gap between White, Black, and Hispanic students, 97 percent of the public cited more parent involvement (Rose & Gallup 2004, p. 49).

Parents share the sentiments expressed by the public in the Gallup Polls. In a survey conducted by the American Association of School Administrators (AASA), 96 percent of parents cited the role of the parents as critical for student success and 87 percent believed that too few parents get involved (AASA 1999). In a more recent study conducted by the National PTA, 58 percent of the respondents said having schools put plans in place to improve parent involvement would be an effective means for improving student achievement (PTA 2003). These findings mirrored those of the Pew Research Center study in which seventy-nine percent of parents surveyed said high parent involvement was a sign of a good school (2000).

Despite calls to enlist parents as part of the teaching process, and despite the fact that parent involvement is seen by so many as desirable and even essential, many of the nation's schools have yet to move "beyond the bake sale" (Henderson, Marburger, and Ooms 1989) in terms of their primary

For your consideration . . .

1. Parents should be recognized as the most important teachers of their children.   YES   NO

2. Leadership in the school has a major role to play in parent involvement.   YES   NO

3. Parents have a right to be involved in some aspect of decision making for their child and the school.   YES   NO

4. Teachers have a responsibility to encourage input from families and to help parents become better teachers of their children.   YES   NO

5. Good family involvement makes success for the child easier.   YES   NO

6. Parents and other family members should feel as if the school is "their school."   YES   NO

7. Schools should actively encourage frequent, open, and two-way home-school communication.   YES   NO

8. Parent involvement is important at all grade levels.   YES   NO

9. Schools should encourage involvement from community members in achieving the academic goals of the school.   YES   NO

10. Involving parents and community members in the education of children makes a positive difference.   YES   NO

expectations for parents. Candy bar sales and spaghetti dinners often dominate agendas at meetings of parent-teacher organizations that are far too often attended by only a handful of parents and, at the most, one or two teacher representatives. And, in too many schools, the only opportunity for parents to gain knowledge about the curriculum and ways they can support their child's learning is a one-shot open house held at the start of each new school year.

Why have so many schools yet to extend invitations to parents to be part of the teaching team? Are their definitions of parent involvement limiting their progress and, as a result, student achievement? What is a realistic and appropriate definition of parent involvement? A thorough understanding of these issues and of the research in the area of parent involvement is critical if schools truly desire home-school partnerships that impact positively on students. In this chapter you will become acquainted with important legislation related to parent involvement, examine national standards for parent/ family involvement, and gain an understanding of key research, paying particular attention to those programs that yielded the greatest benefits in terms of student achievement, motivation, and desire to learn. Before continuing your reading, I invite you to take a few moments to respond to the questions on page 3. There are a number of assumptions that we, as educators, hold about families and about involving parents in their children's education. It is important to examine these underlying assumptions to determine whether they are contributing to or distracting from the building of a strong relationship with all families. The answers you give may help you identify your beliefs regarding parent involvement, as well as the practices you support in your school or district.

*N*O CHILD LEFT BEHIND AND PARENT INVOLVEMENT

The *No Child Left Behind* legislation which was signed into law in 2001 signaled a clear and growing commitment to the role of families and included important provisions for engaging families (Henderson & Mapp 2002). Three years later, the U.S. Department of Education clarified and further elaborated upon these provisions by issuing its clearest and most comprehensive statement on parental involvement, *Parental Involvement: Title I, Part A Non-Regulatory Guidance* (April 2004). Representing the first time in the history of the Elementary and Secondary Education Act that federal education officials have specifically defined "parental involvement," this fifty-five-page document focuses on parents of students who qualify for Title I compensatory education and details how states and school districts should communicate with parents under the No Child Left Behind Act. While the guidelines represent interpretative advice on the No Child Left Behind law, each State Education Agency (SEA) must, in its annual evaluation of each local education agency receiving Title I, Part A funds, determine if the responsibilities with respect to parental involvement are being carried out. These results are to be publicized and disseminated to each local education agency, teachers, and other staff, parents, students, and community members within the state.

What is parental involvement under *No Child Left Behind?* In its 2004 document, *Parental Involvement,* the Department of Education cites the following statutory definition of parental involvement: ". . . the participation of parents in regular, two-way, and meaningful communication involving student academic learning and other school activities, including ensuring—

> ❧ that parents play an integral role in assisting their child's learning;
>
> ❧ that parents are encouraged to be actively involved in their child's education at school;
>
> ❧ that parents are full partners in their child's education and are included, as appropriate, in decision making and on advisory commit-

tees to assist in the education of their child. . . ." [Section 9101(32), ESEA.]

In Section D-7 (Parental Involvement 2004) we see clarification of eligibility for participation in parent involvement programs: ". . . *all* parents in a school-wide program are eligible to participate in parent involvement activities. However, given that the focus of a schoolwide program is to raise the achievement of the lowest-achieving students, a schoolwide program should ensure that its parent involvement activities include the parents of the lowest-achieving students, in order that they may better assist in the education of their child" (D-7, p. 24).

NATIONAL STANDARDS FOR PARENT AND FAMILY INVOLVEMENT

National PTA

Long recognized as a leader in helping schools and districts create strong relationships with parents and families, the National Parent Teacher Organization (PTA) developed voluntary guidelines to assist educators in forming "dynamic parent involvement programs that are meaningful, well planned, and long-lasting" (National PTA 2001). *The National Standards for Parent/Family Involvement Programs, An Implementation Guide for School Communities,* developed in 1997 and revised in 2004, have been endorsed by over 100 professional education and parent/family involvement organizations, adopted by many state Boards of Education and school districts nationwide, and incorporated into educational legislation (National PTA 2004). The six standards are as follows:

- ⤴ *Standard I. Communicating:* Communication between home and school is regular, two-way, and meaningful.

- ⤴ *Standard II. Parenting:* Parenting skills are promoted and supported.

- ⤴ *Standard III. Student Learning:* Parents play an integral role in assisting student learning.

- ⤴ *Standard IV. Volunteering:* Parents are welcome in the school, and their support and assistance are sought.

- ⤴ *Standard V. School Decision Making and Advocacy:* Parents are full partners in the decisions that affect children and families.

- ⤴ *Standard VI. Collaborating with Community:* Community resources are used to strengthen schools, families, and student learning.

Available in a number of languages other than English, the standards also include questions for assessing individual school's efforts with respect to each of the six areas (see Appendix 1).

National Association for the Education of Young Children (NAEYC)

The NAEYC Academy for Early Childhood Program Accreditation administers a national, voluntary accreditation system through which the quality of early childhood programs can be assessed. Program Standards 7 and 8 relate to parent and community involvement (NAEYC 2004):

➤ *Standard 7:* The program establishes and maintains collaborative relationships with each child's family to foster children's development in all settings. These relationships are sensitive to family composition, language, and culture.

➤ *Standard 8:* The program establishes relationships with and uses the resources of the children's communities to support the achievement of program goals.

Teachers and staff working in programs for young children can use these standards, and their accompanying criteria (see Appendix 2) to evaluate their knowledge and understanding of the families with whom they work, the procedures through which they communicate with each other and with families, and the degree to which they nurture families and serve as advocates for children (NAEYC 2004).

NAEYC also reviews associate, baccalaureate, and graduate degree early childhood programs for institutions accredited by the National Council for Accreditation of Teacher Education (NCATE). NAEYC grants national recognition to those programs that are found to be in compliance with NAEYC's professional preparation standards. Standard 2, Building Family and Community Relationships, of these accreditation criteria states: "Candidates know about, understand, and value the importance and complex characteristics of children's families and communities. They use this understanding to create respectful, reciprocal relationships that support and empower families and to involve all families in their children's development and learning" (NAEYC 2001, 2002, 2003).

Association for Childhood Education International (ACEI)

In a manner similar to the way NAEYC reviews degree programs for early childhood, ACEI reviews elementary education programs seeking NCATE accreditation. Standards 5.3 and 5.4 relate to parent and community involvement and are as follows:

➤ *Standard 5.3. Collaboration with Families:* Candidates know the importance of establishing and maintaining a positive collaborative relationship with families to promote the intellectual, social, emotional, and physical growth of children.

➤ *Standard 5.4. Collaboration with Colleagues and the Community:* Candidates foster relationships with school colleagues and agencies in the larger community to support students' learning and well-being.

ACEI cites as the source document for Standard 5.3, the *National PTA Standards for Parent and Family Involvement* (ACEI 2002). Rubrics detailing elements of each of the standards are available from ACEI and can be used to ascertain whether teacher education candidates possess the knowledge and skills necessary for building positive and collaborative relationships with all families.

*T*YPES OF PARENT INVOLVEMENT

Although a number of researchers in parent involvement have attempted to identify essential characteristics for successful programs (Epstein 1987; Henderson, Marburger, and Ooms 1989; Marcon 1999; Walberg 1984; Ho Sui-Chu & Willms 1996; Williams 1998; Williams & Chavkin 1989), the six types of parent involvement developed by Joyce Epstein and her colleagues at Johns Hopkins University (2002) are the most widely used (Henderson & Mapp 2002). The six types of involvement included in their research-based framework are: (1) parenting, (2) communicating, (3) volunteering, (4) learning at home, (5) decision making, and (6) collaborating with the community. A description of each type is included in Figure 1.

*R*EVIEW OF RESEARCH

Over three decades of research provide unequivocal support for the involvement of families in the education of their children (Henderson & Mapp 2002). When one considers the complex nature of families and the many variables that cannot be controlled or accounted for, it is surprising to find so many research studies conducted in the area of parent involvement. There is a solid base of research supporting a joint effort of parents, teachers, students, and the community to increase the effectiveness of the education programs (Boethel 2003, 2004; Epstein 2001, 2001a; Epstein & Sanders 2000; Henderson & Berla 1994; Henderson & Mapp 2002; Hiatt-Michael 2001). Studies published since 1995 have focused primarily on one of the following three broad areas:

1. the impact of family and community involvement on student achievement;

2. effective strategies to link schools, families, and communities; and

3. organizing efforts by parents and communities to improve schools (Henderson & Mapp 2002).

The majority of researchers conducting studies in parental involvement utilized the six-step framework developed by Joyce Epstein and her colleagues at the Center on Family, School, and Community Partnerships at Johns

Framework for Parent Involvement

TYPE ONE: Parenting
Teachers and other school staff help parents and other family members, as appropriate, with parenting skills, emphasizing child and adolescent development and establishing home conditions conducive to learning. Through these activities, schools gain important information about the families' backgrounds, cultures, and goals for their children.

TYPE TWO: Communicating
Teachers, principals, and other school staff establish two-way communication between school and home, sharing information about school programs and student progress.

TYPE THREE: Volunteering
Teachers, principals, and other school staff arrange activities and schedules so that families can be involved as audiences and volunteers. Efforts are in place to recruit, train, and utilize volunteers at the school or in other locations.

TYPE FOUR: Learning at Home
Teachers and other school staff design interactive at-home learning activities and help parents understand how they can assist their children's learning by becoming involved in homework, goal setting, and other curriculum-related activities.

TYPE FIVE: Decision Making
Teachers, principals, and other school staff encourage family involvement in school councils, improvement teams, committees, and parent organizations where decision making, governance, and advocacy activities take place.

TYPE SIX: Collaborating with the Community
Teachers, principals, and other school staff coordinate resources and services for families within the community, and encourage the involvement of local businesses, agencies, cultural and civic organizations, and institutions of higher education in supporting schools, students, and their families.

Figure 1

Hopkins University to form their definition of parent involvement. In the studies, student achievement was typically defined and measured through teacher ratings, report card grades, grade point averages, enrollment in advanced classes, standardized test scores, more classes passed and credits earned, enrollment in more challenging academic programs, better attendance, and improved behavior (Henderson & Mapp 2002). Findings from key research studies are presented below and are organized around a series of True/False statements to which you may wish to reply prior to reading about each one.

True or False

1. Schools that engage families in supporting their children's learning both at school and at home are linked to higher student achievement.

True. Research shows a strong link between family involvement and student benefits. These benefits include higher academic achievement, higher grade point averages, and scores on standardized tests, more classes passed, better attendance and social skills and improved behavior both at school and home (Henderson & Mapp 2002). Henderson and Mapp (2002) conducted an extensive review of fifty-one studies categorized into the three broad areas cited above. With respect to effects on student achievement, they found children of parents who participated in programs and activities to help them promote learning at home and who provided consistent at-home support throughout the grades had higher achievement.

In a three-year study of 1,200 kindergarten through grade three students in an urban district, Izzo and his colleagues (1999) found parent involvement, both at home and at school, to be positively related to student achievement, with home activities having the widest range of gains on math and reading tests. Marcon (1999) studied skill ratings of 700 African American preschoolers in Washington, D.C. and found that the children of parents with high levels of involvement, regardless of income level or background, had higher scores. In a retrospective study of 700 eighth-grade students in Chicago, Miedel and Reynolds (1999) found that 70 percent of the parents interviewed had been engaged in activities offered by the Chicago Parent Centers. These researchers found that those children whose parents took part in a greater number of parent involvement activities during the years between first and eighth grade tended to demonstrate higher reading scores, spend less time in special education, and successfully progress through the grades without retention.

Jordan, Snow, and Porche (2000) studied the effects of Project EASE (Early Access to Success in Education), a literacy program in Minnesota offering home and school activities for kindergarten children and their families. In the four lower-income schools studied, children were found to make significant gains on language scores-scores which were positively correlated with the number of activities a family completed. In two experimental studies of a program to develop math skills in Head Start children, Starkey and Klein (2000) found that when given proper training and materials, parents were willing and able to work with their children and, as a result, the children developed greater knowledge and skills in math. A ten-year study conducted in Turkey of a program based on HIPPY, the Home Instruction Program for Preschoolers, found both immediate and long-term benefits. Not only did the children in the program make greater initial progress, seven years after program completion, children from HIPPY were earning higher scores in reading, math, and in social development (Kagitcibasi et al. 2001). Older children benefit as well. In studies of interactive home learning activities in language arts, science, and math conducted by Joyce Epstein and her colleagues at Johns Hopkins University, the more TIPS (Teachers Involving Parents in Schoolwork) activities students completed, the higher their grades (Epstein, Simon, and Salinas 1997a; VanVoorhis 2001, 2003; VanVoorhis & Epstein 2003).

In a study commissioned by the U.S. Department of Education, Westat and Policy Studies Associates (2001) looked at the impact of standards-based reform practices implemented by 71 Title I schools. They found that teacher outreach in the form of telephone calls, meetings, and sending home materials for parent-child interaction was consistently linked to student gains in both reading and math. In fact, in schools where teachers reported high levels of outreach to families of low-performing students, test scores grew at a rate 40 percent higher than in schools where low levels of outreach was reported. Similarly, a study of the effects of parent involvement on Title I students in grades two through eight in a West Virginia district showed students whose parents regularly attended parent education workshops held at the school made greater gains in reading and math on district standardized tests (Shaver and Walls 1998).

In a study of eighty Baltimore schools, those schools with more highly developed partnership programs also showed improved attendance and enhanced students' learning opportunities (Epstein, Clark, Salinas, and Sanders 1997; Epstein & Salinas 2004). With respect to attendance, Epstein and Sheldon (2000) reported that schools affiliated with the National Network of Partnership Schools at Johns Hopkins University who engaged in home visits and workshops to help parents understand and act on attendance reported a decrease in the percentage of students missing over twenty days of school. Parents were also given a contact person at school to call as needed.

2. The greatest predicator of student achievement is family income.

False. The greatest predictor of student achievement is family involvement in which the family (1) creates a home environment that encourages learning, (2) expresses high expectations for their child's achievement and future, and (3) becomes involved in their child's education at school and in the community (Henderson & Berla, 1994). Families, regardless of income level, can engage in these kinds of activities which make a real difference in their children's academic achievement and success in life.

3. Parents' education is significantly correlated with parent involvement.

True and False. Epstein and Scott-Jones (1993) found that parents' education was not significantly correlated with parent involvement unless teacher practices were considered. Where teachers were leaders in involving families, parents at all educational levels were frequently involved in learning activities at home. In other studies, researchers found that parents who believe that teachers and schools are trying to involve them in their children's education are more involved at school and at home. Conversely, parents who believe that school practices do not foster parental involvement are less likely to be involved at either the home or the school, regardless of parents' education or income level (Dauber & Epstein 1993; Epstein 1986).

4. All families, regardless of cultural background, education, and income level, can, and often do, have a positive effect on their children's learning.

True. All types of families, regardless of cultural backgrounds, education, and income levels, are and can be involved in their children's education (Henderson & Mapp 2002; Mapp, 2002). While research does show that children from higher-income families tend to do better in school, students of all backgrounds gain from the involvement of their parents (Henderson & Mapp 2002). In her 2003 synthesis of research in parent involvement related to diverse student populations, Boethel states: "Families from racial, ethnic, and cultural minorities are actively involved in their children's schooling, although their involvement may differ somewhat from those of White, "mainstream" U.S. families" (p. v).

Researchers have reported consistent findings with respect to the high aspirations that most minority and low-income families have for their children (Aspiazu, Bauer, & Spillett 1998; Auerback 2002; Fan 2001; Halle, Kurtz-Costes, & Mahoney 1997; O'Connor, 2001). These findings held true for both multiracial and single population families, as well as for low-income Latino, African American, and White families, and for Asian immigrant families.

Noted in several studies is the fact that families' and schools' aspirations for success are not always the same (Azmitia & Cooper 2002; Goldenberg, et al. 2001; Scribner, Young, & Pedroza 1999). According to Boethel (2003) "Families tend to be concerned about the whole child, while schools tend to focus on academics. Though this difference is likely to be true regardless of family background, it may have extra significance for relationships between schools and families of minority and low-income students (pp. 27–28). Lopez (2001) reported that parents of Latino children who scored in the top 10 percent of their class described themselves as being "highly involved in their children's education, emphasizing the importance of hard work and a good education" (p. 8). This was despite the fact that these families did not routinely attend school functions. As Lopez states: "For these families, 'involvement' was seen as teaching their children to appreciate the value of education through the medium of hard work" (p. 8). In several studies, Asian, Hispanic and African American parents were found to be as active in their middle and high school students' education as White parents (Catsambis 1998; Ho Sui-Chu & Willms 1996; Keith and Keith 1993). Ho Sui-Chu and Willms also found no significant differences between the involvement of higher-income and two-parent families and that of lower-income and single-parent families.

Low-income and families of color were found by a number of researchers to respond well to training and home visits designed to assist them in helping their younger children learn (Epstein, Simon, and Salinas 1997; Mathematica 2001; Shaver and Walls 1998; Starkey and Klein 2000; VanVoorhis 2003; Westat/Policy Studies Associates 2001). Hoover-Dempsey, et al. (2001) found that parents were willing to help students with homework tasks if they believed they had a role to play. Clark (1993), in his survey of 1,171 third-grade children of all backgrounds in Los Angeles, found that high achievers came from many different family backgrounds; whereas low achievers tended to have younger parents who did not go to college, did not work outside the home, and were low-income. According to his findings, the way children spent their time at home predicted their success in school. While parents of all income and education levels reported talking to their children about homework, reading to their children, and making sure they did their assignments, the families with high achievers reported spending more time in home learning activities. Clark identified four variables that explained 47 percent of the variation between low- and high-achievers in his study: (1) the parents knowing about homework that was assigned, (2) the accuracy of the parents' perception of their child's active engagement in their assignments, (3) the child's ability to use a dictionary, and (4) the parents' expectations for their child's education.

"Hard-to-reach" families have been the target of research in many studies (Boethel 2003, Henderson & Mapp 2002, Epstein and Scott-Jones 1993; Epstein 1992); Epstein and Dauber 1991). As stated by Epstein (1992) "The hard-to-reach include those whose physical, social, or psychological distance from the school place extra barriers in the school's or family's path, and make communication and interaction even more difficult than usual" (p. 1145). Families described as hard-to-reach include single parents, parents who are less educated, language-minority parents, parents with low incomes, the homeless, and parents with personal problems such as alcoholism, drug use, or mental illness. Parents whose age differs significantly from the norm, such as very young parents—especially adolescent parents—as well as older parents, may also be more difficult to involve. Additionally, families who are new to the community and those of students who are bused great distances may also fall into this hard-to-reach category.

Positive attitudes towards parent involvement are significantly correlated with more success in working with "hard-to-reach" parents. Teachers with more positive attitudes hold regular conferences with all students' parents, communicate with parents about school programs, and provide parents with both good and bad reports of students' progress. These teachers believe they share similar beliefs with parents about being involved in their children's education and therefore they offer more types of activities to involve all families and make more contacts with parents believed by other teachers to be hard-to-reach (Epstein and Dauber 1991). Conversely, teachers who see themselves as "different" from the parents are associated with weaker parent involvement programs. These teachers tend to make fewer contacts with parents and to conduct fewer types of activities to involve families (Epstein 1991).

With respect to involving all families, research findings to date indicate the necessity for teachers and parents to come to know one another and to develop shared goals and beliefs about the role each plays in the education of children. Although schools cannot eradicate the serious social and economic problems that many families face, they can play an important role in the lives of children and parents from these traditionally disadvantaged or hard-to-reach families.

5. When families are involved in their children's school, they give the school and the teacher higher ratings.

True. Characteristics of teachers most often evaluated by parents as "good teachers" have been identified in studies conducted by Epstein (1985, 1986). Teachers who work hard to provide parents with ideas for home-learning and who communicate frequently with parents are recognized by them as being better teachers. Similarly, principals were found to rate those teachers who frequently involve parents in the education of the children as higher in overall teaching ability (Epstein 1985).

6. As students progress through school, the involvement of their parents tends to decrease.

True. Research efforts present a very clear picture of the sharp decline in parental involvement after the elementary grades. Many parents who are actively involved in the education of their children during the preschool and primary years become less involved as their children progress through the grades. Research shows a decline in parental involvement at each grade level and a significant drop at the middle and high school levels (Eccles & Harold 1993; Epstein 1992; George 1995).

Researchers have cited several reasons for this decline, including school size and organizational structure, teacher and parental attitudes that students need less help as they progress in school (Epstein & Connors 1995; Rutherford 1997), and lack of guidance in how to develop meaningful relationships with families (Chavkin 1995). The larger and more impersonal structure of many middle schools can also serve as a barrier to parent involvement. Unlike most elementary schools, middle school students have several teachers so parents do not have one individual with whom they can communicate about their child's progress. At the same time, teachers' practices to inform parents and to involve them in the education of their children dramatically decrease in the middle school years (Sanders 2000). As a result, middle school teachers communicate less frequently with parents than do elementary teachers. Teachers in semi-departmentalized and departmentalized classrooms with many more students to teach than in self-contained classrooms, and teachers of academic subjects other than English and reading also use fewer parent involvement strategies (Epstein 1991).

Another reason for the decrease in parent involvement in the middle and high school years may be related to parents' sense of efficacy, that is, their ability to effectively help their older learner do well in school, be happy and safe. In a national study of 900 families with children aged 10 to 17, Shumow and Lomax (2001) found that parents who felt a stronger sense of efficacy, or effectiveness, monitored their children more closely and were more involved in their education. Researchers have found, however, that teachers and administrators at all levels can effectively involve families if they have the right support (Sanders & Epstein 2000; Sanders, Epstein, & Connors-Tadros 1999).

7. Parent involvement efforts are as important at the middle and high school levels as they are at the early childhood and elementary levels.

True. Building strong relationships with parents and families is critical at all levels, yet many middle and high schools need to increase their present efforts. Henderson and Mapp (2002) stated: "Most programs that engage families in supporting children's learning are aimed at families with young children, from birth through preschool. More programs are needed at the elementary level and especially in the middle and high school" (p. 62). Parents of middle-grade students report receiving less information or guidance from schools—during a time when they most need assistance (Useem 1990; Epstein, 2001). In a statement for a House Subcommittee Hearing on Educational Research and Development, Epstein stated (1989, pp. 3–4):

> Many parents begin to lose touch with their children's schools, do not understand middle school and high school programs, or teachers' expectations and requirements for their children. Many parents begin to lose touch with their children when they do not understand early and later adolescent development, or the learning, social, and personal problems their children face, or how to maintain home conditions that support learning in appropriate forms across the grades. This may be an especially important problem for parents of inner-city youngsters, because continued, knowledgeable parental guidance and understanding is crucial for children who face a host of competing problems in their communities.

Simon (2000) found that family involvement increases with support and encouragement from the school. Parents who were contacted by school staff members were more likely to attend workshops and other school events and activities, help their teenager with homework, and talk with their teenager about school. Involving families also increased students' English and math report card grades and achievement scores, and improved attendance and behavior.

Trusty (1999) found that eighth-grade students who said their parents talked with them about school and supported their learning were more likely to pursue higher education. In a study of the effects of contrasting designs for science homework at the middle-school level, Van Voorhis (2001) found that students who worked with their parents to complete interactive home assignments reported dramatically higher family involvement and higher science grades. Researchers Gutman and Midgley (2000) studied low-income African American students' transitions from elementary to middle school in an effort to determine facilitating factors. Findings included a combined effect of parent and school support, in addition to student factors: (1) parents talking to students about school, checking homework, attending events, and volunteering; (2) teachers taking the time to help students and to offer support, rather than criticism; and (3) students feeling a sense of belonging and of being accepted, respected, and included at school.

Practices found to be effective with parents of middle and high school students included: (1) interactive homework that involved parents in their children's learning (Epstein, Simon, and Salinas 1997a; VanVoorhis 2001, 2003; VanVoorhis & Epstein 2003), (2) workshops on topics of interest to parents (Starkey & Klein 2000; Westat 2000; Sanders, Epstein & Connors-Tadros 1999; Simon 2000), (3) regular calls from teachers to share information about children's progress (Westat 2001), (4) at-home learning packets and parent training in using these with their children (Starkey & Klein 2000; Westat 2001), and (5) conferences and meetings to talk about children's progress (Westat 2001).

8. Conducting home visits is appropriate only at the early childhood level.

False. Although home visitation is a commonly used approach in serving families with young children, schools are reporting positive results with home visiting programs for elementary and middle school students (Delisio 2004; Steele-Carlin 2001; Knapp 1999). Teachers and principals attribute better academic achievement, improved discipline, and increased parental involvement in the classroom-to-home visits (Knapp 1999). Home visits have also been cited as an important tool in school reform, particularly in low-income, urban districts and those with immigrant families (Delisio 2004).

Home-visiting programs reach as many as 550,000 children and families annually in the U.S. Researchers have assessed a variety of outcomes of home-visiting programs (Gomby et al. 1993, 2003; Powell 1994). Benefits include positive changes in the interaction of parents with their children; positive adaptations to the home environments; and benefits in cognitive, behavioral, and motor development of the children served (Gomby et al. 1999; Mathematica 2001). More recent data suggests, however, that the most successful programs are those that are linked with other services, especially those involving direct service to children (Gomby, 2003).

Home-visiting in communities where parents are generally reluctant or unable to come to school or participate in school activities serve to foster cooperation and forge bonds between teachers and parents. As teachers reach out to parents, parents begin to view schools as less threatening places, and parents are more inclined to reciprocate by becoming involved in school activities (Nielson 1991). Traveling to different homes also affords the opportunity for teachers to discover resources for curriculum enrichment. Parents find it easier to come to school if they have already shared with the teacher a particular interest or ability such as gardening, carpentry, sewing, or preparing ethnic foods (Fox-Barnett and Meyer 1992).

Home visitations have been a part of early childhood programs for many years. In the 1960s and 1970s, home-visiting was a part of early intervention programs for children with special needs (Powell 1990), and in 1972, home visiting within Head Start began, with an emphasis on providing health, education, and social services to children and their families (Zigler and Freedman 1987). Early Head Start programs serve families with infants and toddlers.

Through these programs, mothers learn ways to stimulate their children's mental, physical, and emotional development at home. A variety of early education, parenting education, and health and family services are provided either through home visits or classes at a central location (Henderson & Mapp 2002). In a study of 3000 children and families, early Head Start children scored higher on cognitive development scales, used more words, and spoke in more complex sentences than did children in the control group (Mathematica 2001). Other well-known programs include the federal Even Start program first funded in 1989, the Home Instruction Program for Preschool Youngsters (HIPPY) program (Baker, Piotrkowski & Brooks-Gunn 1999), and the Parents As Teachers (PAT) program (Wagner & Clayton 1999). These programs provide early childhood education to promote school readiness and emphasize age-appropriate activities for language, intellectual, social, and motor development. Although differences in home visiting programs exist, researchers have identified some common characteristics of successful early childhood home-visiting programs. These include the provision of multiple services, use of professionals, and program duration (Gomby 2003; Gomby et al. 1993; Olds and Kitzman 1993; Ramey and Ramey 1993). Planning for a home visit depends on the goals of the program, which may be to strengthen relationships, to teach parents effective strategies to use with their children, or to bring educational materials into the home. Fox-Barnett and Meyer (1992) advocate child-centered home visits, or those which have as their purpose spending some time together with the child in the home environment and helping the parent and child feel good about themselves.

9. Schools with effective partnership programs share the responsibility for children's education with parents and community members.

True. In their synthesis of studies, Henderson and Mapp (2002) stated: "Effective programs to engage families and community embrace a philosophy of partnership. The responsibility for children's educational development is a collaborative enterprise among parents, school staff, and community members" (p. 51). Research has shown that partnership programs should be part of a broad-based plan to support student achievement. Studies of community-based tutoring programs, after-school learning programs, and literacy programs have shown significant gains in student achievement (Dryfoos 2000; Invernizzi, et.al 1997; Moore 1998; Wang, Oates, & Weishew 1997). Clark (2002) examined out-of-school activities for 1,058 students representing a range of achievement levels. Those scoring at or above the 50th percentile reported spending a minimum of nine hours a week in reading, writing, and study guided by adults; whereas, those scoring below the 50th percentile reported spending much more time talking on the phone, "hanging out," playing games, and watching television.

Mentoring programs involving one-on-one support for students have also been found to affect students' school attendance, performance, attitude, and interpersonal relationships. Research findings suggest that students with mentors are less likely to use drugs, skip school, or engage in school violence

(Banicky & Noble, 2000; Jekielek, Moore, Hair, & Scarupa 2002; Northwest Regional Education Laboratory, 1998). Shelley Prince, school counselor and coordinator for the mentor program at Parklawn Elementary School in Alexandria, Virginia states: "The backbone of the program is community involvement: local residents willing to make a connection with young people, gain their trust, foster mutual respect, and make a sustained, intensive, personal commitment" (2004, p. 84).

Engaging parent and community volunteers in ways that support schools and benefit students is another way to improve attendance and increase specific skills (Epstein 2001; Burke 2001). Millions of dollars of services are contributed annually by public school parents and family members (National PTA 2004). According to Epstein, principals at all levels should "support the organization, training, and purposeful assignment of volunteers as part of a comprehensive program of school, family, and community partnerships" (p. 5).

A key factor in forming and sustaining an effective three-way partnership is the quality of the relationship. Researchers have found that how parents and community members are viewed and treated by school personnel is critical—and can predict the quality of a school (Payne & Kaba 2001; Mapp 2002; Pena 2000; Starkey & Klein 2000; Sanders & Harvey 2000; Lareau & Horvath 1999; Scribner, Young, & Pedroza 1999). How schools promote a sense of community among educators and families was studied by Belenardo (2001) who found the leadership style of the principal and teachers' communications with families about students' academic work and ways they could help at home were related to teachers' and parents' feelings of a strong sense of community.

10. Support from the administration and an expectation for teachers to involve parents is critical for successful parent involvement programs.

True. According to the Coalition for Community Schools (CCS) "The research shows that high-performing schools are guided by strong leadership and clear vision and create an atmosphere of trust among staff and parents" (p. 2). Research shows that principals who encourage parents to share their perceptions of the school send the message that parent involvement can assist in improving the school (Inger 1993, Vandergrift & Green 1993, Vatterott 1994). Similarly, Sanders and Harvey (2000) found that the principal's support and vision for involvement was a critical factor for successful partnerships. The administration sets the stage by sharing an expectation for teachers to involve parents and by securing the resources necessary for effective involvement.

Sanders and Simon (1999) found that schools can build excellent partnership programs when they have the support of district and school administrators, staff, and parents. This finding held true regardless of school location or socioeconomic level of families or grade levels served.

According to the National PTA (2004, p. 35):

The principal or program director plays a pivotal role in making parent and family involvement a reality. Teachers and other staff sense the level of priority administrators give to involving parents. If principals collaborate with parents, teachers will be more likely to follow suit. Without administrative leadership, long-term progress in family-school partnerships is difficult to achieve since genuine change requires systemic solutions and coordinated efforts with consistent leadership support.

11. Building and maintaining comprehensive parent involvement programs is a costly endeavor.

False. Effective parent involvement programs do not have to be costly. According to the National Network of Partnership Schools, a variety of federal and state sources exist to support partnership programs and staff. These include Title I, Title VI, Title VII, and Safe and Drug Free Schools allocations. In addition, many districts and schools report investment of local dollars and those from foundations and community organizations as important to their partnership efforts (Sanders 2001). In a 1999 examination of data collected from over 100 schools, Sanders found the mean school budget for partnerships to be $4,065. The schools in the study varied with respect to funding sources, with some schools raising funds to support activities and other using grant money to hire full or part-time staff to lead and/or assist in parent involvement efforts (1999). Epstein, et. al. (1999) used data from members of the National Network of Partnership Schools to estimate a "per pupil expenditure" needed to support parent involvement at the school, district, and state levels. According to their calculations, healthy partnership efforts could be established at all levels for approximately $20 per student per year. Even when one considers rising costs due to inflation, parent involvement is surely a reasonable expenditure considering the proven benefits.

12. Schools need only to reach out to parents to boost student achievement.

False. While the research in parent involvement is, without doubt, encouraging and more researchers are continuing to find positive effects of parent involvement on achievement, parent involvement rarely stands alone. In their synthesis of research in parent involvement, Henderson and Mapp (2002) issue a caution for schools and districts: "It takes more than engaged parents to produce high student achievement. Many studies of high-performing schools identify several key characteristics associated with improvement. These include high standards and expectations for all students and curriculum, as well as instruction and assessments aligned with those standards. Other standards include effective leadership, frequent monitoring of teaching and learning, focused professional development, and high levels of parent and community involvement" (24).

SUMMARY

The research findings to date are unequivocal. Involving parents in the education of their children results in increased student performance at all grade levels, regardless of educational background or social class. Further, both children and parents develop more positive attitudes about school. From research we have learned that parents can have a very positive impact on the education of their children and that teachers who make frequent attempts to involve all parents are regarded by parents and principals alike as "good teachers." We have also learned that teachers who are leaders in the use of parent involvement strategies are more likely to reach parents regarded by other teachers as hard-to-reach.

Effective family involvement programs open the lines of communication between home and school, support parents in their attempts to help their children in home-learning activities, and recognize the importance of building strong partnerships. While home-school partnerships cannot eliminate the many stresses and demands faced by both families and school personnel, working together can reduce conflict and increase the probability that learning will occur for all children.

LOOKING AHEAD

This chapter contained key research in parent involvement, including studies concerning involvement with families of varying cultural, ethnic, racial, and socio-economic groups and other hard-to-reach families. In the next chapter, "Understanding Families: Barriers and Bridges to Involvement," we examine reasons why many parents do not become involved in their child's school.

REFERENCES

American Association of School Administrators (2000). *Presentation of findings from focus groups and a survey of parents of public school children—October 1999.* www.aasa.org/issues_and_insights/parents_public/00public/sld001.htm.

Aspiazu, G. G., Bauer, S. C., & Spillett, M. (1998). Improving the academic performance of Hispanic youth: A community education model. *Bilingual Research Journal, 22*(2), 103–123.

Association for Childhood Education International (2002). *Rubrics for NCATE standards: Professionalism.* http://acei.org/rubrics5c.htm

Auerbach, S. (2002). "Why do they give the good classes to some and not to others?" Latino parent narratives of struggle in a college access program. *Teachers College Record, 104*(7), 1369–1392.

Azmitia, M. C., & Cooper, C. R. (2002). *Navigating and negotiating home, school, and peer linkages in adolescence.* Santa Cruz, CA: CREDE, Center for Research on Education, Diversity & Excellence. http://crede.ucsc.edu/resaearch/sfc/3.3_final.html

Baker, A. J. L., Piotrkowski, C. S., & Brooks-Gunn, J. (1998). The effects of the Home Instruction Program for Preschool Youngsters (HIPPY) on children's school performance at the end of the program and one year later. *Early Childhood Research Quarterly, 13*(4), 571–588.

Banicky, L., & Noble, A. J. (2000). *Mentoring students* (Education Policy Brief, 5). Newark, DE: University of Delaware. *www.udel.edu/chep/edbriefs/mentoring.pdf*

Belenardo, S. (2001). Practices and conditions that lead to a sense of community in middle schools. *NASSP Bulletin, 85*(627), 33–45.

Boethel, M. (2003). *Diversity: School, family, & community connections.* Austin, TX: National Center for Family and Community Connections with Schools.

Boethel, M. (2004). *Readiness: School, family, & community connections.* Austin, TX: National Center for Family and Community Connections with Schools.

Burke, M. S. (2001). Recruiting and using volunteers in meaningful ways in secondary schools. *NASSP Bulletin, 85*(627), 46–52.

Catsambis, S. (1998). *Expanding knowledge of parental involvement in secondary education—Effects on high school academic success* (CRESPAR Report 27). Baltimore, MD: Johns Hopkins University.

Chavkin, N. F. (1995). Comprehensive districtwide reforms in parent and community involvement programs. In B. Rutherford (Ed.), *Creating family/school partnerships.* Columbus, OH: National Middle School Association.

Clark, R. (2002). Ten hypotheses about what predicts student achievement for African American students and all other students: What the research shows. In W. R. Allen, M. B. Spencer, & C. O'Conner (Eds.), *African American education: Race, community, inequality, and achievement: A Tribute to Edgar G. Epps.* Oxford, UK: Elsevier Science.

Coalition for Community Schools (2003). *Making the Difference: Research and Practice in Community Schools.* Washington, DC: Coalition for Community Schools, Institute for Educational Leadership. *www.communityschools.org* Accessed 2/3/05.

Dauber, S., & Epstein, J. L. (1993). Parents attitudes and practices of involvement in inner-city elementary and middle schools. In N. F. Chavkin (Ed.), *Families and schools in a pluralistic society.* Albany, NY: State University of New York Press.

Delisio, E. R. (2004). Home visits forge school, family links. *Education World,* 2/10/2004. *http://www.education-world.com/a_admin/admin/admin342.shtml*

Dryfoos, J. G. (2000). *Evaluations of community schools: Findings to date.* Washington, DC: Coalition for Community Schools. *http://www.communityschools.org/evaluation/evalprint.html*

Eccles, J. S., & Harold, R. D. (1993). Parent-school involvement during the early adolescent years. *Teachers College Record, 94*(3): 568–587.

Epstein, J. L. (1985). A question of merit: Principals' and parents' evaluations of teachers. *Educational Researcher, 14*(7), 3–10.

Epstein, J. L. (1986). Parents' reactions to teacher practices of parent involvement. *The Elementary School Journal, 86*(3), 277–294.

Epstein, J. L. (1989). *Prepared statement for the House Subcommittee on Select Education Hearing on Educational Research and Development Applications.* Baltimore, MD: The Johns Hopkins University.

Epstein, J. L. (1991). Effects of teacher practices of parent involvement on student achievement in reading and math. In S. Silver (Ed.) *Advances in reading/language research: Literacy through family, community, and school interaction.* Greenwich, CT: JAI Press.

Epstein, J. L. (1992). School and family partnerships. In M. Aklin (Ed.), *Encyclopedia of Educational Research,* 6th ed. New York: Macmillan.

Epstein, J. L. (2001). New directions for school, family, and community partnerships in middle and high schools. *National Association of Secondary School Principals Bulletin, 85*(627), 5.

Epstein, J. L. (2001a). *School, family and community partnerships: Preparing educators and improving schools.* Boulder, CO: Westview Press.

Epstein, J. L., Clark, L., Salinas, K. C., & Sanders, M. G. (1997). *Scaling up school-family-community connections in Baltimore: Effects on student achievement and attendance.* Paper presented at the Annual Meeting of the American Educational Research Association, Chicago, IL.

Epstein, J. L., & Connors. (1995). School and family partnerships in the middle grades. In B. Rutherford (Ed.), *Creating family/school partnerships.* Columbus, OH: National Middle School Association.

Epstein, J. L., & Dauber, S. (1991). School programs and teacher practices of parent involvement in inner-city elementary and middle schools. *Elementary School Journal, 91*(3), 289–303.

Epstein, J. L., & Salinas, K. L. (2004). Partnership with families and communities. *Educational Leadership, 61*(8), 12–18.

Epstein, J. L., & Sanders, M. G. (2000). Connecting home, school, and community: New directions for social research. In M. T. Hallinan (Ed.), *Handbook of the Sociology of Education* (pp. 285–306). New York, NY: Kluwer Academic/ Plenum Publishers.

Epstein, J. L., Sanders, M. G., Clark, L. A., & Van Voorhis, F. E. (1999). *Costs and benefits: School, district, and state funding for programs of school, family, and community partnerships.* Paper presented at the 1999 annual meeting of the American Sociological Association, Chicago.

Epstein, J. L., Sanders, M. G., Simon, B. S., Salinas, K. C., Jansorn, N. R., & Van Voorhis, F. L. (2002). *School, family, and community partnerships: Your handbook for action* (2nd ed.). Thousand Oaks, CA: Corwin.

Epstein, J. L., & Scott-Jones, D. (1993). Schools, family, and community connections for accelerating student progress in elementary and middle grades. In H. M. Levin (Ed.), *Accelerating the education of at-risk students.* Philadelphia, PA: Falmer.

Epstein, J. S., & Sheldon, S. B. (2000). *Improving student attendance: Effects of family and community involvement.* Paper presented at the annual meeting of the American Sociological Association, Washington DC.

Epstein, J. L., Simon, B. S., & Salinas, K. C. (1997a). Involving parents in homework in the middle grades. *Research Bulletin No. 18. http://www.pdkintl.org/edres/resbul18.htm*

Fan, X. (2001). Parental involvement and students' academic achievement: A growth modeling analysis. *The Journal of Experimental Education, 70*(1), 27–61.

Fox-Barnett, M., & Meyer, T. (1992). The teacher's playing at my house this week! *Young Children, 47*(5), 45–50.

George, P. (1995). Search Institute looks at home and school: Why aren't parents getting involved? *High School Magazine, 3*(5), 9–11.

Goldenberg, C., Gallimore, R., Reese, L., & Garnier, H. (2001). Cause or effect? A longitudinal study of immigrant Latino parents' aspirations and expectations, and their children's school performance. *American Education Research Journal, 38*(3), 547–582.

Gomby, D. S., Culross, P. L., & Behrman, R. E. (1999). Home visiting: Recent program evaluations. *The Future of Children, 9*(1).

Gomby, D. S., Larson, J. D., Lewit, E. M., & Behrman, R. E. (1993). Home-visiting: Analysis and recommendations. In R. E. Behrman (Ed.), *The future of children: Home visiting, 3*, 6–22.

Gomby, D. S. (2003). *Building school readiness through home visitation.* Sacramento, CA: First 5 California Children and Families Commission.

Gutman, L. M., & Midgley, C. (2000). The role of protective factors in supporting the academic achievement of poor African American students during the middle school transition. *Journal of Youth and Adolescence, 29*(2), 223–248.

Halle, T. G., Kurtz-Costes, B., & Mahoney, J. L. (1997). Family influences on school achievement in low-income, African American children. *Journal of Educational Psychology, 89*(3), 527–537.

Henderson, A. T., & Berla, N. (1994). *A new generation of evidence. The family is critical to student achievement.* Washington, DC: Center for Law and Education.

Henderson, A. T., & Mapp, K. L. (2002). *A new wave of evidence: The impact of school, family, and community connections on student achievement.* Austin, TX: National Center for Family & Community Connections with Schools, Southwest Educational Development Laboratory.

Henderson, A. T., Marburger, C. T., & Ooms, T. (1989). *Beyond the bake sale: An educator's guide to working with parents.* Columbia, MD: National Committee for Citizens in Education.

Hiatt-Michael, D. (2001). *Promising practices for family involvement in school.* Greenwich, CT: Information Age Publishing, Inc.

Ho-Sui-Chu, E., & Willms, J. D. (1996). Effects of parental involvement on eighth-grade achievement. *Sociology of Education, 69*(2), 126–141.

Hoover-Dempsey, K. B., Battaito, A. C., Walker, J. M., Reed, R. P., DeJong, L. M., & Jones, K. P. (2001). Parental involvement in homework. *Educational Psychology, 36*(3), 195–209.

Inger, M. (1993). Getting Hispanic parents involved. *The Education Digest, 5*, 32–34.

Invernizzi, M., Rosemary, C., Richards, C. J., & Richards, H. C. (1997). At-risk readers and community volunteers: A 3-year perspective. *Scientific Studies of Reading, 1*(3), 277–300.

Izzo, C. V., Weissberg, R. P., Kasprow, W. J., & Fendrich, M. (1999). A longitudinal assessment of teacher perceptions of parent involvement in children's education and school performance. *American Journal of Community Psychology, 27*(6), 817–839.

Jekielek, S. M., Moore, K. A., Hair, E. C., & Scarupa, H. J. (2002). *Mentoring: A promising strategy for youth development.* Washington, DC: Child Trends.

Jordan, G. E., Snow, C. E., & Porche, M. V. (2000). Project EASE: The effect of a family literacy project on kindergarten students' early literacy skills. *Reading Research Quarterly, 35*(4), 524–546.

Kagitcibasi, C., Sunar, D., & Bekman, S. (2001). Long-term effects of early intervention: Turkish low-income mothers and children. *Applied Developmental Psychology, 22*, 333–361.

Keith, T. Z., & Keith, P. B. (1993). Does parental involvement affect eighth-grade student achievement? Structural analysis of national data. *School Psychology Review, 22*(3), 474–496.

Knapp, D. (1999). *Parents grateful that teachers make house calls. CNN.com.* September 7, 1999. http://www.cnn.com/US/0090/07/teacher.home.visits/

Lareau, A., & Horvat, E. M. (1999). Moments of social inclusion and exclusion: Race, class, and cultural capital in family-school relationships. *Sociology of Education 72*(1), 37–53.

Mapp, K. L. (2002). *Having their say: Parents describe how and why they are involved in their children's education.* Paper presented at the Annual Meeting of the American Education Research Association, New Orleans, LA.

Marcon, R. A. (1999). Positive relationships between parent school involvement and public school inner-city preschoolers' development and academic performance. *School Psychology Review, 28*(3), 395–412.

Mathematica Policy Research, Inc., & Center for Children and Families at Teachers College, Columbia University (2001). *Building their futures: How Early Head Start programs are enhancing the lives of infants and toddlers in low-income families.* Washington, DC: Administration of Children, Youth, and Families, Department of Health and Human Services. *http://www.acf.dhhs.gov/programs/core/ongoing_research/ehs/ehs_reports.html*

Miedel, W. T., & Reynolds, A. J. (1999). Parent involvement in early intervention for disadvantaged children: Does it matter? *Journal of School Psychology, 37*(4), 379–402.

Moore, D. R. (1998). *What makes these schools stand out: Chicago elementary schools with a seven-year trend of improved reading achievement.* Chicago, IL: Designs for Change. *http://www.designsforchange.org/pdfs/SOScomplete.pdf*

National Association for the Education of Young Children (2004). *Final Draft Accreditation Performance Criteria Program Standards. http://www.naeyc.org/accreditation/naeyc_accred/draft_standards/com.html*

National Association for the Education of Young Children (2001). *National Standards for Early Childhood Professional Preparation: Initial Licensure Programs. http://www.naeyc.org/faculty/pdf/2001.pdf*

National Association for the Education of Young Children (2002). *National Standards for Early Childhood Professional Preparation: Advanced Licensure Programs. http://www.naeyc.org/faculty/pdf/2002.pdf*

National Association for the Education of Young Children (2003). *NAEYC National Standards for Early Childhood Professional Preparation: Associate Degree Programs. http://www.naeyc.org/faculty/pdf/2003.pdf*

National PTA (2004). *National Standards for Parent/Family Involvement Programs, An Implementation Guide for School Communities. http://www.pta.org*

National PTA (2003). *Results of National PTA Survey of American Voters. http://www.pta.org/ptawashington/survey.asp#4*

National PTA (2001). *Setting the Standard: An Update on How the National Standards for Parent/Family Involvement Programs Have Been Implemented Across the Nation. http://www.ptta.org/parentinvolvement/standars/natstand_jan01.asp*

Nielson, S. (1991). Enhancing home-school links through home visits. *Educational Horizons, 70*(4), 206–10.

Northwest Regional Education Laboratory (1998). *Student mentoring: What does the research say?* Portland, OR: Author. *www.nwrel.org/request/sept98/index.html*

O'Connor, S. (2001). Voices of parents and teachers in a poor white urban school. *Journal of Education for Students Placed at Risk, 6*(3), 175–198.

Olds, D. L., & Kitzman, H. (1993). Review of research on home visiting for pregnant women and parents of young children. *The Future of Children, 3*, 53–92

Payne, C. M., & Kaba, M. (2001). *So much reform, so little change: Building-level obstacles to urban school reform.* Northwestern University, 2.

Pena, D. C. (2000). Parent involvement: Influencing factors and implications. *The Journal of Educational Research, 94*(1), 42–54.

Pew Research Center (2000). *Straight Talk From Americans—2000. http://www. pewcenter.org/doingcj/research/r_ST2000nat2.html#educ*

Powell, D. R. (1990). Home-visiting in the early years: Policy and program design decisions. *Young Children, 45*(6), 65–73.

Powell, D. R. (1994). Evaluation of family support programs: Are we making progress? In S. L. Kagan, & B. Weissbourd (Eds.), *Putting families first: America's family support movement and the challenge of change* (pp. 442-470). San Francisco: Jossey-Bass.

Prince, S. R. (2004). The magic of mentoring. *Educational Leadership, 61*(8), 84–86.

Ramey, C. T., & Ramey, S. L. (1993). Home visiting programs and the health and development of young children. *The Future of Children, 3*, 129–139.

Rose, L. C., & Gallup, A. M. (2004). The 36th Annual Phi Delta Kappa/Gallup Poll of the Public's Attitudes Toward the Public Schools. *Phi Delta Kappan, 86*(1), 41–52.

Rose, L. C., & Gallup, A. M. (2003). The 35th Annual Phi Delta Kappa/Gallup Poll of the Public's Attitudes Toward the Public Schools. *Phi Delta Kappan, 85*(1), 41–52.

Rutherford, B., Anderson, B., & Billig, S. (1997). *Parent and community involvement in education*. Washington, DC: U.S. Department of Education, Office of Educational Research and Improvement.

Sanders, M. G. (1999). School membership in the National Network of Partnership Schools: Progress, challenges and next steps. *Journal of Educational Research, 92*(4), 220–230.

Sanders, M. G. (2000). Creating successful school-based partnership programs with families of special needs students. *The School Community Journal, 10*(2), 37–56.

Sanders, M. G. (2001). Schools, families, and communities partnering for middle level students' success. *NASSP Bulletin, 85*(627), 53–61.

Sanders, M. G., & Epstein, J. L. (2000). Building school, family and community partnerships in secondary schools. In *Schooling students placed at risk: Research, policy, and practice in the education of poor and minority adolescents*. Mahway, NJ: Erlbaum.

Sanders, M. G., Epstein, J. L., & Connors-Tadros, L. (1999). *Family partnerships with high schools: The parents' perspective*. Report 32. Baltimore: Center for Research on the Education of Students Placed At Risk, Johns Hopkins University.

Sanders, M.G., & Harvey, A. (2000). *Developing comprehensive programs of school, family, and community partnerships: The community perspective*. Paper presented at the American Educational Research Association, New Orleans, LA.

Sanders, M. G., & Simon, B. (1999). *Progress and challenges: Comparing elementary, middle and high schools in the National Network of Partnership Schools*. Paper presented at the annual conference of the American Educational Research Association, April, Montreal, Quebec, Canada.

Scribner, J. D., Young, M. D., & Pedroza, A. (1999). Building collaborative relationships with parents. In P. Reyes, J. D. Scribner, & A. Paredes-Scribner (Eds.), *Lessons from high-performing Hispanic schools: Creating learning communities* (pp. 36–60). New York, NY: Teachers College Press.

Shaver, A. V., & Walls, R. T. (1998). Effect of Title I parent involvement on student reading and mathematics achievement. *Journal of Research and Development in Education, 31*(2), 990-997.

Shumow, L., & Miller, J. D. (2001). Parents' at-home and at-school academic involvement with young adolescents. *Journal of Early Adolescence, 21*(1), 68–91.

Simon, B. (2000). *Predictors of high school and family partnerships and the influence of partnerships on student success.* Unpublished doctoral dissertation, Johns Hopkins University.

Starkey, P., & Klein, A. (2000). Fostering parental support for children's mathematical development: An intervention with Head Start families. *Early Education and Development, 11*(5), 659–680.

Steele-Carlin, S. (2001). Teacher visits hit home. *Education World.* 10/09/2001. *http://www.educatioworld.com/a_admin/admin/admin241.shtml*

Trusty, J. (1999). Effects of eighth-grade parental involvement on late adolescents' educational experiences. *Journal of Research and Development in Education, 32*(4), 224–233.

U.S. Department of Education (2002). *Testing for results: Helping families, schools and communities understand and improve student achievement.* U.S. Department of Education: Washington.

U.S. Department of Education (2004). *Parental involvement: Title I, Part A Non-Regulatory Guidance.* U.S. Department of Education: Washington DC.

Vandergriff, J., & Greene, A. (1993). Involving parents of the at-risk: Rethinking definitions. *Education Digest, 58*, 18–21.

Vatteroff, C. (1994). A change in climate: Involving parents in school improvement. *Schools in the Middle, 3*, 12–16.

Van Voorhis, F. L. (2003). Interactive homework in middle school: Effects on family involvement and students' science achievement. *Journal of Educational Research, 96*(9), 323–339.

Van Voorhis, F. L. (2001). Interactive science homework: An experiment in home and school connection. *NASSP Bulletin, 85*(627), 20–32.

Van Voorhis, F. L., & Epstein, J. L. (2002). *Teachers involve parents in schoolwork: Interactive homework CD.* Baltimore: Center on School, Family, and Community Partnerships, Johns Hopkins University.

Wagner, M. M., & Clayton, S. L. (1999). The Parents As Teachers Program: Results from two demonstrations. *The Future of Children, 9*(1), xx.

Walberg, H. J. (1984). Families as partners in educational productivity. *Phi Delta Kappan, 65*(6), 397–4000.

Wang, M. C., Oates, J., & Weishew, N. L. (1997). Effective school responses to student diversity in inner-city schools: A coordinated approach. In Haertel, G. D., & M.C. Wang (Eds.), *Coordination, cooperation, collaboration* (pp. 175–197). Philadelphia, PA: The Mid-Atlantic Regional Educational Laboratory at Temple University.

Westat and Policy Studies Associates (2001). *The longitudinal evaluation of school change and performance in Title I schools.* Washington, DC: U.S. Department of Education, Office of the Deputy Secretary, Planning and Evaluation Service. *http://www.ed.gov/offices/OUS/PES/esed/lescp_highlights.html*

Williams, D. B. (1998). *Parent involvement gender effects on preadolescent student performance.* Paper presented at the Annual Meeting of the American Education Research Association, San Diego, CA.

Williams, D., & Chavkin, N. (1989). Essential elements of strong parent involvement programs. *Educational Leadership, 47*, 18–23.

Zigler, E. F., & Freedman, J. (1987). Head start: A pioneer in family support. In E. F. Zigler et al. (Ed.), *America's family support programs.* New Haven, CT: Yale University Press.

Understanding Families: Barriers and Bridges to Involvement

A signature was needed on an Individual Education Plan (IEP) and the school had not been able to get the parent to come in for a conference. One day as the little girl was waiting after school for her mother to pick her up, the principal and special education teacher waited with her to ask the mother to come in for a conference. When the mother pulled up, she explained that her boss would not let her leave, so she only had time on her break to pick up the child and take her to work with her. The little girl was to wait in the lobby until the mother got off work. The woman was obviously afraid that she would be in trouble with her boss, so no conference was held then. On the way back into the school building, the principal and teacher talked of all of the barriers present in this situation that prevented the mother from being involved in her child's education. This woman was not an irresponsible parent, or even one that did not care. She simply had a more pressing problem—one of putting something to eat on the family's table.

*I*NTRODUCTION

In the previous chapter we discussed the positive effects that a strong parent involvement component can have on the performance of children in school. Yet, do we really take this powerful research seriously? Are we *really* convinced that this investment of time, energy, and money will yield results as great as these indicated in the research literature? A look at the policies and programs that currently exist in many schools would lead us to think not. Too few schools do more than go through the motions of involving parents in the instruction of their children. To be sure, there are the traditional, almost ceremonial programs and events that get parents into school once or twice yearly: the open houses and the parent-teacher conferences. There may even be a parent-teacher organization; however, involvement directed toward helping adults become better partners in their children's education is not very common.

As Henderson and Mapp (2002) point out: "Supporting more involvement at school from all parents may be an important strategy for addressing the achievement gap" (p. 7). Yet, in far too many schools, the most we ask of parents is that they show their child that learning is important by being informed of what is going on at school, by attending events in which their child is participating, or by putting pressure on their child when more effort in schoolwork is needed. While these activities yield some benefits and may represent an initial step toward increased involvement, research indicates that parents who are given strategies to use at home and who are provided with home-learning activities to work with their children make the greatest contributions to their children's learning.

Despite strong research evidence of the positive effects parent involvement can have on students' achievement, attitudes about school, and behavior, why is it that so many schools have yet to involve parents in the education of their children in ways proved by research to be most effective? What barriers exist that prevent schools and parents from forming strong partnerships?

BARRIERS TO EFFECTING STRONG FAMILY INVOLVEMENT

The first step in building strong and effective partnerships involves identification of the barriers that play a significant role in the school and in the homes of the families that make up the school population or clientele. This is no simple task; the reasons—or barriers—why most schools have not developed strong partnerships are many and varied. Most reasons, or barriers, can be divided into two main groups: barriers erected by schools and barriers erected by families. Let's look first at the barriers erected by schools—the ones most changeable within the jurisdiction of school personnel.

BARRIERS ERECTED BY SCHOOLS

The U.S. Department of Education requires schools receiving funds under Title I, Part A to identify barriers to increased parent involvement ". . . with particular attention to parents who are economically disadvantaged, are disabled, have limited English proficiency, have limited literacy, or are of any racial or ethnic minority background" (2004, p. 12). Each school's findings are to be used to design strategies for more effective parental involvement.

I routinely ask teachers enrolled in graduate courses in education to list reasons why parents aren't more involved in their children's education. Many of the reasons given represent barriers erected by schools: (1) lack of time; (2) parents may interrupt the routine of the classroom; (3) parents might criticize the instructional program; (4) fear of giving up power, control, or authority to the parents; (5) lack of communication skills to work with parents; (6) use of "educationese" that tends to intimidate parents; (7) lack of understanding of the various cultural groups represented by the families; or (8) inability to speak the home language and having to talk through an interpreter, which makes communication difficult.

More often than not, teachers discuss barriers presented by parents and families with the most common of these being time. Rebecca Larson, an elementary teacher in Bettendorf, Iowa was one of many teachers who voiced this concern: *"I think that the lack of time is one barrier that parents face in their involvement with schools/districts. Parents are pulled in many directions with work, children's activities, and maintaining a home. They sometimes feel that if they can't give a large amount of time to the school then maybe it won't be a valuable contribution."*

Similarly, Dawn Cheesman, a primary grade teacher in Viola, Illinois shared: *"I feel that some parents are not involved in their child's education because they may be a single parent and work a shift where they are not at home to help their child in the evenings with homework or to attend family nights, parent teacher conferences, etc. Also, some parents are not educated enough to feel that they can help their child."*

With regard to parents' education and abilities, Angela Maher, speech and language pathologist in the Mt. Pleasant, Iowa school district stated: *". . . some parents don't feel equipped to involve themselves in the educational process. We have heard the statements, 'I don't know what to do,' or 'I don't know how to help.' They may be intimidated by professionals, or feel 'dumb' in comparison to someone with a college degree. Many of these parents may have had negative educational experiences themselves and simply want to avoid it all. They look at school as being a 'necessary evil.'"*

Other teachers, like Jennifer Steinke, a reading interventionist in the south side of Des Moines, Iowa where most of the students are ESL, mention cultural or language barriers: *"My ESL parents are still learning English themselves and have to talk to a translator not the teacher, and the teacher then talks to the translator."*

Teachers do express concern about the lack of parent involvement, as can be seen from this statement by Elise Howard, a middle school teacher in Galesburg, Illinois: *"I think that in our building there appear to be two things that tend to keep parents/guardians away. First, many parents have incredibly busy schedules. When they work multiple jobs, in addition to having to complete a variety of other often unrelated tasks while caring for their children, they seldom have much free time to come in to speak with our team about their child. We have had to wait several weeks on end before finally having an opportunity to meet with some of our student's parents. The other thing that tends to make parents avoid us is an idea that when a phone call or letter arrives from school, they automatically think it is in reference to something negative. If teachers never make a call or write something positive to our students' parents/guardians, then parents are, understandably, wary when they do receive a call. It is terrible that they should assume there is a problem, when something might not even be wrong at all. This has been our team's goal over the last two years—to make more positive home contacts. This will hopefully eliminate the tension some parents feel when they see our school's number on their caller I.D."*

Many teachers, like Elise, mention ways their schools are trying to overcome barriers. Kelly Wickham, a literacy coach in the Springfield, Illinois school system stated: *"Most parents don't understand 'educationese' and feel intimidated. We've tried to work on using a more common language during conferences."*

Connie Pitzer, a special education teacher in Iowa shared: *"Some parents have actually said they are intimidated by the clothes the teachers wear. They feel that it elevates the level of the teacher, and the parents feel inferior when they have to meet with staff. At one school, they moved to a more casual dress code in an after-school enrichment program attended by parents and children to make the parents feel more comfortable."*

Amy Schwiderski, a middle school teacher in Jacksonville, Illinois shares a personal strategy for overcoming barriers: *"I find it is all about breaking the barriers early on. I have a back-to-school conference with each family individually so we are all on the same page from the start. I try to make them feel comfortable with me, so when a tough situation does arrive, we can work it out together."*

Some teachers mention barriers that come from the school administrators, who—through their actions or words—let parents know they are not welcome in the schools. Janice Johnson, a special education teacher in Knoxville, Illinois shared her views about the importance of supporting parents in their attempts to help their children succeed in school: *"In my experience, the most successful school districts are the ones that are able to guide parents in their zest in assisting students in their education experience and are recognized for their involvement in education. I believe it takes a 'village to raise a child,' as not one person is capable of reaching every child."*

*L*ACK OF KNOWLEDGE/SKILL IN PARENT INVOLVEMENT

The reasons cited above are not unique to this group of teachers. They are, in fact, rather common reasons or excuses for not increasing the level of parent involvement in a classroom, school, or program. Several of the barriers teachers mentioned are a result of lack of knowledge or skill in working with parents. This represents one of the most common barriers to the establishment of a strong home-school partnership. Lack of pre-service and/or in-service education in the area of family and community involvement accounts for many misconceptions about the role of both parents and teachers. Additionally, a lack of communication skills often results in many misunderstandings that might have been avoided. As mentioned above, many times teachers speak in "educationese," using words such as *phonetic* or *math manipulatives,* or acronyms such as SRA and IEP. While this language is part of the everyday language of educators, it is often not understood by parents and serves to reinforce age-old barriers that send the erroneous message: *Parents are not teachers.*

Vast gaps exist between what research indicates are effective practices in parental involvement and what teachers and schools currently do. Pre-service and in-service opportunities in parent involvement are critical to developing partnerships. As teachers, we need to view our role as one of managing many types of resources—including parent involvement—in order to help all students succeed to the best of their abilities. Unfortunately, many in-service programs in the area of parent involvement focus exclusively on communicating with parents. While communication is important, this is a limited view of parent involvement-involvement that should also include sharing strategies for helping parents become better teachers of their own children.

ATTITUDES AND BELIEFS ABOUT PARENTS

Cultural attitudes held by school personnel about the role of parents, language barriers, parent cliques, parents' educational levels, attitudes of school staff, and family issues such as childcare, have all been found to influence the involvement of parents in activities organized by the school (Pena 2000). Researchers have noted that teachers tend to define parent involvement in terms of at-school activities, whereas parents reported that the time they spent supporting children's learning at home was of greater importance (Scribner, Young, & Pedroza 1999). According to Pena (2000), parents interviewed in her study reported feeling "patronized" by the teachers and principal, unwelcome in the school, and judged negatively because of their need for assistance. Parents' recommendations for improving parent involvement in the school included ". . . changing the attitudes of school staff to 'make the parents feel more welcome'; taking parents' interests into consideration when planning activities; recognizing that even if parents cannot be present at school, helping their children at home is also a valuable contribution; and providing parents with knowledge about how to be involved in a range of involvement opportunities" (p. 54).

Several studies have examined the discrepancy between teachers and parents reports of involvement (Lopez 2000, Mapp 1999, Scribner, Young, and Pedroza 1999). Findings by Scribner, Young, and Pedroza prompted this conclusion: "the meaning of parent involvement is defined through the eyes of the beholder, especially in terms of differing perceptions of activities, relationships, and roles" (p. 41). Researchers studying risk factors related to parent involvement found that teachers' perceptions of parents' education levels were negatively associated with parents' involvement at school (Kohl, Lengua, and McMahon 2000).

*T*HE INCREASING DIVERSITY OF FAMILIES

"The need to improve academic achievement among 'diverse' student populations—notably African American, Latino, Native American, immigrant and language minority students, and students from poor families-is one of the most persistent and challenging issues that education faces" (Boethel 2003, p. v). Not surprisingly, many teachers report the increasing diversity of families as a barrier for parent involvement. Single parents, two working parents, blended families, parents sharing custody, parents who work at night, homeless parents, military parents, and so on all have needs that schools must take into account when they attempt to interact with and involve parents. According to the National PTA: "Not only are programs called upon to serve culturally diverse populations, but the structures and supports for families are continually changing as well. The predominant scenario in most households includes both parents working outside the home. In addition, single-parent families are on the rise, as well as the number of grandparents who serve as primary caregivers for their grandchildren. These patterns of change in family structure indicate that the current needs of families are indeed diverse, requiring heightened sensitivity to the increasing demands of home life" (p. 35).

Racial, Ethnic, and Cultural Diversity

Approximately 40 million U.S. residents are Black or Black and at least one other race. The Black population in the United States increased 4.4 percent or 1.6 million between 2000 and 2003. This was higher than the overall increase of 3.3 percent for the population as a whole (U.S. Census Bureau 2005). Five states have over 2 million Black residents: Florida, California, Texas, Georgia, and New York whose estimated Black population in 2003 was almost 4 million. The largest Black population (1.4 million) is concentrated in Cook County, Illinois. Los Angeles, California's Black population also exceeds 1 million (U.S. Census Bureau 2005). According to the January 24, 2005 *Facts for Features* publication of the U.S. Census Bureau, there are 8.9 million Black families living in the United States. Nearly one-half are married-couple families, and there are five or more family members in the household of approximately 20 percent of the families. Approximately 10 percent of Black children live in a household maintained by a grandparent.

Almost 10.5 million students attending elementary and high school in the United States are foreign-born or have at least one foreign born parent. The Hispanic population is by far the largest with over 5.5 million children enrolled compared to Asian and Pacific Islanders who represent almost 2 million children enrolled in our nation's schools (U.S. Census Bureau 2005a). Less than 60 percent of the Hispanic population had earned a high school degree in 2003, compared to over 85 percent of the White, 80 percent of the

Black, and over 86 percent of the Asian and Pacific Islander population with high school degrees (U.S. Census Bureau 2005a).

Seven states in the U.S. have more than 1 million Hispanic residents: Arizona, California, Florida, Illinois, New Jersey, New York, and Texas. From 1990 to 2003, the Hispanic population in the United States increased from under 22 million to over 40 million, and in 2003 more than 1 in 8 individuals living within the United States were of Hispanic origin (U.S. Census Bureau 2005a). Second-generation Latinos—immigrant children born in the United States—are emerging as the largest component of the Hispanic population. As a result, the number of second-generation Latinos in U.S. schools will double and the number in the U.S. labor force will triple by 2020 (Suro & Passel 2003). In their report funded by the Pew Hispanic Center, Suro and Passel stated: ". . . in the current decade and for the foreseeable future there will be very sizeable impacts from the number of native-born Latinos entering the nation's schools and in the flow of English-speaking, U.S.-educated Hispanics entering the labor market" (p. 2).

Almost 7 million people in the U.S. have a multiracial identity (U.S. Census Bureau). Multiracial children, like all children, have a strong need for a positive identity. Francis Wardle, executive director of the Center for the Study of Biracial Children and father of four biracial children states: "Multicultural education aspires to help all students develop positive cross-cultural attitudes, perceptions, and behaviors. It is based on the belief that individual student identity and positive self-esteem are based on a child's pride in, knowledge of, and loyalty to their cultural group's history and achievements. However, this approach cannot accommodate children who do not fit neatly within traditional categories and, therefore, these children are placed in a no-man's-land regarding racial and ethnic self-esteem" (p.6). Wardle recommends that schools learn how to provide information and support to multiracial and multiethnic families, work closely with interracial parents to find out how they choose to address this issue, and receive training in meeting the needs of all children and families, including "those who do not fit into the existing racial and ethnic boxes" (p. 6).

Children in Poverty

In ours, the wealthiest nation in the world, over 12 million children are poor, hungry and/or at risk for hunger, living in the worst housing conditions, or are homeless (2000 U.S. Census). According to the National Center for Children in Poverty (2005), 37 percent of children in the United States (27 million) live in low income families, 16 percent of which (over 11 million) are living in homes that are below the federal poverty level ($13,861 for a family of three) and 6 percent of which (5 million) live in extreme poverty ($6,930 or less for a family of three). Many children experience hunger and food insecurity, the point in the month in which money, food stamps or other resources used for food are depleted. In 2002 one out of every six families with children was "food insecure" (U.S. Department of Agriculture 2002).

According to the Children's Defense Fund (2004), "Children who are poor are more likely to die in infancy; have a low birth weight; lack health care, housing, and adequate food; and receive lower scores in math and reading" (p. 2).

Over the past decade, the number of homeless families with children has increased significantly with preschool and kindergarten children comprising the largest group of homeless children (U.S. Department of Education 2000). According to the education subtitle of the Stewart B. McKinney Act, the term 'homeless child and youth' (A) means individuals who lack a fixed, regular, and adequate nighttime residence . . . and (B) includes: (i) children and youth who are sharing the housing of other persons due to loss of housing, economic hardship, or a similar reason; are living in motels, hotels, trailer parks, or camping grounds due to lack of alternative adequate accommodations; are living in emergency or transitional shelters; are abandoned in hospitals; or are awaiting foster care placement; (ii) children and youth who have a primary nighttime residence that is a private or public place not designed for or ordinarily used as a regular sleeping accommodation for human beings, (iii) children and youth who are living in cars, parks, public spaces, abandoned buildings, substandard housing, bus or train stations, or similar settings, and (iv) migratory children . . . who qualify as homeless for the purposes of this subtitle because the children are living in circumstances described in clauses (i) through (iii) (McKinney-Vento Act sec. 725(2); 42 U.S.C. 11435(2)).

Factors most often cited for the rising growth in homelessness are a growing shortage of affordable rental housing and a simultaneous increase in poverty. Persons living in poverty are most at risk of becoming homeless, and demographic groups who are more likely to experience poverty are also more likely to experience homelessness. Some of these families reside in shelters where the average stay is nearly a year (Santos, 2002). In 1998, almost half of the children in shelters were under the age of five and school-age children encountered difficulties in enrolling and attending school, obtaining records from previous schools, and having the necessary clothing and supplies. Additionally, when children move and change schools often they experience absences that may result in retention. While only 5 percent of school children repeat a grade because of frequent absence, 21 percent of homeless children do so (Better Homes Fund 1998). Many families are separated as children of homeless parents are placed into foster care or with relatives and friends in order to save them from the ordeal of homelessness or to permit them to continue attending their regular school.

People who become homeless do not fit one general description. The U.S. Conference of Mayors conducted a study of the homeless in 25 cities in 2003. The homeless population in these cities was 49 percent African-American, 35 percent Caucasian, 13 percent Hispanic, 2 percent Native American, and 1 percent Asian (U.S. Conference of Mayors, 2003). According to the Children's Defense Fund (2004), larger numbers of White non-Hispanic children reside in poverty, even though the overall proportion of

Black and Hispanic children who are poor is far higher. Geographic location plays a major role in determining the ethnic makeup of homeless populations. Data compiled by the U.S. Department of Agriculture reveals more people experiencing homelessness are found in rural areas and are much more likely to be White, Native Americans and migrant workers (U.S. Department of Agriculture, 2002). Single women living in poverty and those experiencing physical abuse are also represented among the homeless. Violence has a tremendous impact on families with children. Women who live in poverty and are in abusive relationships often have to choose between abuse and homelessness (Zorza, 1991, 2001). Some homeless children may have experienced or witnessed violent behavior and abuse, while others may be fearful that they will be abducted by an abusive parent or that their mother will be harmed.

According to the Better Homes Fund (1999), deep poverty and housing insecurities are especially harmful during the earliest years of childhood. Homeless children are more than twice as likely to become ill, and have higher rates of asthma, ear infections, stomach problems, and speech problems. They also experience more mental health problems, such as anxiety, depression, and withdrawal, and are four times as likely to have developmental delays (National Center for Children in Poverty 2005). Only 15 percent of homeless preschool children attended preschool in 2000 (U.S. Department of Education) compared to 57 percent of low-income preschool children enrolled (National Center for Education Statistics 1999). In a review of the literature on educating preschoolers, the National Research Council (NRC) concluded:

> Young children who are living in circumstances that place them at greater risk of school failure-including poverty, low level of maternal education, maternal depression, and other factors that can limit their access to opportunities and resources that enhance learning and development-are much more likely to succeed in school if they attend well-planned, high-quality early childhood programs. (Bowman, Donovan, & Burns, 2001, p. 8).

Having homeless students in the classroom can be quite challenging for teachers; however, school attendance is important for homeless children because it can provide them with a sense of stability which, in turn, helps them cope with homelessness. The parents of homeless children are sometimes depressed, under-nourished, ill, or so involved in acquiring work or a home that they are able to give their children little positive attention. These children may try to compensate for this lack of attention through inappropriate behavior at school. Educators must be cognizant of the difficulties encountered by these children and their families in homeless situations and understand that focusing on academic goals may not be possible until the students' social and psychological needs have been met. Supports that some schools have put in place to help students in poverty include providing various types of homework support, assigning students to the same teacher(s) for two or more years, teaching students strategies for coping in school, and offering parental training opportunities via videotape (Payne 2001).

In her book, *A Framework for Understanding Poverty,* Ruby Payne distinguishes between generational poverty—that which has existed for two or more generations, and situational poverty—short-term poverty caused by circumstance. According to Payne "An individual brings with him/her the hidden rules of the class in which he/she was raised. . . . schools and businesses operate from middle-class norms and the hidden roles of middle class" (p. 11). Some of the hidden rules of poverty shared by Payne include: "The noise level is high (the TV is always on and everyone may talk at once), the most important information is non-verbal, and one of the main values of an individual to the group is an ability to entertain" (p. 18). Payne helps educators understand these and other hidden rules and ways to teach students the rules of school and work they need in order to be successful.

The National PTA seeks to affirm diversity and calls for programs serving parents and families to be aware of and sensitive to the changes in our society. They state: "As our society increases in the numbers and groups of diverse populations represented, only those programs willing to be flexible, sensitive, and supportive to the parents, children, and families they serve will be determined effective and worthwhile" (p. 35).

TIME CONSTRAINTS

There's no way to skirt the issue of time-the most often cited reason for lack of parent involvement. Teachers have heavy demands on their time, and the added burden of preparing workshop materials, directions, and/or materials for home-learning activities, and other parent involvement projects can be daunting. Unfortunately, teachers who say that they "just don't have time" to promote the concept of parents as partners don't realize that this just may be the most effective tool they have to increase student learning.

Family involvement takes time. The challenge we face is to find ways to devote the time that is necessary for building solid, lasting partnerships with all families.

BARRIERS ERECTED BY HOMES

Although research indicates that parents *do care* about their children and *do want* to be involved in their children's education, there are some barriers to building strong partnerships which have been erected by the home. The tendency for schools to view barriers as unalterable variables that cannot be addressed by the school is erroneous. Many school staffs have worked successfully to overcome barriers erected both by schools and by homes. These barriers must be attended to in order for schools to truly develop lasting relationships with all families.

NEGATIVE ATTITUDES TOWARD SCHOOL

When parents have developed negative associations with and expectations about school, building a bridge from the school to the home is a difficult— but *absolutely necessary*—task. Sometimes parents themselves were not successful in school. They may have struggled with academic tasks, perhaps being labeled "disabled" or "lazy." They may have had behavioral difficulties that resulted in negative reports to their parents and/or alienation from their classmates. Although these events would have taken place many years earlier, to some parents the events may seem as if they happened only yesterday. Just walking through the door of the school elicits negative images and feelings of frustration! It is not difficult to imagine what these parents must be going through when they are asked to visit the school for a conference with a teacher or principal. Other parents may have had more recent unpleasant experiences, such as parents of children with special needs who do not understand the school's evaluation and placement procedures for the child, or parents of children who experience chronic behavioral difficulties resulting in frequently negative contacts with the school. Sometimes these negative—and even hostile—attitudes about school affect more than one generation in a family, and grandparents become convinced that their grandchildren may be hurt they way they were hurt when they were in school many years before. Gutman and McLoyd (2000) found that parents who experienced negative interactions with the school appeared to be "more wary" of school personnel and their intentions and parent involvement offerings (p. 14).

Schools must work hard to reach parents for whom the image of school is a negative one. Signs welcoming parents as they enter the building, rather than ones that read "Stop! All Visitors Must Report to the Office" might be one place to start to develop a "family-friendly" building. Being sure that families can find their way around the school—and that they can easily locate the school office and their child's classroom—is another way to reduce the stress that families sometimes feel when they enter a school. Speaking to family members in words they can understand and asking for their opinions and ideas as well as their assistance with home-learning activities are other ways to begin to chip away at old barriers and build new bridges between the home and school. Lindle (1989) suggests that a "personal touch" is the most enhancing factor in school relations. Parents appreciate teachers who convey a special interest in their children and share successes as well as problems in both academic and social areas. This sentiment is echoed by Anita Lovell, an elementary school teacher who states:

Early + often

> I think it is important to get the parents involved before school starts. One measure would be for teachers to contact each parent personally through phone conversation and or e-mail before the students step foot in the classroom on the first day of school. To get the lines of communication open

from the get go is a big asset in reassuring concerned parents. My past experiences as a parent have been that when a teacher contacts me, it is usually because my child has exhibited an inappropriate act or behavior. Not enough positive feedback is given to break down the barriers for parents to get involved. Inviting parents to come in to be guest readers or guest speakers is one of the easiest ways to get the parents involved. Once parents feel comfortable talking and mingling with teachers and administrators, their involvement typically increases. Parent involvement is not only necessary for the schools, but also for the children involved.

TIME AND ECONOMIC RESTRAINTS

Lack of time is frequently mentioned by parents and teachers as a barrier to greater involvement. In fact, in its report of findings from focus groups and a nationwide survey, the Public Education Network (2001) stated: "Nearly three in five parents (57 percent) say time is a barrier (with 33 percent calling it a major barrier)" (p. 23). Single-parent families and low-income families are further constrained by their lack of dollars for fast food, reliable transportation, and other such "time-savers" that two-wage-earner families use to "buy" time for other activities (Levine & Trickett 2000, Mapp 1999, McGrath & Kuriloff 1999, Richman-Prakash, West, & Denton 2002, Starkey & Klein 2000). Some studies have addressed strategies for addressing this barrier. These include flexible scheduling of activities and events; locating family involvement centers in highly accessible areas, such as public housing projects; and using community organizations to provide transportation, child care, and other assistance to make it possible for families to be involved in the education of their children (Aspiazu, Bauer, & Spillet 1998, Birch & Ferrin 2002, Johnstone & Hiatt 1997).

PARENTS' EDUCATIONAL LEVELS AND ABILITIES

Many parents express concern over their ability to help their children with at-home learning activities. Kohl, Lengua, and McMahon (2000) studied family risk factors impacting parent involvement. Not surprisingly, parents' education level was found to be negatively associated with parents' involvement at school. Mestina Vancil, a first-grade teacher in Galesburg, Illinois, expressed concern about inappropriate expectations teachers may have for some parents:

> In our school I feel that the most prevalent barrier is intimidation. Most of our parents are of very low education background. Many are jobless, on government intervention programs, and are poor readers. I feel that many of our parents don't get involved because they are intimidated by the things we are asking them to do. If we ask the parent to read with the child for

30 minutes a night and they can't read, what does that do to their self-esteem as a parent?"

Many families report a lack of knowledge about the curriculum and subjects their children are studying (Aspiazu, Bauer, & Spillet 1998, Azmitia & Cooper 2002, Pena 2000). Parents of older elementary children, in particular, may feel inadequate to help their children in reading and math at home. To overcome this barrier, schools need to offer families strategies for helping their children with at-home learning activities. Providing workshops and videos to help parents understand how to use at-home learning materials, and sending home materials with clearly stated directions for parent-child interaction can help to address this barrier.

LANGUAGE BARRIERS

Language differences have become an increasing barrier to parent involvement (Adger 2001, Aspiazu, Bauer, & Spillet 1998, Paratore, Melzi, & Krol-Sinclear 1999, Pena 2000). Kim (2002) found a positive relationship between the English proficiency of parents and their involvement both at home and at school. *Parental Involvement, Title I Part A* (USDE 2004) calls for schools to "implement effective means of outreach to parents of limited English proficient students to inform those parents of how the parents can be involved in the education of their children; and be active participants in assisting their children to attain English proficiency, achieve at high levels in core academic subjects, and meet the challenging state academic achievement standards and state academic content standards expected of all students" (p. 13). Each school is to provide information to parents in an "understandable and uniform format, including alternative formats upon request, and, "to the extent practicable," in a language that parents understand (p. 13).

Schools that are addressing this barrier are conducting meetings and other school events in the language(s) with which families are most comfortable, have a bilingual teacher or other translator available for parent conferences, and make written communications, such as the school handbook and newsletters, available in parents' home language. When this is not feasible, schools are enlisting the help of "cultural carriers," individuals within the community who can communicate with the family on behalf of the teacher and school. These individuals often take an active role in helping parents understand school policies and procedures, classroom routines, and other important information necessary for their child's success in school.

THE FAMILY SYSTEM

In many schools across our nation, the barriers that serve to separate homes and schools are slowly being replaced by bridges created to link the two. As educators, we have been called upon to understand the family system as a whole and to work to provide a variety of services within the educational setting. Some programs have experimented with "one-stop shopping" services where families can receive—right in the school building—a variety of services—medical, dental, counseling, GED classes, and so forth. Many schools are providing before- and after-school programs with educational enrichment and tutoring opportunities. These programs are often linked to other programs within the community, such as the park district and YMCA.

As stated in the Accreditation Performance Criteria (2004) developed by the National Association for the Education of Young Children (NAEYC), "Young children's learning and development are integrally connected to their families" (p. 1). In order for us to establish collaborative relationships with the parents and families of the children with whom we work, we must possess an understanding of families and the rules, roles, and boundaries established by and adhered to by the members of each individual family unit.

Family systems theory is one way to describe the emotional processes that regulate human functioning in families. Used most often by therapists and counselors, family systems theory recognizes the family as a natural unit or system in which the emotional functioning of each member affects the functioning of all of the other members (Bowen, 1985). Children are greatly affected by their relationship with their family; therefore, a rudimentary knowledge of family systems is important.

In a family system, each member is part of the whole system, as well as a unique individual. Each family member assumes a role and resides within the family structure according to established rules (Nichols & Swartz 2002). Family roles define the expectations of each individual's behavior and functioning within the family unit. Stereotypical adult roles include "breadwinner," "homemaker," and "caretaker." There may also be established roles for "gardener," "cook," "housecleaner," "mechanic," "dog walker," and so forth. The roles of the children within the family vary according to gender and birth order, and when there is an "only child," the role has unique aspects not seen in families with siblings. Roles assumed by children in a family might include "the babysitter," "the sports hero," "the brainy or studious one," or the "talented one," to name a few. One person usually fulfills more than one role, and roles vary from one culture to another according to cultural norms.

In healthy families, roles are generally interchangeable as each family member experiences times when they need help, as well as times when they are capable of helping others. Parents share equal power with each other while allowing input, as appropriate, from children. There is no doubt within these families as to who the parents are and who the children are. Fathers and mothers have a healthy self-concept, good communication skills, and flexible roles.

In dysfunctional families, roles assumed by family members are less flexible and generally serve to maintain the equilibrium within the family.

For example, in homes where an addiction is present there is often an "enabler" who allows the substance abuse to continue by making excuses for the addict's behavior. Sometimes, another family member, usually a child or youth, begins to excel in school, sports, or the arts to create a positive family image for the world outside. There may also be a "scapegoat" whose unacceptable behavior draws attention away from the substance abuse problem. This role is sometimes assumed by the addict in a "cover-up" attempt designed to show other family members that the problems are a result of poor behavior, rather than addiction. At the same time, another member may serve as the "family clown" who uses comedy to try to divert attention away from the problems within the family. And, all too often, there is also someone functioning in the role of the "lost child." This is the individual who never causes a problem and is relatively invisible within the family.

Family rules are those spoken and unspoken guidelines that govern communication and other activities, including how members of the family communicate with each other and with others outside the family. All families have established rules and boundaries or limits that guide their actions and decisions. These rules, like the roles members assume, differ from one culture to another. Healthy families typically operate within an open family system where the interchange of information and activity is subject to change based on outside influences and family decision-making. Conversely, closed family systems work to prevent outside information and activity from entering and changing the family. Much energy is often spent trying to maintain the status quo and there are few, if any, connections outside of the family. In these dysfunctional families, the behaviors and roles of the family members are limited so as to isolate the family from the community (Nichols & Swartz 2002). These are, indeed, our "hard to reach" families, who view change as potentially uncomfortable or threatening.

Turnbull and Turnbull (1990) have designed a four-component family systems framework which includes family characteristics, family interaction, family functions, and the family life cycle. The first component, *family characteristics,* includes information about the size and make-up of the family. Knowing how many adults and children are in the home, whether there are step-parents and step-children, and the role of a non-custodial parent is seen as important, as is learning about the family's cultural background, socioeconomic status, and any other personal characteristics of the family which may have an impact, such as a family member with a chronic illness or disability. How family members communicate and work with one another is a major focus of the second and third components, *family interaction* and *family functions.* Finally, the fourth component, *family life cycle,* looks at stages of family life: newly married couples, families with young children, families with school-age children, families with young adults, and families with middle-aged parents.

SUMMARY

Administrators, teachers, and other school personnel erect powerful barriers that serve to hinder the creation of strong and effective partnerships with parents and family members. In this chapter we discussed some of the more prevalent barriers, as well as some possible reasons why they exist. Treatment was also given to the barriers erected by parents and family situations. There is an increasing move toward recognition of the family as a complete unit. Effective teachers will do all they can to learn about and understand the families of the children in their classrooms and schools. Recognizing and respecting differences that exist in all families will assist us in not only removing barriers, but in building bridges to link home and school.

LOOKING AHEAD . . .

The next several chapters will share many strategies for communicating with families and for involving them in their children's education in ways well-supported by research. Before continuing in your reading, perhaps it would be beneficial for you to consider your own school situation. Answering the questions listed below may provide you with important insights into the barriers that prevent your school from building bridges to each student's home.

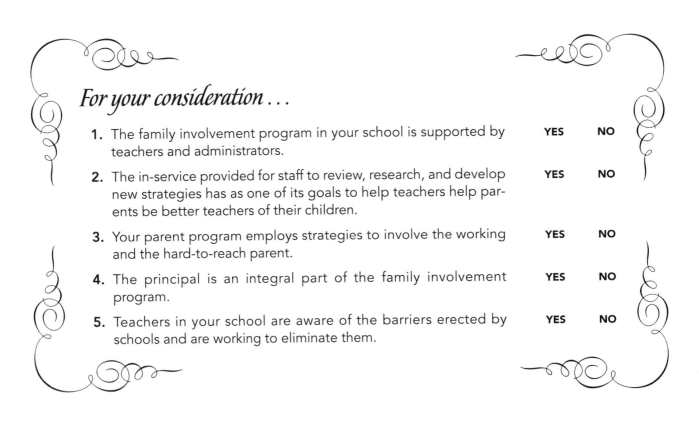

For your consideration . . .

1. The family involvement program in your school is supported by teachers and administrators.   **YES   NO**

2. The in-service provided for staff to review, research, and develop new strategies has as one of its goals to help teachers help parents be better teachers of their children.   **YES   NO**

3. Your parent program employs strategies to involve the working and the hard-to-reach parent.   **YES   NO**

4. The principal is an integral part of the family involvement program.   **YES   NO**

5. Teachers in your school are aware of the barriers erected by schools and are working to eliminate them.   **YES   NO**

REFERENCES

Adger, C. T. (2001). School-community-based organization partnerships for language minority students' school success. *Journal of Education for Students Placed at Risk, 6*(1&2), 7–25.

Aspiazu, G. G., Bauer, S. C., & Spillet, M. (1998). Improving the academic performance of Hispanic youth: A community education model. *Bilingual Research Journal, 22*(2), 103–123.

Better Homes Fund (1999). *Homeless children: American's new outcasts.* Better Homes Fund: Newton Centre, MA. *http://www.tbhf.org/factsheet.html*

Birch, T. C., & Ferrin, S. E. (2002). Mexican American parental participation in public education in an isolated Rocky Mountain rural community. *Equity & Excellence in Education, 35*(1), 70–78.

Boethel, M. (2004). *Readiness: School, family, & community connections.* Austin, TX: National Center for Family and Community Connections with Schools.

Bowen, M. (1985). Society, crisis and systems theory. In *Family therapy in clinical practice* (pp. 413–459). Northvale, NJ: Jason Aronson.

Bowman, B., Donovan, M., & Burns, M. (2001). *Eager to learn: Educating our preschoolers.* Washington, DC: National Academy Press.

Children's Defense Fund (2004). *Defining poverty and why it matters for children.* Washington, DC: Children's Defense Fund. *www.childrensdefensefund.org*

Children's Defense Fund (2003). *Child poverty: Characteristics of poor children in America. www.childrensdefensefund.org*

Gutman, L. M., & McLoyd, V. C. (2000). Parents' management of their children's education within the home, at school, and in the community: An examination of African-American families living in poverty. *The Urban Review, 32*(1), 1–24.

Henderson, A. T., & Mapp, K. L. (2002). *A new wave of evidence: The impact of school, family, and community connections on student achievement.* National Center for Family & Community Connections with Schools. Austin, TX: Southwest Educational Development Laboratory.

Johnstone, T. R., & Hiatt, D. B. (1997). *Development of a school-based parent center for low income new immigrants.* Paper presented at the annual meeting of the American Educational Research Association, Chicago, IL.

Kim, E. (2002). The relationship between parental involvement and children's educational achievement in the Korean immigrant family. *Journal of Comparative Family Studies, 33*(4), 529–540.

Kohl, G. O., Lengua, L. J., & McMahon, R. J. (2000). Parent involvement in school: Conceptualizing multiple dimensions and their relations with family and demographic risk factors. *Journal of School Psychology, 38*(6), 501–523.

Levine, E. B., & Trickett, E. J. (2000). Toward a model of Latino parent advocacy for educational change. *Journal of Prevention & Intervention in the Community, 20*(1&2), 121–137.

Lindle, J. C. (1989). What do parents want from principals and teachers? *Educational Leadership, 47*(2), 12–14.

Mapp, K. L. (1999). *Making the connection between families and schools: Why and how parents are involved in their children's education.* Unpublished doctoral dissertation, Cambridge, MA: Harvard University.

McGrath, D. J., & Kuriloff, P. J. (1999). "They're going to tear the doors off this place": Upper-middle-class parent school involvement and the educational opportunities of other people's children. *Educational Policy, 13*(5), 603–629.

National Association for the Education of Young Children (2004). Final Draft Accreditation Performance Criteria Program Standards. *http://www.naeyc.org/ accreditation/naeyc_accred/draft_standards/com.html*

National Center for Education Statistics (1999). *National household education survey.* Washington, DC: National Center for Education Statistics. *www.nces.ed.gov*

National Center for Children in Poverty (2005). *Basic facts about low-income children in the United States.* National Center for Children in Poverty. New York: Columbia University.

National Coalition for the Homeless (2001). *Welfare to What II: Findings on Family Hardship and Well-being.* National Coalition for the Homeless. Washington, DC. *www.nationalhomeless.org*

National PTA (2004). *National Standards for Parent/Family Involvement Programs, An Implementation Guide for School Communities. http://www.pta.org*

Nichols, M., & Schwartz, R. (2002). *Family Therapy: Concepts and Methods* (5th ed.). Boston: Allyn and Bacon.

Paratore, J. R., Melzi, G., & Krol-Sinclair, B. (1999). *What should we expect of family literacy? Experiences of Latino children whose parents participate in an intergenerational literacy project.* Newark, DE: International Reading Association.

Payne, R. K. (2001). *A framework for understanding poverty.* Highlands, TX: Aha! Process, Inc.

Pena, D. D. (2000). Parent involvement: Influencing factors and implications. *The Journal of Educational Research, 94*(1), 42–54.

Public Education Network/Education/Education Week (2001). *Action for All: The public's responsibility for public education. www.publiceducation.org/*

Richman-Prakash, N., West, J., & Denton, K. (2002). *Differences in parental involvement in their children's school among children of poverty.* Paper presented at the annual meeting of the American Educational Research Association, New Orleans, LA.

Santos, F., & Ingrassia, R (2002). Family surge at shelters. In *New York Daily News,* August 18th, 2002. Available at: *www.nationalhomeless.org/housing/families article.html*

Scribner, J. D., Young, M.D., & Pedroza, A. (1999). Building collaborative relationships with parents. In P. Reyes, J. D. Scribner, & A. Paredes-Scribner (Eds.), *Lessons from high-performing Hispanic schools: Creating learning communities* (pp. 36–60). New York: Teachers College Press.

Starkey, P., & Klein, A. (2000). Fostering parental support for children's mathematical development: An intervention with Head Start families. *Early Education and Development, 11*(5), 659–680.

Suro, R., & Passel, J. S. (2003). *The rise of the second generation: Changing patterns in Hispanic population growth.* Washington, DC: Pew Hispanic Center.

Turnbull, A. P., & Turnbull, H. R. (1990). *Families, professionals, and exceptionality: A special partnership* (2nd ed.). Columbus, OH: Merrill Publishing Company.

Urban Institute, The (2000). A new look at homelessness in America. Washington, DC: The Urban Institute. www.urban.org

U. S. Census Bureau, (2005). *Facts for features.* Washington, DC: U.S. Census Bureau. *www.census.gov*

U.S. Census Bureau (2005a). *Statistical abstract of the United States: 2004-2005.* Washington, DC: U.S. Census Bureau. *www.census.gov*

U.S. Census Bureau (2003). *Thresholds for 2002 by size of family and number of related children under 18 years.* Washington, DC: U.S. Census Bureau. *www.census.gov*

U.S. Census Bureau (2002). *Poverty in the United States 2001.* Washington, DC: U.S. Census Bureau. *www.census.gov*

U.S. Conference of Mayors (2003). *A status report on hunger and homelessness in American's Cities.* Washington, DC: U.S. Conference of Mayors.

U.S. Department of Agriculture (2002). *Annual report: Expenditures on children by families.* Washington, DC: USDA.

U.S. Department of Education (2000). *Education for Homeless Children and Youth Report to Congress.* Washington, DC: USDE. *www.ed.gov*

U.S. Department of Education (2004). *Parental Involvement: Title I, Part A Non-Regulatory Guidance.* Washington, DC: U.S. Department of Education.

Wardle, F. Helping multiracial and multiethnic children escape no man's land. *Our Children Magazine, 25*(6), 6.

Zedlewski, S. R., Giannarelli, L., Morton, J., & Wheaton, L. (2002). *Extreme poverty rising, existing government programs could do more.* Washington, DC: The Urban Institute. *http://www.urban.org/UploadedPDF/310455.pdf*

Zorza, J. (2001). Woman battering: A major cause of homelessness. *Clearinghouse Review, 25*(4) (1991). Qtd. in *National Coalition Against Domestic Violence,* "The Importance of Financial Literacy," October.

Sharing Policies and Procedures: Creating Effective Handbooks and Websites

The parent handbook is often the family's first written communication from the school. While conveying policies and procedures is certainly an important goal, we need to examine our handbooks from the perspective of the parents who will be reading them. Unfortunately, many school handbooks sound more like a military manual than a booklet that reassures parents their children will be in good hands! Full of do's and don'ts, many handbooks follow an alphabetical order that places any mention of parent contact with the school near the end. In this chapter are ideas and examples for using your handbooks as a welcoming tool for establishing a home-school partnership. Also included in this discussion will be use of school web sites to share a plethora of information and ideas with families.

INTRODUCTION

Some school handbooks resemble an army manual more than a booklet to reassure parents their children are in good hands. The school handbook may be the first encounter families have with the school . . . It should project a warm welcome and a partnership philosophy, and have a personal flavor to it. Policy statements are important, but overall, the school handbook should look more like an advertisement for the school and less like an institutional manual.

The research on parent involvement indicates that teachers and parents can create viable partnerships by exchanging information, sharing in decision making, collaborating in the child's learning, and supporting each other in their respective roles (Henderson & Mapp 2002). In the previous two chapters research relating parent involvement to student achievement and to changes in attitudes and behaviors of students, parents, teachers, and principals was reported. Barriers that hinder the creation of strong and effective partnerships was also discussed. This chapter will include information to assist schools and teachers in developing handbooks containing policies and procedures that provide the foundation for a family-centered school. Central to the development of these policies and procedures is the recognition of various parent and teacher roles and behaviors that make for successful partnerships. Some general policy suggestions and strategies for engaging parents and teachers in supportive and collaborative roles will be included along with guidelines for developing an effective handbook.

SHARED BELIEFS ABOUT PARENT INVOLVEMENT

Through a partnership arrangement, parents, teachers, and principals can be actively involved in collaborative efforts supporting maximum learning for all children. The concept of partnership is based on the premise that collaborating partners have some "common basis for action and a sense of mutuality that supports their joint ventures" (Swick 1991, 1). Certainly, supporting children's learning is a common goal for both parents and school personnel. As in any partnership, all parties involved must exhibit certain characteristics and ways of behaving toward one another. Certain attributes are correlated with successful partnerships. For parents, these attributes include warmth, sensitivity, nurturance, the ability to listen, consistency, a positive self-image, a sense of efficacy, personal competence, and effective interpersonal skills (Swick 1991). Attributes for teachers include warmth, openness, sensitivity, flexibility, reliability, and accessibility (Comer and Haynes 1991).

Integral to the adoption of policies and procedures for parent involvement are the related beliefs held by school personnel. The following assumptions or beliefs form the basis for developing partnerships with all families (Knight 1987).

- ❧ Parents are their children's first and most important teachers.

- ❧ Parents love their children and want the best possible education for them.

- ❧ Parents will participate in ways they can in light of their cultural, family, and personal priorities.

- ❧ Parents participate when they feel accepted, cared about, and respected by school personnel.

- ❧ Students benefit from their parents' active involvement in schooling.

- ❧ A parent involvement program is only as successful as the school leadership and staff believes it can be.

The determination of specific beliefs or assumptions about parent involvement is an important first step for school staff members charged with the task of developing policies and procedures reflective of a strong family-centered focus.

GENERAL POLICY SUGGESTIONS

Clearly, leaders at the federal and state levels have become increasingly aware of the necessity for involving parents in the education of their children. Title One, Head Start, and other federal programs mandate consultation and collaboration with parents. These mandates, in turn, affect state and district policies requiring parent involvement for other programs and other grade levels, as well. Forming policies and procedures uniquely suited to each school system and school is the task of school leaders, with input from teachers, administrators, parents, students, and the community. There are, however, some key concepts that need to be reflected in the policies and procedures that are adopted. The National Coalition for Parent Involvement in Education (NCPIE) suggests that policies provide ways for parents to become knowledgeable about the opportunities that exist for parent involvement and the provision of regular communications from the school concerning the school programs and their children's specific progress in relation to the goals and objectives of those programs. Further, policies relating to opportunities for parents to assist in the instructional process at school and at home and opportunities for involvement of parents of children at all ages and grade levels should be included. Finally, all policies should reflect a recognition of diverse family structures, lifestyles, cultures, education levels, and language differences. With respect to the continued development of teachers, NCPIE suggests policies that provide for professional development for teachers and principals to enhance their effectiveness in working with parents. And to foster strong ties within the community and to better meet the needs of the family populations served by the school, NCPIE suggests policies mandating linkages with social service agencies and community groups.

CHARACTERISTICS OF EFFECTIVE SCHOOL HANDBOOKS

Every school has a need to convey to parents some general policies and procedures. Handbooks containing this information are very useful to parents who need basic information about how the school is run: arrival and dismissal times, the school calendar, the lunch program, codes of conduct, and so on. Unlike many other documents and notices sent home throughout the year, this one has a chance of being read! Parents who are new to the school are often insecure about what they can expect from the school. Parents of returning students want to know about the schedule for the current year and about any staff program and policy changes. Handbooks provide this information and much more. Still, schools miss an enormous opportunity when they don't utilize the handbook as a public relations tool—an advertisement, so to speak—for all the good programs and traditions ongoing in the school.

Like any informational literature to be distributed to a wide public audience, school handbooks should be neatly presented and easy to read. Wide margins, appealing graphics, and use of varying fonts and type styles serve to make the handbook attractive. Clear headings and subheadings, as well as the inclusion of a table of contents, assist readers in readily locating necessary information. The content should be as brief and direct as possible, yet adequately present the necessary information. And, probably most important, the information should be presented in language that is clear, concise, and free from educational jargon.

SUGGESTED CONTENTS

The school handbook is a good tool to use for communicating general information about the school to parents, students, school personnel, and members of the community. It can also serve as a vehicle for sharing the school's philosophy, mission statement, and purpose, as well as conveying a strong commitment toward forging educational partnerships with families and members of the community. The handbook should, above all, *convey a positive tone and message,* rather than project a negative or authoritarian attitude. For example, although behavior codes should be explicitly stated in the handbook, a listing of forty-two rules at the beginning of the handbook does little to establish a warm feeling of partnership.

A letter of introduction or welcome from the building principal is a nice first entry. The letter, printed just inside the front cover, could give an overview of the year to come and perhaps reveal some schoolwide purposes or goals. In it the principal may explain the school philosophy and mission statement. Most of all, though, the letter should serve as a personal welcome for the parents and students (see Figure 3.1).

If your school has a parent-teacher organization, you may want to ask the president, the volunteer coordinator, or another officer to provide a letter of welcome for inclusion in the handbook. This letter may outline activities for the coming year, a schedule of meetings and special activities, and information about services available to fellow parents, as well as information about joining the parent-teacher organization.

Your faculty, or a representative committee, will want to discuss topics for inclusion in your school handbook. Although some topics are unique to an individual school or district, Figure 3.2 lists a sample table of contents of common topics.

The contents for a preschool center handbook would be somewhat different. In Figure 3.3 is the table of contents of the parent handbook for the

---

**Canton Elementary Schools
CUSD #66**
Canton, Illinois 61520

Welcome Back to School

This year will provide students an exciting, productive educational experience. Many plans have been made to ensure all students experience success at school. You will find the students and staff very helpful. Teachers at our schools are very dedicated and plan many special activities to help students learn in both traditional and non-traditional ways.

We are very proud of our schools and hope that you respect our schools. We all work as a team to help keep the buildings clean and safe.

Our sincere wish is for a wonderful school year. Our office is available to assist both students and parents with any questions or concerns that might occur during the school year. Please remember to use Infonet, an automated phone system available 24 hours a day for your use in communicating with both our school and staff members. Additional information on Infonet can be found in the handbook.

We wish all students a safe, productive, and rewarding school year!

Sincerely,

Mrs. Boelkes   Mrs. Stephenson   Mrs. Kruse
Eastview Principal   Lincoln Principal   Westview Principal

> *"It is the mission of the Canton Union School District #66 to motivate and to provide all students opportunities to reach their maximum academic, social, and physical potential in order to become responsible, successful participants in a changing global society."*

http://www.cantonusd.org

Figure 3.1

Western Illinois University Infant and Preschool Center. Note the entries under the heading "Parent Involvement." As in the suggested handbook for an elementary school, the curriculum philosophy would be clearly explained (see Figure 3.4).

An area of the handbook that requires especially careful wording is the behavior, or discipline, section. The Canton Elementary School Handbook (see Figure 3.5) is an excellent example of how a strong message can be conveyed in a positive tone.

Table of Contents

Welcome to YOUR school: A Letter from the Principal
Working as Partners: School Philosophy
Mission Statement and Purpose
Curricular Approach
Special Programs
    After-school program
    Bilingual program
    Title One reading and math
    Guidance counselor
    Special education resources
    Speech and language program
Home-School Connections
    Home-learning activities
    Conferences
    Parent education opportunities
    Parent resource library
    Reporting pupil progress
    Parent advisory council
    School volunteer program
    Home school organization
    Parents-helping-parents program
Routine Policies, Procedures, and Regulations
    Attendance
    Grading system
    School lunch and nutrition program
    Transportation schedules and regulations
    Health and immunization policies
    Emergency and safety procedures and policies
    Student fees
Behavior Codes
Sample Daily and Weekly Schedules
School Calendar
School Staff
District Staff and School Board Members
Community Resources

Figure 3.2

Table of Contents

Figure 3.3

Curriculum Philosophy

Our curriculum is designed to be appropriate for the age span of the children within the group with attention being given to children's individual needs, interests, and developmental levels. The development of positive self-esteem and a positive attitude toward learning are a primary emphasis.

We view learning as an interactive process between the child and her/his environment. The curriculum is designed to provide for children's exploration and manipulation of the environment through meaningful interaction with adults, other children, and materials.

The teachers' knowledge of child development will aid them in observing and recording each child's needs, interests, and developmental progress. Materials and experiences are then planned to meet these needs and stimulate learning in all developmental areas—physical, social, emotional, and intellectual—using an integrated approach.

Learning activities and materials are concrete, real, and/or representational, and relevant to the lives of young children. As children develop understanding and skills, the teachers will provide a variety of activities and materials of increasing difficulty, complexity, and challenge. Child-initiated, child-directed, and teacher-supported play is an essential component of our program.

Multicultural and nonsexist experiences, materials, and equipment are provided for children of all ages.

Daily learning experiences include the following:

- **ART:** Use of various art media such as Playdo, finger paints, water colors, crayons, and easel paints assist the child in self-expression, creativity, and in the development of fine motor coordination.

- **DRAMATIC PLAY:** Dramatic play gives each child the opportunity to better understand family and community roles.

- **MUSIC:** Ample time is allowed for singing, movement, and experimentation with instruments and rhythm. Listening to music serves as a way to relax the child and provide smooth transitions to other activities. Children are exposed to a variety of music throughout the day.

- **LITERATURE AND LANGUAGE ARTS EXPERIENCES:** Books are readily available to all children. Children are frequently read to individually or in small groups. In addition, special time is set aside for puppets and stories with various media such as flannel boards, videos, and story tapes. Children are encouraged to dictate stories as well as to experience many print-related activities.

- **LARGE AND SMALL MUSCLE ACTIVITIES:** Physical exercise and the development of motor skills is experienced daily. A variety of equipment is used. Small muscles are developed through various manipulative materials.

- **MATHEMATICS:** Number concepts, measurement, geometry, patterns, and relationships are introduced through hands-on experiences and daily living routines. Children have many opportunities to count, compare and classify throughout the day. Problem-solving, reasoning, and communication are emphasized.

- **SCIENCE:** Children are curious about the world around them. By building on this natural interest, we can take advantage of events in our classroom as well as outdoors. By taking field trips and providing science projects, we allow opportunities for experimenting, observing, estimating, classifying, ordering, measuring, predicting, collecting, and problem-solving. Classroom pets are an important element of the science curriculum.

- **SOCIALIZATION:** Small group experiences help children learn how to get along with others. Emphasis is put on assisting the children in the expression of feelings, needs, and ideas. As children grow in social and communication skills, teachers encourage them to solve problems through discussion and negotiations.

Infant and Toddler Group

Very young children learn about their environment through their senses (seeing, hearing, tasting, smelling, and touching), through their own actions, and through their social interactions with adults and peers. The staff develop warm, positive relationships with each child, helping her/him feel safe and emotionally secure. The development of a trusting relationship with the staff is critical to the very young child's sense of self and is the foundation for the development of independence. Infants and toddlers learn through their own experiences, trial and error, repetition, imitation, and identification. Our staff provide experiences that help children gain confidence in their own abilities, thus helping develop positive self-esteem. Relationships with people are emphasized.

Children this age are mastering and building on their vocabulary. Through their experiences with simple books, pictures, music, puzzles, and tactile experiences, as well as active play such as jumping, running, and dancing, they learn about themselves and the world around them.

PARENT INVOLVEMENT

Parents have both the right and the responsibility to share in decisions about their children's care and education. During the early years, children are largely dependent on their families for identity, security, care, and a general sense of well-being. Communication between families and teachers helps build mutual understanding and provides consistency for children. Mutual sharing of information and insights about the individual child's needs and developmental strides helps both the family and the program. Teachers encourage parents to observe and participate in their child's education.

Communication with Teachers

Parents and teachers have the opportunity to exchange information regarding the children twice daily, during arrival and departure. This is important to provide

Figure 3.4

continuity between the child's family environment and the center environment. The staff are available and happy to answer questions, discuss important information, or help with problems parents may be experiencing. Since arrival and departure times are sometimes hectic, we can arrange for more in-depth discussion at a time that is more relaxed. The staff welcome parents' comments and suggestions.

Visits

All parents are welcome to visit their children any time during the day. This helps parents and children feel more secure with the center and the staff. Visitation is especially encouraged for very young children. If separation is a problem, and you feel uncomfortable coming in your child's room, the observation booth provides a good solution. We have several parents every year who bring their lunch and eat with their child or eat their lunch while observing in the booth.

Observations

The center has an observation booth located between the preschool room and the infant/toddler room. Parents, friends, and students are welcome to observe at any time. The special one-way glass allows anyone to watch unobserved by the children or staff, as long as the observation room remains dark and the lights remain on in the room being observed. Microphones are set in the ceilings of each room with speakers in the booth to allow those in the booth to hear what is being said in the room. The controls for the microphones are on the south wall. We encourage you to take advantage of this opportunity.

Parent Conferences

The staff observe and monitor your child's developmental progress throughout the year. Parents and/or teachers may request a conference at any time, however, we do encourage you to attend at least two conferences each year. Appointments for all conferences will be arranged at a time suitable to the parent and at a time the teacher has no other responsibilities.

Conferences are held for the purpose of discussing your child's development and learning. The first conference will include an informal sharing of your expectations for your child in our program. At following conferences, we will share with you developmental information about your child that has been observed by our staff, as we continue to learn more about your child through information and insights you share with us.

We also ask for parents to evaluate the program, (i.e., what they like, what they would like added, and any concerns they may have), by completing questionnaires provided at the end of each semester.

We want you to feel free to come and talk with us at any time throughout the year when you may have a concern.

Assessment

Center staff engage in assessment of the children throughout the year. The preschool room uses the Work Sampling Illinois Assessment Guidelines. The infant-toddler room uses the Infant and Toddler Child Observation Record. Teachers will provide you with information relating to this assessment at the first parent teacher conference and throughout the year.

Newsletters

Parents receive weekly newsletters from the child's teachers. These newsletters contain information concerning the day-to-day events and activities ongoing in the classroom. In addition, a monthly newsletter is distributed. These monthly newsletters contain short informative articles and tips for parents, as well as news pertaining to all children in the center. Parents are welcome to submit ideas for the newsletters.

Family Social Events

We hold several events throughout the year to give our families an opportunity to meet informally and to come to know the families of their children's friends, as well as the staff's families. This allows everyone the chance to get better acquainted. These events may include, but are not limited to, an open house before school opens for the fall session, a family potluck in the fall, a family event in December, and a brown bag lunch the last week of school. Many of our family nights are planned and implemented by early childhood methods classes. This provides the college students with valuable experience, as well as offering families a night of unique learning activities. We usually have a large number of families participating in these events. We encourage parents to offer ideas for other events.

Participation

We frequently need volunteers to help with field trips or special events. In addition, we encourage parents to share with the children a special skill, hobby or information about their culture or their job. Please let your child's teacher know of ways you would like to volunteer your time. All parent participation is valued and appreciated.

Parent Library

The center has a resource library housed in the preschool room. We have books, magazines, videotapes, and pamphlets available for check out. These cover a wide variety of parenting topics. A list of materials available for checkout can be obtained from the office. To check out an item, simply ask your child's teacher. Our staff will be happy to show you to the Parent Library or answer any questions about it.

Parent Discussion Groups

Discussion group meetings are offered periodically. These are planned and facilitated by staff and the Early Childhood Education faculty with suggestions from parents as to the topics. Meetings are offered at various times so that all parents have the opportunity to participate. The number of meetings will depend upon parent interest and participation.

Figure 3.4 (cont.)

Discipline: The elementary staff at CUSD #66 is committed to establishing a school climate which nurtures learning and assures the safety and welfare of all students and staff. Our staff promotes student growth in abilities, attitudes, and habits in order to help our students develop a strong sense of self-worth achievement and assume the responsibility of their actions. In addition, our District strives to provide a positive, supportive atmosphere to engage students to become responsible, life-long learners. Our disciplinary approach relies upon behaviors expected in the "real world" that enable people to become successful members of society. The school's expectations for students and staff are:

Be Responsible – Use Self-Control. Be Safe.

Be Caring – Care About Others.

Be Honest – Tell the Truth at All Times.

Be Respectful – Respect Others and Property.

Students meeting these expectations may be recognized in a variety of ways, which may include the following:

- Monthly Buzzy Bee Award (4th grade students)
- Character Coupons – Drawings held for monthly lunch with the principal
- Special recognition at assemblies

Each classroom teacher may have separate celebrations within the classroom to reward students for making good choices. Students and parents will be informed of classroom expectations and incentives at the beginning of the year. Teachers will send home a copy of the disciplinary expectations and parents are encouraged to review the information with their child. A signed copy of the plan must be returned to school.

When it is necessary to use corrective measures for students who have difficulty practicing responsible behavior, the corrective measures taken by teachers or administrators will involve discussion, mutual problem-solving, and conflict management to promote positive behavioral changes. In addition, the following techniques may be utilized:

- **Parental contact**
- **Loss of privileges**
- **Restitution**
- **Behavioral plans or journals**
- **Restricted lunch**
- **Time out from the group**

To help provide a safe environment for all students, the following behaviors will not be tolerated:

- Physical aggression
- Harassment-verbal, physical or sexual

- Property damage school or peer property
- Gross insubordination
- Possession of dangerous, illegal items, or weapons

If a student chooses to engage in any of the above, the student will be sent to the office and a parent contact will be made. The consequences include but are not limited to:

- **Removal from the classroom for a period of time (Time out)**
- **Loss of privileges**
- **Behavior plan**
- **Restitution**
- **Restricted lunch**
- **Detention**
- **Seizure of contraband**
- **Parent/student conference with the principal**
- **Suspension or expulsion**
- **Police involvement**
- **Suspension of bus riding**

Disciplinary measures are intended to help students understand their obligations to themselves and others in the school setting and the roles of law and school district policy and regulations in meeting these obligations.

Explanations for Students and Parents:

Loss of privileges: This will be related to the behavior. For instance, if a child has a problem at recess, then that child could lose a recess privilege for a day.
Restitution: The theory of restitution is that the child needs to restore the environment to its original state before the incident. If a student colors on his/her desk then he/she will clean the desk after school or before earning recess.
Behavioral Plans or Journals: Behavior plans or journals may be used to assist the students in making appropriate choices.
Restricted Lunch: Students may be assigned to a restricted lunch by the principal as a consequence. Students need to report to the office to meet the restricted lunch supervisor. They should bring any work that they need to complete. A behavior plan will be completed during lunch recess time with the supervisor.
Time Out: Time-out is a strategy used to help a student regain control by removing him/her from the group. This cooling-off period is usually followed up with an oral or written problem-solving exercise.
Suspension: Temporary removal from school or from riding a school bus for up to 10 days. A suspended student is prohibited from being on the school grounds and from participating in school activities.

Figure 3.5

DEVELOPING THE HANDBOOK: A SUGGESTED PROCESS

In the last section we discussed forming a handbook committee comprised of the whole faculty, or a representative group, and the principal. Additionally, inviting one or two parents to serve on the handbook committee to provide the parental perspective is a good idea. Some schools find it helpful to survey parents for topics they would like to see addressed in the handbook. Although the committee may find it necessary to narrow the topics included so as not to produce a document that is unwieldy, having as much input as possible will be helpful to you at this stage in your work.

Once topics have been identified, the committee can discuss and clarify the information to be presented in the handbook for each topic. Following consensus on each of the major issues, topics may then be divided among the group members who will assume responsibility for writing a draft of what might appear in the handbook. Or one person may be responsible for creating a draft of the entire handbook, which would then be brought before the committee for review and suggestions for revision. Either way, the entire group needs to have an opportunity to review and approve the final draft.

Some thought will need to go into how best to print and bind the handbook, with consideration given to readability and attractiveness, as well as cost. With computer word processing and desktop publishing programs readily accessible in practically every school, the cost involved in preparing an appealing, reader-friendly document should be minimal. With respect to binding, some schools simply duplicate their handbook on 8½ × 11 inch sheets of white paper and staple the pages together. Others use half sheets, folded in "book" form. Still other schools elect to have their handbooks bound in some way that allows for the addition and/or substitution of pages throughout the year. Cost, again, is a factor. Although initial costs are greater, binding that allows for alterations may be more cost effective in the long run if changes and additions are expected. Either way, an attractive cover printed on heavier card stock and in the school colors serves to publicize your school in a positive way.

With respect to printing the handbook, as school populations become increasingly diverse, the need for translating important school documents into languages other than English becomes a real consideration. Parents for whom English is a second language can perform a great service to schools and to fellow parents by translating the school handbook.

DISSEMINATING THE HANDBOOK

A final issue to be addressed by the group is the distribution of the handbook. How and when the handbook will be shared with parents and key community members bears careful thought and discussion. Some schools distribute the handbook during school registration at the start of a new school year, knowing that they are likely to reach the greatest number of parents at this time. Other schools give each family a handbook during a "back-to-school" night or "orientation" meeting held prior to or during the first weeks of the school year. Handbooks are sometimes mailed to parents not in attendance at this first meeting.

Key consideration should be given to parents' use of the handbook. You may decide to feature the handbook at a classroom, school, or parent organization meeting held during the first week of school. References can then be made to various sections in the handbook, with the principal, teachers, other school personnel, and parent leaders present to share additional information and to answer questions.

Disseminating your school handbook to community agencies/organizations, real estate agencies, health care providers, and so forth is often a good public relations tactic. Much of the voting public no longer has school-age children. Sharing in-depth and accurate information is important, and the cost involved in sending out twenty-five or so additional handbooks is minimal compared to the benefits that could be gained. Think of places where large numbers of individuals are likely to visit, such as doctors' and dentists' offices. One handbook placed in a health clinic has the potential for being read, or at least browsed through, by hundreds of individuals each month!

Finally, school board members and central office staff members should receive a copy of your school handbook. Attached to the handbooks disseminated to these individuals might be a letter from the principal in which the *process* through which the handbook was developed and distributed is briefly described. The sharing of this information helps school board members and district leaders better understand the seriousness with which your school addressed this task and the commitment you feel toward the end product.

EVALUATING AN EXISTING SCHOOL HANDBOOK

The survey appearing in Figure 3.6 may be useful to school personnel and parent leaders who wish to evaluate an existing handbook. Recognizing the uniqueness of each school and its parent population, before responding to the survey the committee may wish to study the items included and suggest other pertinent questions that should be added. Responses to the survey can be compiled and used to assist the committee in revising the handbook to better meet the needs of the parents and the school staff.

CLASSROOM HANDBOOKS

Classroom teachers can also follow the recommendations discussed above for developing a personalized handbook for their own classrooms. The information in a classroom handbook would compliment the district handbook by providing a warm welcome to the classroom and explaining classroom rules and procedures. In Appendix 3 is a handbook prepared by Lynn Traser, a third-grade teacher in Macomb, Illinois.

SCHOOL WEBSITES

With today's technology, one generally expects to find information about each local school and district on the World Wide Web. Websites that are easy to locate and navigate, and that provide helpful and up-to-date information can be a tremendous parent communication tool, as well as one for promoting positive public relations. A search of sites currently located on the Web can reveal many good examples, as well as some poor ones.

Survey of Existing School Handbook

	YES	NO	UNDECIDED	COMMENTS
1. The school handbook is effective in communicating general information about the school program.	☐	☐	☐	
2. The school handbook adequately conveys the school philosophy, mission statement, and purpose.	☐	☐	☐	
3. The school handbook conveys a strong commitment to developing strong home-school partnerships.	☐	☐	☐	
4. The school handbook conveys a positive image for the school.	☐	☐	☐	
5. The school handbook is attractive.	☐	☐	☐	
6. The school handbook is easy to read.	☐	☐	☐	
7. The school handbook is effectively organized, making it easy to locate needed information.	☐	☐	☐	
8. The school handbook is written in clear, concise language that is free from educational jargon.	☐	☐	☐	
9. The school handbook conveys a positive tone and message rather than a negative or authoritarian attitude.	☐	☐	☐	
10. The school handbook reflects shared beliefs and consensus as to the policies, procedures, and regulations described.	☐	☐	☐	
11. The school handbook includes information about all of the topics that should be included in our handbook.	☐	☐	☐	
12. The school handbook includes adequate, up-to-date information about each topic covered.	☐	☐	☐	
13. The school handbook is available in languages other than English, as needed.	☐	☐	☐	

Figure 3.6

Many of the guidelines discussed above for creating handbooks is applicable to the development of a school or classroom Website. Certainly, all Websites affiliated with a particular school system should be presented in an attractive and user-friendly format, provide accurate and timely information, be regularly updated, and convey a positive tone and message. District Websites should include a letter from the Superintendent, general information about the district and each of its schools, calendar, and contact information for district office staff. Also included should be links to each of the school Websites, and links to important documents such as the district's Parent Involvement Plan and any other district-wide efforts for improvement. Most district Websites also include the district mission statement. In Figure 3.7 is an excerpt reprinted with permission from Dr. Fran Karanovich, Superintendent of Macomb CUSD 185 in Illinois, a district that supplies parents with a link to the district's curriculum maps for their classes. The district also provides parents with an access code for viewing their child's grades, attendance, any disciplinary actions taken, and even lunchroom expenditures.

School Websites should compliment the district site and include a welcome letter from the principal, general information about the school and its staff, calendar and information about upcoming events, information about the parent teacher organization, copy of school handbook, and copy of school newsletter. Middle and secondary schools also have information about the

---

Welcome to Macomb CUSD 185's Curriculum Maps!

The Internet has allowed us at the Macomb CUSD #185 to share our curriculum with you each and every day. Gone are the days when school districts put together curriculum maps manually, which took hours of filling out forms, gathering, collating, and duplicating this data, so that it could be distributed and shared with the teachers and community. By contracting with WestJam Enterprises' Curriculum Mapper software package, our district teachers use computers to create curriculum maps for their classes. These curriculum maps serve as a guide for teachers to follow through the school year, just like drivers use road maps as a guide to follow as they travel through a state or a country.

Here is how you can look up a curriculum map:

Step 1: Internet Explorer, Netscape Navigator & AOL browsers all work fine. Because the Curriculum Mapper uses the latest Internet technology, you need version 5.17 (AOL version 8.0) of Internet Explorer or Netscape Navigator to go to this site: http://www.curriculummapper.com/cmap/logon.asp Use the information below to enter your *User ID & Password.* (Note: passwords are case sensitive.) Click the "Enter" button.

Step 2: You will now come to a very brightly colored page. At the top of the page, click on the line that says: "Click Here to Enter Curriculum Mapper." You will now come to a page that says **You are currently logged in as GUEST with (your school name).**

Step 3: Move your cursor to the column on the left side of the screen to "Maps." A drop down menu will appear. Click on "School Overview." You may now view all courses within your school but may not alter or add any information. If you would like to contact a particular teacher, you may click on his/her name and your e-mail program will automatically start. **Online help is available by clicking the "?" on any screen.**

Figure 3.7

school counseling services, and extracurricular activities, including the sports program. Many schools also include links to helpful sites for students and parents, as well as links to attendance, test scores, and grades. There should also be a link to the district office, as well as to the other schools in the district. Photos, when added and updated frequently, encourage parents to visit the site to see their children involved in school activities.

Many teachers, or teams of teachers working together, have developed their own classroom, team, or grade-level Websites. These sites typically provide an introductory welcome letter from the teacher(s), information about the curriculum, classroom newsletter, links to resources needed by the students, and information about special events, such as field trips and parent conferences. In Figure 3.8 is an example of the introductory page from a Website developed by Brian Lexvold at Crestview Middle School in the Cougar Park School District located in Highlands Ranch, Colorado. On the site Mr. Lexvold has included links to many resources that students will need throughout the year. An example of a project in World History is included in

---

8ᵀᴴ Grade Social Studies 2004-2005 - Mr. Lexvold

August 12, 2004

Dear Parents, Guardians, and Students:

    As the school year begins, I would like to extend a warm welcome. I am looking forward to a rewarding academic year.

OVERVIEW
    In eighth grade your student will be studying the Eastern Hemisphere in social studies. This year-long survey course is sequenced geographically starting with Africa and concluding with Japan. This class will explore issues relevant to history, geography, economics, and government. To do this we will use readings, notes, videos, projects, simulations, exams, as well as other assignments.
    Students are expected to review each day's materials and work on assigned work nightly regardless of the due date. To help on cumulative work, including open note <u>semester finals</u>, students are required to keep and organize *all* work. Students wishing to checkout materials overnight may do so after school. Many classroom resources (maps, instructions, grading scales, examples, study guides...) are also available on the resource page of my Website, www.lexvold.com.

STANDARDS
    Students will be assessed on the Chronology (Standard 6) and Location and Place (Standard 3) checkpoints listed below:

  3. LOCATION AND PLACE:
    3.1 Knows the location of major physical features, countries, and cities of the United States and Eastern Hemisphere.
    3.2 Knows how to read, use, and construct thematic and regional maps.

  6. CHRONOLOGY:
    6.1 Understands the chronological organization of historical events.

In addition to your own discussions at home, your student's progress on the standards will be discussed extensively during student-led conferences and you should expect a written standards progress report in November and February. Answers to frequently asked questions regarding standards are available at my Web site: www.lexvold.com.

EXTRA-CREDIT
    There is a limited opportunity to earn extra-credit in my class. Extra credit is awarded for outstanding <u>academic</u> achievement on *regular* assignments as opposed to doing "extra" assignments.

BEHAVIOR
    To achieve a positive learning environment, I expect each student to demonstrate respect and courtesy to <u>all</u> members of the Cresthill community. In a busy school such as ours, these skills are equally important both inside and outside the classroom. Please take time to review the Student Handbook and your own behavioral expectations with your student.

I look forward to a productive year and encourage your involvement and support.

Sincerely,

Brian M. Lexvold
Brian M. Lexvold

Figure 3.8

Figure 3.9. The website also includes information from and about the team of teachers with whom Mr. Lexvold teaches. On the site parents and students can find links to weekly grades for each team member's class, the grading policy, calendar with dates listing when progress reports are to be sent home, information about student-led conferences, and more.

EVALUATING AN EXISTING WEBSITE

In Figure 3.10 you'll find a survey for evaluating school or classroom Websites. These criteria may also be useful for administrators wishing to develop guidelines for Website development within their district and its schools and classrooms. For example, many districts prohibit personal information about staff and parent volunteers and student last names and contact information from being used on sites that are not password-protected. Similarly, links to personal home pages of students or staff are not generally allowed. Some districts have requirements for regular Website maintenance to ensure that the most up-to-date information is being provided and that all links are working properly. Others specify requirements for use of photos and other graphics. These and other guidelines should be discussed and agreed upon so that all Websites associated the district or school are representative of a strong partnership approach.

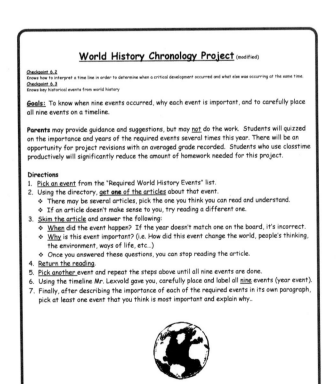

World History Chronology Project (modified)

Checkpoint 6.2
Knows how to interpret a time line in order to determine when a critical development occurred and what else was occurring at the same time.
Checkpoint 6.3
Knows key historical events from world history

Goals: To know when nine events occurred, why each event is important, and to carefully place all nine events on a timeline.

Parents may provide guidance and suggestions, but may <u>not</u> do the work. Students will quizzed on the importance and years of the required events several times this year. There will be an opportunity for project revisions with an averaged grade recorded. Students who use classtime productively will significantly reduce the amount of homework needed for this project.

Directions
1. <u>Pick an event</u> from the "Required World History Events" list.
2. Using the directory, <u>get one</u> of the articles about that event.
   ❖ There may be several articles, pick the one you think you can read and understand.
   ❖ If an article doesn't make sense to you, try reading a different one.
3. <u>Skim the article</u> and answer the following:
   ❖ <u>When</u> did the event happen? If the year doesn't match one on the board, it's incorrect.
   ❖ <u>Why</u> is this event important? (i.e. How did this event change the world, people's thinking, the environment, ways of life, etc...)
   ❖ Once you answered these questions, you can stop reading the article.
4. <u>Return the reading</u>.
5. <u>Pick another</u> event and repeat the steps above until all nine events are done.
6. Using the timeline Mr. Lexvold gave you, carefully place and label all <u>nine</u> events (year event).
7. Finally, after describing the importance of each of the required events in its own paragraph, pick at least one event that you think is most important and explain why..

Figure 9.9a

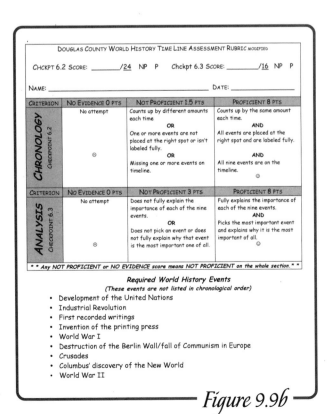

DOUGLAS COUNTY WORLD HISTORY TIME LINE ASSESSMENT RUBRIC MODIFIED

CHCKPT 6.2 SCORE: _____ /24 NP P   Chckpt 6.3 SCORE: _____ /16 NP P

NAME: _____   DATE: _____

CRITERION	NO EVIDENCE 0 PTS	NOT PROFICIENT 1.5 PTS	PROFICIENT 8 PTS
CHRONOLOGY CHECKPOINT 6.2	No attempt ☺	Counts up by different amounts each time **OR** One or more events are not placed at the right spot or isn't labeled fully. **OR** Missing one or more events on timeline.	Counts up by the same amount each time. **AND** All events are placed at the right spot and are labeled fully. **AND** All nine events are on the timeline. ☺
CRITERION	NO EVIDENCE 0 PTS	NOT PROFICIENT 3 PTS	PROFICIENT 8 PTS
ANALYSIS CHECKPOINT 6.3	No attempt ☺	Does not fully explain the importance of each of the nine events. **OR** Does not pick an event or does not fully explain why that event is the most important one of all.	Fully explains the importance of each of the nine events. **AND** Picks the most important event and explains why it is the most important of all. ☺

* * *Any NOT PROFICIENT or NO EVIDENCE score means NOT PROFICIENT on the whole section.* * *

Required World History Events
(These events are not listed in chronological order)
- Development of the United Nations
- Industrial Revolution
- First recorded writings
- Invention of the printing press
- World War I
- Destruction of the Berlin Wall/fall of Communism in Europe
- Crusades
- Columbus' discovery of the New World
- World War II

Figure 9.9b

Survey of Existing Website

	YES	NO	UNDECIDED	COMMENTS
1. The Website is effective in communicating general information about the district/school/classroom program.	☐	☐	☐	
2. The Website conveys a positive image for the district/school/classroom.	☐	☐	☐	
3. The Website has a title and contact information on the homepage.	☐	☐	☐	
4. A consistent style is used on the main pages of the Website.	☐	☐	☐	
5. A consistent navigation system is used on all Websites affiliated with the district.	☐	☐	☐	
6. Each page includes a link to the main homepage and to the school and district page, as applicable.	☐	☐	☐	
7. The Website uses "web safe" colors so they display properly, and color schemes or backgrounds that make the information difficult to read are avoided.	☐	☐	☐	
8. Graphics are used judiciously and serve to enhance, rather than detract from the information being conveyed.	☐	☐	☐	
9. Animated GIF files are used very sparingly and are relatively small so as not to delay the "load time" of the Webpage.	☐	☐	☐	
10. A consistent font, such as "Arial and "Times New Roman" on the PC, or "Helvetica" and "Times" on Macintosh, are used for regular text entries.	☐	☐	☐	
11. The Website includes helpful information for parents and students, including, but not limited to information about the staff, curriculum, calendar, school activities, parent involvement opportunities, and pertinent information regarding school policies and procedures.	☐	☐	☐	
12. The Website is maintained and updated on an ongoing basis to ensure that all information is current and all links are working properly.	☐	☐	☐	
13. Personal contact information about staff, parent volunteers, and students is not included on sites available to the general public.	☐	☐	☐	
14. Pages posted to the main site follow the same guidelines as the main site and no links to personal homepages of staff or students are included.	☐	☐	☐	
15. Guest books, chat areas, and message boards are avoided.	☐	☐	☐	
16. No unauthorized use of copyrighted material appears on the website.	☐	☐	☐	

Figure 3.10

SUMMARY

The process of writing a handbook or developing a Website that reflects a strong partnership approach and makes a warm and reassuring first impression on the reader is not an easy one. Developing statements of philosophy, mission, and purpose that portray a family-centered approach to schooling, deciding on topics to be included, and reaching consensus for information to be shared about each topic require a deep commitment on the part of the school personnel and parent leaders involved in the process. A caution: do not succumb to the tendency to shortchange this process. Your final product—a well-written and carefully constructed handbook or Website that accurately communicates important information about your district, school, or classroom—can best be realized through a shared decision-making approach.

LOOKING AHEAD . . .

In this chapter, criteria for evaluating existing handbooks and Websites were examined and ideas for creating new ones were explored. In the next chapter, we'll begin to address tools for communicating with families and members of the community, beginning with the development of effective letters and newsletters.

REFERENCES

Boethel, M. (2003). *Diversity: School, family, & community connections.* Austin, TX: National Center for Family and Community Connections with Schools.

Boethel, M. (2004). *Readiness: School, family, & community connections.* Austin, TX: National Center for Family and Community Connections with Schools.

Comer, J. P., & Haynes, N. M. (1991). Parent involvement in schools: An ecological approach. *Elementary School Journal, 91*(3): 271–77.

Henderson, A. T., & Mapp, K. L. (2002). *A New Wave of Evidence: The Impact of School, Family, and Community Connections on Student Achievement.* Austin, TX: National Center for Family & Community Connections with Schools, Southwest Educational Development Laboratory.

Knight, B. J. (1987). *Parent involvement assumptions.* Position paper. Manhattan Beach, CA: Manhattan Beach Intermediate School.

National Coalition for Parent Involvement in Education. A Framework for family involvement. *www.ncpie.org/DevelopingPartnerships/* Last accessed on 3/1/05.

Swick, K. (1991). *Teacher-parent partnerships to enhance school success in early childhood education.* Washington, DC: National Education Association.

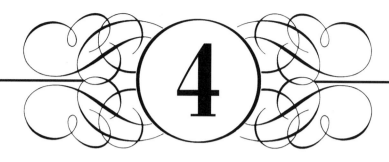

Read All About It! Creating Effective Written Communications for Classrooms and Schools

Strong home-school partnerships require ongoing communication. Well-constructed classroom and school newsletters can be an effective tool for keeping parents up-to-date about school issues and events. And, in this age of accountability, they provide concrete evidence of the efforts of teachers and principals to inform and involve all parents in the education of their children.

INTRODUCTION

Goals for home-school communication include the design of effective forms of communication to reach parents and the provision for two-way communication. This chapter provides criteria for effective letters and newsletters, two good tools for communicating to parents the ongoing activities in a particular classroom, program, school, or district. Then, in the chapters that follow, strategies and tools that serve to initiate two-way communication between the home and school will be discussed.

FRIENDLY LETTERS

Some teachers set the stage for communication by sending a letter to each student and his or her family prior to the start of the new school year. This letter serves as a welcome to the classroom and an introduction to the teacher. It is also an opportunity for the teacher to set expectations and goals, describe the classroom procedures, share reading lists and projects, and describe opportunities for families to be involved in the classroom. Included also might be the telephone numbers where the teacher can be reached and best times for parents to call. In schools where the classroom roster is not available prior to the first day of school, some teachers prepare a letter to send home with the children on the first day of school. This letter often serves as the family's first contact with the teacher and as such should convey a warm, personal introduction. Reproducible letters found in commercial publications may have some helpful ideas, but they do not convey the desired personal touch. When teachers write their own letters, they can use language appropriate for their parent population and include information unique to their own background and classroom. Some teachers find writing letters to parents to be an effective way to share information about the curriculum and strategies for parents to use at home. In Figure 4.1 we see an example of a letter sent home prior to the first week of school by third-grade teacher Lynn Traser. This letter conveyed personal information about the teacher, showed her interest in getting to know each student, and provided information about the first day of school. Letters like the one shown in Figure 4.2 could also be made available to parents and students prior to the start of a new school year. Notice the list of school supplies included, along with ideas for fun summer learning at home.

EWSLETTERS

Writing friendly letters to parents is an excellent way for teachers to share their impressions about classroom happenings. As suggested in the last section, letters can provide a warm, personal touch between the teacher and the students' families. When a variety of information is to be shared, such as announcements about upcoming events, needed supplies and materials, and/or home-learning activities, the use of the friendly-letter format is not as effective as a newsletter format. One reason for this is that parents have to reread the entire letter when they want to review information about just one particular item (for example, the date for an upcoming field trip or the title of a suggested book that can be obtained at the library). Included in this section will be a variety of styles and types of newsletters developed for dissemination by classrooms and by schools.

Format and Style

Newsletters can be formatted in a variety of ways. Principal Byron Sondgeroth's Ingersoll Middle School Newsletter in Figure 4.3 and the Eastview News prepared by Kim Boelkes, principal shown in Figure 4.4 are both examples of newsletters typed in two- and three-column formats, respectively. The use of columns and a smaller font size for the body of each article

August 19, 2004

Dear Skylar,

My name is Mrs. Traser and I am very happy that I am going to be your third grade teacher. I've had a great summer but am ready to go back to school because I'm anxious to meet you and love teaching. I also love thunderstorms, reading, watching movies, listening to music, and taking care of my animals and my family. My husband, Scott, and I have two children who are both in high school.

Are you anxious to start back to school? What is your favorite thing to do at recess? What do you want me to know about you? I can't wait to talk to you on Monday and begin to get to know you. Maybe you can answer some of my questions.

When you come to school on Monday, please go to the gym. I will be watching for you. Our class will sit together until the principal dismisses us, and then I will show you how to line up and walk down the hallway to the classroom. When we get to our classroom I will help you find the desk with your name on it, and you can put your backpack under your desk. We will put your supplies away after we've done our morning jobs.

This is going to be your best school year ever and I can't wait to see you on Monday.

Sincerely,

Mrs. Traser

Figure 4.1

Welcome to 6ᵗʰ grade!

Dear Students,

We look forward to meeting you at the end of August. We have a great school year ahead of us with many new experiences and topics to explore. To keep your brain working over the summer, try to do some of the following activities:

- Read a few novels and discuss them with your family or friends.
- Practice basic math facts, including use of fractions and decimals.
- Visit some local museums and historical places (New Salem, Lincoln's home, Mark Twain's home, and many others)
- Look at the stars and try to locate the Big Dipper, Orion, and other constellations.
- Write letters to friends & family, keep a diary, write in a journal, etc.

To make your 6ᵗʰ grade year a success, you will need to have the following supplies. Some of these will be used in all classes and others are only for a specific subject.

ALL CLASSES: One large binder, paper, dividers, pens, pencils, and 4 computer disks
LANGUAGE ARTS: 200 index cards (3x5 size), folder and two spiral-bound composition notebooks.
MATH: One 5-subject spiral notebook and graph paper.
SOCIAL STUDIES: One folder and colored pencils or markers.
SCIENCE: One folder, one spiral-bound notebook, and safety goggles.
WISH LIST: If you would like to supply your teachers with a little something extra on the first day, we would welcome tissues, masking tape, and/or AAA batteries.

Thank you so much for coming to school ready to learn on the first day. We look forward to seeing you soon!

Your 6ᵗʰ grade teachers

Figure 4.2

or entry allows for more information to be included without having the page appear crowded. Notice the use of a masthead or headline with school or classroom name and date. This part of the newsletter should remain consistent throughout the year to assist readers in easily distinguishing the newsletter from other communications that are sent home by the school. If the format of the newsletter and the pictures and print used on the masthead are changed from month to month, parents and other community members to whom the newsletter is sent have a more difficult time identifying the newsletter. You might also consider always using paper of the same color, keeping in mind that paper that is too brightly colored—hot pinks, greens, yellows, oranges, and fluorescent colors—is very hard on the readers' eyes.

Each entry or article needs to be well-spaced, and the use of bold print and larger font sizes for headings or titles of individual entries helps the reader easily locate specific information. "Bullets" can be used to emphasize important points. Similarly, some entries can be enclosed in boxes, and simple graphics can be used to create interest and make the newsletter more appealing to readers.

Office and classroom computers, now readily available, contribute to better-quality newsletters and significantly decrease the time needed to prepare them. It doesn't take a computer expert to use one of the many desktop publishing programs available for preparing newsletters.

Figure 4.3a

Figure 4.3b

Figure 4.4

As with any school or classroom communication tool, the needs of the audience must be considered. For a newsletter to be effective, parents must be able to *read it* or have access to someone who can read it to them. Use of clear, simple sentence structure and nontechnical language will serve to make the newsletter more readable by groups with varied reading levels. Also, while articles do need to be interesting, state the main facts—who, what, when, where—at the very beginning of the article. Another language-related caution must also be taken into account. In our increasingly diverse population, many families need to have written communications available to them in languages other than English. Although this takes time, the effort will be greatly appreciated by non-English-speaking family members. Sometimes parents or older students can translate the newsletters for the teacher. If so, this promotes the spirit of volunteerism, as well as partnership.

Uses and Contents of Newsletters

Just as newsletters can be formatted in a number of ways, they can serve many purposes. Some teachers send home a weekly, biweekly, or monthly newsletter for informing parents of classroom activities, projects, field trips, and so forth. Major topics of study, concepts, skills, titles of books, due dates for assignments, and other important information can be shared as well. In many classrooms, students routinely contribute to the classroom newsletter by writing news articles about classroom or school events, or by sharing original poems, short stories, and/or reports. Using parents as audiences often motivates children to produce better products. And having student work appear in the newsletter helps give parents a sense of what other children are doing in the classroom and makes parents more aware of what is expected of the students in terms of writing. Sometimes upper-grade students assume full, or almost full, responsibility for planning, writing, editing, and publishing the newsletter. In these classrooms the teacher usually has a "From the teacher . . ." column in each edition.

Some teachers use the classroom newsletter, or certain portions of it, as a vehicle for sharing strategies that parents could use to help their children learn. Study tips for spelling, a strategy for how to help when a child comes to an unknown word in reading, notetaking strategies, and so on provide valuable information aimed at helping parents help their own children. In the newsletter shown in Figure 4.5, Kristin Johnson shares five ways parents can help their young children learn the importance of sharing.

Other content suggestions for classroom newsletters include current achievements of students, reminders of school rules and procedures, notes about class curricular goals, and parent follow-up activities, photographs, and "want ads," or a list of supplies needed for special projects. Specialized handouts prepared for parents and suggestions for parent/child home-learning activities always make good attachments and can also be used to fill up any blank pages when the newsletter is photocopied back-to-back.

Pre-K News

Lincoln Elementary School
Mrs. Johnson
October 2004

Looking Back...
The theme for September was "Apples." We were very busy and had a lot of fun in the classroom! Below is a list of some of the activities we did in September.
- Painted with apples.
- Tasted a variety of apple products.
- Made a graph to determine which apple product the class liked best.
- Visited Murphy's Apple Orchard.
- Made a book about apples.

Looking Ahead...
The theme for October will be "Fall." We will be reading a lot of books about the Fall season. The children will also be involved in many activities that relate to the "Fall" theme. We will be doing activities that involve leaves, pumpkins, and nuts. We will also be working on graphing, sorting, getting along with others, and recognizing letter sounds. We are all looking forward to learning about the Fall season!

Accomplishments...
- Keegan can write his name!
- Carly can tie her shoes all by herself!
- Matthew can recognize all of the letters in the alphabet!
- Lily is doing a great job sharing!
- Ryan finished his painting of an apple tree!

☺ Keep up the good work!

There are many children's books in the classroom library that relate to this month's theme. Below is a list of some of the books. I encourage you to come in and check them out!
1. <u>Fresh Fall Leaves</u> by Betsy Franco
2. <u>Fall Leaves Fall!</u> by Zoe Hall
3. <u>It's Pumpkin Time!</u> by Zoe Hall
4. <u>The Biggest Pumpkin Ever</u> by Steven Kroll
5. <u>Fall is Here! I Love It!</u> by Elaine Good

Figure 4.5a

Encouraging Sharing...
Many parents are faced with the agonizing question, "How can I help my child understand that sharing is important?" It is normal for young children to have difficulty with sharing. However, there are a few things that you can do to encourage sharing both at home and at school. You can encourage sharing by...
- Putting your child in charge of the sharing.
  "We only have one cookie, what is the best way to share it?"
- Pointing out the advantages of sharing.
  "If you give her half of your cake, and she gives you half of her cookie, then you'll have two snacks."
- Allowing time for children to think about their actions.
  "When Mary is ready to share, she will let us know."
- Showing appreciation for sharing when it occurs.
  "Thank you for giving me one of your dolls to play with. It is really pretty."
- Modeling sharing yourself.
  "Now I want to give you a drink of my juice."

Source: Parenting With Confidence Inc.

Curl Up With a Good Book...
<u>1-2-3 Magic: Effective Discipline for Children 2 – 12</u> by Thomas W. Phelan
This book addresses the difficult task of child discipline. It describes an effective approach to handling misbehavior both at home and in public places. You can find this book in the school library.

Recipe...
Do you need a recipe for a healthy snack? If you do, below is a great recipe that is easy for both parents and children!
Ingredients (per person):
- 1 Tbsp. spreadable cream cheese
- 1 dried apple ring
- 1 tsp. applesauce
- 1 cinnamon graham cracker square
"Stack the cream cheese, applesauce, and apple ring on top of a cinnamon graham cracker square. Now, bite into Fall!

Want Ads...
We need volunteers for the field trip to the pumpkin patch on October 29th. We will leave at 9:00 a.m. and return at 11:45 a.m. Please, let me know if you are interested in going. We would love to have you!

Figure 4.5b

An alternative to the traditional classroom newsletter comes from Baskwill (1992), who designed "Ask Me About"—a newsletter for the parents of the children in her early childhood class. Since parents have many questions about school (such as "What did you do today?") and children typically respond with "Nothing" (or worse yet "We just played") Baskwill developed a newsletter designed to give parents "insider's information" so they would know which questions to ask of their children. Before sending home each weekly newsletter, Baskwill discusses it with the children so they leave expecting to discuss school activities with their family members. An "Ask Me About" section could be a regular feature of any classroom newsletter and one that parents would probably look forward to reading. Note the "Be sure to ask your child about . . ." section in Mandy Ricco's newsletter shown in Figure 4.6.

School Newsletters

In addition to sending home classroom newsletters, many schools also send home a school newsletter to promote a strong school spirit and a sense of "community" within the families. The principal generally has a column or

Mrs. Ricco's 1st Grade

October Newsletter

Captivating Read Alouds!
(Located at our school and public Libraries)

1. The Spider and the Fly by Tony DiTerlizzi. This tricky spider must lure the fly into his web, your family will enjoy the beautiful illustrations and the clever tale.

2. You Read to Me, I'll Read to You by Mary Ann Hoberman. This is a collection of very short stories that are intended to be read aloud between two speakers. The funny characters and sing-song verses are fun to read and hear.

A Parenting Must Read
(Available to borrow from me)

1. Games With Books by Peggy Kale. This book is full of ideas to help you read with your child. The author uses 28 children's books and 89 games to create a fun-filled learning experience.

Parent Information Article

1. www.literacyconnections.com This website gives tips on reading aloud in order to make reading to your child one of your best parenting experiences.

2. www.pbs.org/launchingread This website offers ways to read, write and tell stories together with your child. This will provide an opportunity to applaud your young reader and beginning story writer.

Edible Spiders: Since this month we are learning about insects, we have discussed how spiders are not insects because they have eight legs. You can create the eight legged creatures with oreo cookies(for the body), pull and peel licorice(for the legs), orange wedges (for the head) and white tube frosting for the eyes and fangs.

Be Sure to Ask Your Child About...

Their journal. Each day we take time to write in our journals. You can help your child come up with ideas for future writing and ask them about what they wrote today!

Our homemade insect book. We compiled facts and stories about our favorite insects and made a colorful collection. Everyone will have a chance to bring the book home to share.

Figure 4.6a

Willits Primary School

School Reminders

**Book orders due Oct 3rd
**11:30 Dismissal on Oct 5th
**No School Oct 11th
**Parent/Teacher Conference Oct 18th-22nd
**Family Night Oct 22nd
**Book Fair Oct 25th-29th
**Class Fall Party Oct 29th

Homework

-Each night students should read their leveled book that is sent home with them.

-Every night students should study their "Word Wall" words.

-There will also be additional homework throughout the week on Tuesdays and Thursdays. Please be sure to check their "Daily Folder" and sign the sheet on the back.

-Your child chooses a library book each day to share with you at night.

Classroom News

Math

~~We will be working on ways to make the numbers 1-10. This is the beginning step that will lead towards learning the addition facts.

~~We will also be graphing facts about ourselves and looking at the average.

Word Wall Words

as   are   map   bug   have

Spelling Words

of   the   put

Reading

~~We will be reading books about insects and butterflies.

~~We will make our own books on fall and the seasons.

Writing

~~Students are practicing their D'Nealian handwriting skills.

~~We write in our journals each day and share one entry every week.

Science/Social Studies

~~We will be exploring fall and the changing of the seasons and harvesting.

Help Wanted

• We could use help during our fall party with costumes and treats.

• If you are able to come into the classroom and read aloud to the students we would LOVE to have you!! You can bring your own books or I can provide them for you.

• We are still collecting Box Tops for Education. Our class has collected the most out of the whole school so far, so thank you and keep up the good work!!

Questions

If you have questions or concerns of any kind. I can be reached anytime. If I am not available just leave your name and where I can reach you and I will get back to you as soon as I can. The school phone number is 734-4031 or my home number is 734-5555. My email address is ricco@willitschool.com.

Figure 4.6b

---

letter to the parents. An example from Macomb, Illinois principal, Ed Fulkerson, is shown in Figure 4.7. Also included in the school newsletter is a calendar of upcoming events and information about parent organizations, committees, or advisory groups. In Figures 4.8 and 4.9 are examples of these found in Maureen Hazell's Edison School newsletter. Original writings or artwork created by the students and short, informative articles on high-interest topics such as health and nutrition, learning strategies, and developmental milestones may also be included. In Figure 4.10 is shown an excerpt from Westview School's newsletter with parent tips provided by the district's Behavior Intervention Consultant, Dale Therrien. Many school newsletters contain information about recent or upcoming classroom activities, which helps to broaden family awareness of the school-wide program and serves to acquaint family members with teachers and classrooms other than the ones their children are enrolled in. The Ingersoll Middle School newsletter shown earlier in Figure 4.3 contains a variety of information including details regarding a Spring Book Fair, school attendance rates, end-of-year award programs, a community service project, and more.

October 2004

A message from Mr. Fulkerson...

It's hard to believe that August and September have disappeared and that the fall harvest is upon us. The evenings are turning cooler, the trees are starting to show some color and days are getting shorter. The school year is well into full swing, and I am thankful for the opportunity to work with all the supportive parents, eager students, and professional staff.

Research indicates that the number one indicator of student performance is parent involvement and reading at home. For young children, this is as simple as reading to your child at home and talking about the story. For children who are learning to read, this can entail taking turns reading aloud and talking about passages. For those of you who are doing this, keep it up! For the rest of you, it is never too late to start.

In order to assist in this research, we are delivering our reading services at Lincoln in a different way this school year to most of our first, second, and third graders. (Kindergarten will continue to use the Waterford Early Childhood Reading program.) The reading block has been extended by 10 minutes, and students not only work with their classroom teachers but also with a reading specialist and a program assistant. This allows students an opportunity to work in a smaller group setting that is at the level of each individual student. For those students who need additional support we can offer it! For those students who are excelling we can help them to continue without slowing them down. And for those students right in the middle we can help them by creating smaller groups that enhance achievement. We look forward to continued improvement and are counting on you to help us out at home by actively reading with your child!

Tardiness continues to be a problem at Lincoln for many families. Please help us out. Right now this is your child's job and they need to be here by 7:50 (7:45 if eating breakfast). Help set them up for success in life by emulating the importance of being at their job on time!

Have a great month of October and keep our troops in your thoughts and prayers.

— Figure 4.7 —

P.T.O. NEWS
Saturday Afternoon at the Movies

Edison School students and their families are invited to a Saturday afternoon at the movies in the Edison auditorium at 2:00 p.m. on Saturday, February 12. Please come join us for an afternoon of fun, film, pop, and popcorn! Students must be accompanied by a parent to attend this event. The event is funded by our P.T.O., and all are welcome to attend.

— Figure 4.8 —

Finally, when considering an appropriate length for a newsletter, one sheet printed both front and back is a good length for a weekly newsletter. For monthly newsletters, two pages of paper printed on front and back of each, for a total of four pages, is generally sufficient. If newsletters will be mailed to any of the families or community members, you may want to consider leaving the back page blank for affixing an address label. If no newsletters are to be mailed, or if envelopes will be used, then try to not have *blank*

Strategic Planning Forum
Parents—You are invited!

If you didn't attend the October forum, the Macomb School District invites you to
participate in small discussion groups at the next forum on March 3, from 6:30–8:30 p.m.
in the Macomb High School Library. Your ideas, concerns, and suggestions for a stronger
school district will be gathered along with input from other community members,
students, and staff to help set the direction for a 3–5 year strategic plan for the District.
Forum topics (determined through a survey distributed last spring) include student
learning, teacher quality, district spending/funding, safety, and communication. Please be
a part of this very important process. Your input is sought!

Figure 4.9

Mr. T
Behavior Consultant

Like most of you Westview parents, I don't work in my children's school. And because I
love my children as much as you do yours, I ask them about their day. Are you frequently
disappointed by this conversation in your home: "How was your day?" "Okay." "What
did you do today?" "Nothing."

To get our children to open up, try asking more detailed questions. Experiment with a
few of these, and see if they lead somewhere.
  • Who did you sit next to at lunch?
  • Did you go to art today? What materials did you use?
  • Tell me something about your Accelerated Reader book.
  • Did you earn a CARE card today? What good choice did you make to earn it?
  • Who is your enrichment teacher this week?

Dale Therrien 647-3400 x2530
Canton Union School District No. 66

Figure 4.10

---

pages included. Instead, consider including a list of suggested books, video and
movie reviews, or additional samples of students' work.

Commercial Newsletters

There are several commercial parent newsletters that can be purchased in
bulk for distribution to parents. Although they generally contain good information, we caution schools not to use them as *substitutes* for a classroom or
school newsletter, because commercial newsletters do not project an image
unique to your particular school or classroom. The fact that they are mass
produced is clearly evident to the parents who receive them. Secondly, they
do not include the kinds of personal information that entices many parents
to actually read the newsletter. Finally, if a commercial newsletter is the *only*
regularly written communication device, the message to parents may be that
school staff think that parent involvement is something that can be *purchased*

or that school staff members do not have the time, expertise, or desire to develop their own personal communications to parents.

Having issued these cautions, there are several good commercially available parent communication tools that could be used effectively. For example, the Parent Institute publishes *Parents make the difference!,* monthly newsletters with educational articles and practical ideas for parents to help their children. Two newsletters, a grades K–6 edition and a grades 7–12 edition, are available in English and Spanish. The Parent Institute also has an individual subscription rate that allows the use of their articles in a school's own newsletter or other parent materials. This allows a school staff to take advantage of well-written articles and at the same time to create their own newsletter, one which conveys a warm and *personal* message uniquely suited to their audience and to their particular school situation. The Parent Institute also publishes monthly activity calendars with parent/child interaction ideas for daily home-learning. Some classroom teachers develop similar calendars with activities that reflect the learning taking place in that room. The one shown in Figure 4.11 was created by Michelle Hunt.

*P*RINTING AND DISTRIBUTION

Printing and distributing classroom and school newsletters require careful consideration. Once the time and effort have been expended to create a good newsletter, you want to do everything you can to ensure that it will be read by the target audience. Some teachers and schools drastically reduce the chances that parents will read the newsletter by duplicating it in a sloppy or difficult-to-read way. Use of too-bright or fluorescent paper, too-small print size, ditto-machine duplication, dot-matrix printers, or photocopying that is too light, all reduce the readability and diminish the effectiveness of the newsletter. A black-line copier provides the best results, and use of the same-color paper for each newsletter—a color that is not hard on the eyes—increases recognizability. Access to a copier that allows reductions is helpful since students' work can often be reduced several times without sacrificing quality or readability. Finally, before the newsletter is printed, be sure to have it proofread. Even the most careful writers make typos!

Most newsletters, both classroom and school newsletters, are typically sent home with the students. Increase the chances that the newsletters will reach the parents by sending home the newsletters on the same day of each week or month. In the initial communications—the handbook, Open House, parent meeting—let parents know when to expect the newsletter and the procedure that will be used for distribution. Parents will come to look for the newsletter if they expect it to arrive home with their child each Monday or Friday or first school day of a new month, for example. Having deadlines helps keep teachers and principals from letting this particular commitment slide by without completion, an added benefit to establishing a regular distribution schedule.

JUNE 2005

SUNDAY	MONDAY	TUESDAY	WEDNESDAY	THURSDAY	FRIDAY	SATURDAY
			1 Go for a walk. Talk about temperature and seasons. Find a thermometer and read it together!	2 On a clear night see how many stars you can count. Have Lucky Charms for a bedtime snack.	3 Reread a favorite story, and have your child tell you one thing that happened at the beginning, middle, and end.	4 Go to the grocery store and have your child help you pay. Talk about money!
5 Paint self-portraits while looking in the mirror.	6 Catch fireflies and watch them glow. Read about fireflies.	7 Create "masterpieces" with Playdo and let them dry.	8 Make a leaf drawing by picking a leaf, covering it with a piece of paper and coloring over it.	9 Make pet rocks and give them names.	10 Have your child tell you a story using lunch bag puppets.	11 Make a bird feeder using a pinecone, peanut butter, and bird seed. Watch what happens!
12 Carve your favorite animal out of a bar of soap using a plastic knife.	13 Look through your family photo album. Talk about people who live far away.	14 Take a drive and talk about the colors on a stop light. Go over what each color means.	15 Take a picnic as a family and talk about what you see and do.	16 Put chocolate pudding on a plate and practice writing letters and numbers.	17 Use magnifying glasses and go for a bug hunt!	18 Tell your child four things you love about them. Write it down and give it to them!
19 Father's Day Color a picture or make an award for Dad or Grandpa.	20 Identify the food groups represented in your refrigerator.	21 Read a non-fiction book about a favorite animal.	22 Sing your favorite songs together using your hands and arms to show the action of the words.	23 Using magnetic letters and a cookie sheet help your child spell his/her name. Spell the name of family members.	24 Review the safety rules you have in and around your house.	25 Watch a movie with your child. Afterward, talk about what he/she did or did not like about it.
26 Read, *The Foot Book* by Dr. Seuss. Count how many feet are in your family.	27 Have your child draw a picture. Ask your child to tell you a story about the picture.	28 Have your child help you set the dinner table. Make place cards for the members of your family.	29 Look at a calendar and circle special days. Talk about the days of the week and upcoming events.	30 Read *Beauty and the Beast* and *The Little Mermaid* Compare and contrast the differences.		

Figure 4.11

Some schools send home the newsletters in a laminated brown envelope. Inside the envelope is a sign-off sheet for parents' signatures, indicating receipt of the newsletter. Such a procedure takes some initial planning and setup costs, but it does result in more newsletters getting into the hands of the parents. Few schools mail newsletters to students' homes, for the obvious reasons of cost. Exceptions do exist, and one in particular bears mentioning. As we discussed in previous chapters, the family structure today is very different from that of several years ago. Large numbers of children in each school have two families—and in two homes. Whether or not the parents have a joint-custody arrangement (unless extenuating circumstances as a court order prohibiting or severely limiting visitation exist), *both* parents should be given the opportunity to receive information from the school, including classroom and school newsletters. Oftentimes the child or custodial parent is expected to photocopy information and share it with the noncustodial parent. This is difficult, especially if the parents are experiencing communications problems or if one parent lives in another town. Since additional costs are involved, some teachers and schools issue an invitation for parents in this situation to pay a fee to cover the added costs. Other schools ask that noncustodial parents send self-addressed, stamped envelopes for mailing newsletters and other communication. Schools and classrooms with Websites should routinely post their newsletters on their site. Archiving past newsletters is recommended so parents and community members have these for future reference.

School newsletters should also be disseminated to members of the central office staff and the school board. Staff and board members need to know the efforts being made at your school to foster good relations with parents through increased communication. Reading your school newsletter will also give central office staff and school board members important "inside information" about the beneficial activities taking place at your school.

Regular distribution of the school newsletter in print or electronic format to key businesses, social and religious organizations, government or private social service agencies, and other schools in the area is a worthwhile endeavor. Since the majority of community members may not have children in school, the school newsletter can function as an important public relations tool. Furthermore, sending the newsletter to radio and television stations and to the local newspapers may result in increased coverage for your school events and activities. Any opportunity to increase the public's awareness and knowledge of public education should not be overlooked. *Share the good news!*

*E*VALUATING NEWSLETTERS

It is a good idea to conduct a periodic evaluation of the newsletters sent home. One way to do this is to send home a brief survey in one of your school newsletters. Asking parents if the newsletter is meeting their needs not only conveys respect for parents' opinions but also lets them know that you are willing to make adjustments that will result in better communication. Asking whether the adults *read* the newsletter, as well as asking about the frequency of publication, method of distribution, ease of readability, and helpfulness of content will give you important information and direction for future change. A sample survey is included in Figure 4.12.

Please tell us what you think . . .

Our school newsletter is one tool we use to keep you informed about school events and programs and involved in your child's education. We want this tool to be as effective as possible. Would you please take a few moments to share with us your opinions about our newsletter?

1. Do you receive each monthly edition of the newsletter?
   YES   NO   SOMETIMES
   Comment:

2. Do you read each newsletter?
   YES   NO   SOMETIMES
   Comment:

3. Do you think our newsletter is published
   YES   NO   SOMETIMES
   Comment:

4. Is our newsletter easy to read?
   YES   NO   SOMETIMES
   Comment:

5. Does our newsletter keep you informed about school events and activities?
   YES   NO   SOMETIMES
   Comment:

6. Does our newsletter provide you with helpful ideas to try at home with your child?
   YES   NO   SOMETIMES
   Comment:

7. How could our newsletter be more helpful for you?
   Comment:

Figure 4.12

Time required for constructing letters and newsletters can be kept to a minimum through the use of computers and desktop-publishing software with newsletter options. Advance consideration of newsletter format, color of paper, readability factors, and content to be included greatly increases the probability that the newsletter will be well-received by parents and also reduces time needed for developing subsequent newsletters. In Figure 4.13 is a checklist that may prove helpful as you evaluate your school or classroom newsletter.

Newsletter Evaluation Form

Consider each criterion, then rate your newsletter from 1 (low) to 5 (high) on each item. Have two or more individuals rate the same newsletter, then compare and discuss your ratings and arrive at a consensus for each. List ways to improve those criteria not rated a 5.

FORMAT

❧ Simple, attractive masthead or heading with name and date
   1 2 3 4 5

❧ Good layout with two or three columns
   1 2 3 4 5

❧ Ample space between entries
   1 2 3 4 5

❧ Type or print size not too small—easy to read
   1 2 3 4 5

❧ Good choice of paper color—not hard on the eyes, yet will stand out
   1 2 3 4 5

❧ Good use of attractive graphics
   1 2 3 4 5

❧ Appropriate use of headings and subheadings for each entry
   1 2 3 4 5

❧ High-quality reproduction
   1 2 3 4 5

❧ Appropriate length—one or two pages and printed on both sides of the paper
   1 2 3 4 5

CONTENT

❧ Includes calendar of upcoming events
   1 2 3 4 5

❧ Includes sufficient "news" about school programs and activities
   1 2 3 4 5

❧ Includes helpful home-learning strategies and parent education information/ideas
   1 2 3 4 5

❧ Includes samples of student work, as appropriate
   1 2 3 4 5

Figure 4.13

STYLE
- Entries are written in language appropriate for intended audience
  - 1 2 3 4 5
- Entries are written in simple, direct language
  - 1 2 3 4 5
- Newsletter conveys a warm, personal tone
  - 1 2 3 4 5
- Newsletter is free of spelling and/or grammatical errors
  - 1 2 3 4 5

DISSEMINATION
- Provisions are made for translation of newsletter into languages other than English, as needed
  - 1 2 3 4 5
- Newsletter is disseminated on the same day of each week or month
  - 1 2 3 4 5
- Newsletter is made available to joint custody and non-custodial parents
  - 1 2 3 4 5
- Newsletter is disseminated to local media, key businesses, social service and religious organizations, government service agencies
  - 1 2 3 4 5
- Newsletter is disseminated to members of the central office staff and the school board
  - 1 2 3 4 5
- Measures are taken to increase the probability that all parents receive the newsletter (i.e., sending home in a brown envelope, having a sign-off sheet for parents)
  - 1 2 3 4 5

EVALUATION
- Periodic evaluation of the newsletter is conducted
  - 1 2 3 4 5
- Feedback from evaluations is shared with entire school staff
  - 1 2 3 4 5
- Evaluation data are used to make revisions that will increase the quality and/or effectiveness of the newsletter
  - 1 2 3 4 5

Figure 4.13 (cont.)

Summary

Even though the communication flow is primarily one-way, the advantages of sending home newsletters on at least a monthly basis are far-reaching. A carefully constructed newsletter sends a very positive message to parents and helps them feel confident that the teacher and school staff are knowledgeable and organized. Newsletters serve a variety of purposes, including keeping parents up-to-date about school events and programs, sharing strategies for home-learning, and reporting classroom news.

The questions that follow have been designed to help you think about the major points conveyed in this chapter. The answers you give may help you determine whether or not the newsletters in your school are a true reflection of your beliefs.

For your consideration . . .

1. Each teacher should convey to parents the expectations and goals of the classroom, as well as routine procedures, and special projects or assignments.   YES   NO

2. A school newsletter helps to promote a strong school spirit and a sense of "community" within the families.   YES   NO

3. Newsletters serve a variety of purposes, including keeping parents up-to-date about school events and programs, sharing strategies for home-learning, and reporting classroom news.   YES   NO

4. School leaders should help teachers reduce the time required for constructing letters and newsletters by making available computers and desktop-publishing software with newsletter options.   YES   NO

5. In the case of blended families, when at all possible both parents should be given the opportunity to receive information from the school, including classroom and school newsletters.   YES   NO

6. Using parents as audiences via school and classroom newsletters often motivates children to do better.   YES   NO

7. Having students' work appear in the newsletter helps give parents a sense of what other children are doing in the classroom and makes parents more aware of what is expected of the students in terms of writing.   YES   NO

8. It is a good idea to conduct a periodic evaluation of the newsletters sent home by the school staff.   YES   NO

LOOKING AHEAD . . .

In this chapter the creation of effective letters and newsletters was discussed. In the chapters that follow, varying ways to promote two-way communication between home and school will be explored.

REFERENCE

Baskwill, J. (1992). Ask me about: A newsletter with a difference. *Teaching K–8, 22* (8): 44–45.

Getting to Know You . . .
Open Houses and Parent Programs

When we received the invitation for my daughter's school's annual Open House, I couldn't help being less than enthused. I anticipated the typical routine . . . a brief smile and "hello" to the principal and teacher . . . a quick look at the room . . . a few murmured greetings to fellow parents . . . and a cookie from the table set up in the school gym. WOW! Was I surprised! When we entered the hallway that led to Mrs. Breheny's kindergarten room we were greeted warmly and asked to participate in the graphing activities that were posted on the hallway walls. One graph directed the children to find the clothespin with their name written on it and place it on either the "Yes" or "No" section of a circle graph that asked the question "Do you like bugs?" When we entered the room, the teacher greeted us warmly and explained that the room was set up into learning centers similar to the ones the children would use in kindergarten. The first theme study, bugs, was reflected in the activities currently displayed in each center. We were to visit each center, read the parent information that described the purpose for each center, and participate with our child in the activity. For about forty-five minutes we counted plastic bugs and graphed the total at the math center, constructed playdough creatures at the art center (and also picked up the recipe and volunteered to bring the playdough for the month of December), wrote at the writing center, and listened to a story in the book and listening area. At the end of the hour we had a much clearer idea of the daily routine and had been well-acquainted with not only what our child was learning that year but also why and how.

Too many times Open Houses become just what their name implies. The school is open for parents to walk through and exchange greetings and pleasantries with teachers. The bulletin boards are full and children's work is on display, but attitudes of both teachers and parents often reflect the effort expended on this event—halfhearted! Considered a duty by teachers and parents, even the enthusiasm from the children cannot overcome the fact that very little organization or planning has taken place. Unfortunately, the result is that parents come away with very little new information or insights about the school.

Some teachers, like the one described above, do engage in extensive planning before an Open House. With clear goals in mind they set about creating an atmosphere conducive to good parental involvement. And their efforts are rewarded as parents leave feeling as if they know more about the teacher, the classroom, and the program. These parents are more likely to be receptive to further involvement throughout the year. Camille Breheny, a kindergarten teacher at St. Paul School in Macomb, Illinois, is one such teacher. The Open House described in the opening paragraph was held only for new kindergarten students and their families prior to the first day of school. Later, when the rest of the school hosted their Open House, parents of the kindergarten children were surprised to see how their children had transformed the room. Original writing and works of art covered almost every available space. Displayed on the chart stand and on the front classroom wall were large charts with stories, classroom news, and questions dictated by the children. At each of the learning centers stood chairs covered with large—almost life-sized—creations resembling the children themselves. The children had painted their faces on paper plates and added yarn hair. Mrs. Breheny had taped each paper plate to a clothes hanger which was then attached to a child-sized chair. Finally, an "outgrown" shirt or dress sent from home was pulled over the coathanger and arranged to look as if the child were sitting in the chair. Each learning center was set up with materials that created the illusion of children seated in chairs working at the centers. After touring each center, parents received further information about the program and had an opportunity to view their child's work. This Open House, which sought to recreate the child's normal, everyday classroom environment, was a far cry from traditional ones where parents stood around an "almost too-clean-to-be-believed room" leafing through a stack of papers that had been placed on their child's desk.

The first grade teachers at Fulton Elementary School in Fulton, Illinois developed the survey shown in Figure 5.1. As you can tell, they were seeking information about the home literacy environment, as well as parents' preferences for at-school family activities, such as special classroom visitations called "Dads & Donuts" and "Moms & Muffins." They also included open-ended questions so parents could share their concerns and recommendations.

Hosting an Open House does generate a certain amount of stress. Some teachers naturally approach Open Houses and parent programs as they would a dinner party: *Everything must be perfect.* These teachers must be helped to realize that the emphasis must be on the *children* and *their* work. When the

WELCOME TO FIRST GRADE!

In an effort to better serve the students and parents in first grade, we invite you to take a few minutes of your time to take a survey. By answering the questions below, we will be better prepared to teach the students as well as to offer programs and events that interest you, the parent.
Thank you again for your time,
First Grade Teachers

1. My child is involved in the following activities:

_____   swim lessons   _____   baseball/softball

_____   girl/boy scouts   _____   soccer

_____   wrestling   _____   4 H

OTHER: _____

2. At home, I would find the following reading materials:

_____   books   _____   newspaper

_____   magazines   _____   reading toys (Leap Frog)

OTHER: _____

3. I would attend the following after-school programs:

_____   reading night   _____   Math Night

_____   PTO   _____   Open House

_____   X-Mas Program   _____   Computer Night

_____   Back-To-School Night

4. I would attend the following school-time programs:

_____   Dads and Donuts   _____   Moms and Muffins

_____   Grandparents and Granola

_____   Book Fairs   _____   Holiday Parties

_____   Field Trips   _____   Field Day

5. I would like to see Fulton Elementary School offer:

6. What concerns do you have about your first grader, the teacher, or Fulton Elementary School in general?

Figure 5.1

teacher has done the majority of the work in readying the room, it shows! Most parents have a pretty good idea of what their children are capable of doing on their own—and they know when they are viewing the teacher's work rather than that of the children. Worse still, children have very little owner-ship or interest in projects created largely by the teacher. Some teachers fear that parents will point out unconventional art or spelling—such as a painting of a blue tree by a kindergarten child—and think that the teacher is not doing a good job educating the children. These parents need to be helped to understand age-appropriate expectations and practices. Rather than cover up what the children are really capable of doing on their own, the teacher can use this opportunity to engage parents in informal conversations about the developmental appropriateness of the childrens' work. The teacher may also provide handouts that explain expectations for the children and methods used.

Having a goal—something you want to accomplish through the Open House—makes the event more beneficial for all concerned. For example, the first Open House of the school year at most schools is held every September. The traditional "walk-through" Open Houses are typically referred to as "Meet the Teacher" night. Although attendance is usually good, since the event is held early in the year, the teachers have little time to get to know the students. As a result, the evening serves little purpose other than for teachers to try to match a few names and faces and to share a brief overview of the curriculum. Some schools have changed the focus for their Open Houses and are hosting a "Meet the Parents" night. The goal is to get to know the parents by having them talk and write about their children. Parents are encouraged to think and talk about their children's strengths and to set goals they believe their children need to pursue during the year. Some teachers create surveys and questionnaires that children can fill out with their parents during the Open House. As the children and their parents enter the room, they are greeted warmly by the teacher. They are then directed to the sheet of questions placed on each child's desk. Parents sit with their children to discuss questions such as "What are your child's strongest academic areas?"; "Does your child ever sit down and read by himself/herself?"; "Does your child engage in writing activities at home?"; and "What are your child's interests?" Other questions are designed to find out about the child's particular learning styles. Usually a parent reads the question and then discusses it with the child. Then, either parent or child writes the answer. The questions cause parents to stop and reflect on their children's development and help them begin to acquire the language they need to discuss their child's academic strengths. As teachers walk around the room, they gain valuable knowledge about the parents and the children. At the end of the questionnaire is a place for parents to list, after corroborating with the child, areas of strength, as well as what they need to work on during the year. Sometimes questions such as "What does your child need additional work on academically?" and "What should be your child's three main academic goals for the first nine weeks?" are included to prompt their responses. Through these surveys parents learn how important it is for them to share with the teacher what they know about their child, and they became acquainted with what the teacher looks for in each student. The surveys become a source of discussion during the first parent-teacher conference held in October, and throughout the year they serve as a reminder of goals set by the child and his or her parents.

Open Houses need not be reserved only for the start of the school year. Many schools host at least one other Open House where parents and children have an opportunity to visit all of the classrooms in the school.

The First Day Foundation (*www.firstday.org*) has a free downloadable booklet of ideas for making the first day of school a celebration for the entire community. Some of the ideas included are: inviting parents and community members to a picnic breakfast or lunch on the school grounds followed by a tour of the school; decorating the school with balloons and welcome back banners and posters; hosting an informational meeting for parents; and having booths staffed by the parent/teacher organization, counselors, public health service representatives, and more. Primary and elementary parents may accompany their children to their classrooms, while older students' parents may be invited to attend a pep rally. Area businesses are asked to help fund the event in many districts and parents' employers are asked to grant them permission to attend. Schools that have implemented special first day family and community events have reported increased parent participation and volunteerism due to these special opening of school activities.

Alison Lewsis's school hosts an Open House Carnival/Cookout that is a gigantic success (see Figure 5.2). Parents listen to a twenty- to thirty-minute presentation by the classroom teacher and then gather outside for a cookout with free hotdogs, soda, popcorn, cotton candy, sno-cones, music and more. What a wonderful start to a new year! Later in the year families are invited to a Pajamarama. Children and parents come in their pajamas with their favorite books, teddy bears, blankets, and flashlights. Everyone meets in the gym to share stories, with the town mayor serving as guest reader. Drawings are help for new books. A copy of the letter sent to parents by the school principal appears in Figure 5.3.

It is important that Open Houses, programs, and events serve as an enhancement to instruction and not as an interruption or distraction. When an event such as an Open House is scheduled as a culminating event for a theme study, it becomes a very powerful motivator for children to produce their best work.

To my family,

I am inviting you to come to my school for Open House tomorrow, Tuesday, September 23. You can see my classroom, meet my teacher, and we are going to have hot dogs! There will be a cookout outside on the playground after visiting my school. I am making a video at school and I really want you to come. It starts at 5:15... I hope you can make it!☺

Love,

Figure 5.2

MADISON ELEMENTARY SCHOOL

2435 Maine Street • Quincy, Illinois 62301 • 217-223-6096

Where Everyone Strives to Achieve

JIM BAILEY	**JIL JOHNSON**
Principal	Secretary

To: Madison Parents
Re: Pajamarama
Fr: Jim Bailey
Dt: February, 2005

On Thursday, February 17, Madison School will hold a Pajamarama Read Night. Parents and students are invited to enjoy a night of reading in the Madison School gym.

Festivities begin in the gym at 6:15 p.m. and will continue until 7:30. Participants will be able to share the joy of reading and will also have the opportunity to listen to a guest reader —— Mayor Chuck Scholz.

Please come dressed in your favorite **"Night Clothes"!** Sleeping bags, pillows, flashlights, and stuffed animals are also in order. Don't forget to bring your favorite book(s) to read as a family. **Please remember that all students must be accompanied by their parents, grandparents, or guardians. Sounds like great fun!**

What:	**Madison School Pajamarama Read Night**
When:	**Thursday, February 17, 2005**
Where:	**Madison School Gym**
Time:	**6:15 – 7:30 p.m.**
Dress:	**Pajamas, robes, other appropriate "night clothes", slippers**
What To Bring:	**Sleeping bags, blankets, pillows, stuffed animals, *favorite books*, flashlights**
Rules:	**All students must be accompanied by an adult (parent, grandparent, guardian). Students must stay with adults at all times and not run around throughout the gym or building. The goal is for families to enjoy quiet reading time together.**

Quincy Public Schools - District No. 172

Figure 5.3

Oakwood School in Hannibal, Missouri opens their doors to families and the community to both showcase and celebrate children's academic accomplishments. For example, one year their schoolwide theme was "Celebrating Our Heritage." Children in each classroom began early in the year to think about their past and to talk about what the central focus of their study and subsequent projects would be. Since one of the goals for the Open House was to build a relationship with the community, teachers worked to involve many people from the community as part of the study. The fifth

Madison   Literacy   Week

In addition to the "Pajamarama", the following events are scheduled throughout the week of February 14 – February 17:

Monday, Feb. 14 -   "Valentines Day". Students are encouraged to share and read valentines with each other.

Tuesday, Feb. 15 -   "Favorite Character Day". Students are encouraged (parent discretion) to dress like a favorite "character" from a book. Students are encouraged to bring their books to school for shared reading.

Wednesday, Feb. 16-   "Guest Reader Day" and "Mix and Match Day". Teachers may invite guest readers from the community to read to their classrooms. Students are also encouraged (parent discretion) to wear mis-matched (style/color) clothing and/or crazy hair styles. 3rd grade students are also invited to read to other classrooms – teachers, please arrange individually.

Thursday, Feb. 17-   "We Love To Read In Our Pajamas Day." Students are encouraged (parent discretion) to wear "night clothes" to school (pajamas, robes, slippers, etc.). Regular shoes must be worn to and from school and at recess. Slippers may be worn during the day (when inside) if desired. All classes are encouraged to spend the entire day reading. "Hallway Reading" (stuffed animals, pillows, blankets, water bottles, etc.) is an option. From 2:15 – 2:45, the entire school will participate in D.E.A.R. (Drop Everything and Read). Each student at Madison will be given a free book.

Thursday, Feb. 17-   "Pajamarama". (See full description).
(evening)

Figure 5.3 (cont.)

grade was studying the American colonial period and decided they would tie in a study of the lifestyle of the people of that time and turn their exhibit into a folk life festival for the evening of the Open House. The three fifth-grade classes held their fair in the school library with booths where quilts, candles, bread, noodles, and spiced oranges were being made. Primitive tools, scrimshaw, a spinning wheel, and various kinds of needlework were all being demonstrated. The research conducted by the students involved all of the crafts, and a committee was formed to develop a pamphlet to "advertise" each colony and encourage people to settle there. Representatives from the local Chamber of Commerce taught the children what information was needed in order to promote an area, and an assistant editor for the local newspaper taught them how to create a layout for their pamphlet.

The fourth-grade students were involved in a study of ecology, so they researched and shared the heritage we lose when nature is threatened. For the activity, fossils had been buried in plaster, and children "uncovered" the past at a table equipped with hammers and picks. On the evening of the Open House, results of their study of endangered plants and animals were shared, with the songs of whales as background music.

The third grade studied the history of Ellis Island and all the nationalities that came through the port. Their projects included a study of these people's cultures, their reasons for coming, and what they brought with them. Reports of the studies were displayed along with the flags and emblems from each country involved. Especially enticing were the samples of foods from each country, which were prepared by the students' parents and grandparents.

The second-grade classes were studying African folktales and the contributions of African-American culture to our heritage. Their study included contributions made in the areas of history, music, art, literature, and food.

The first grade studied the state in which they lived—Missouri—and what it was like before becoming a state. They conducted library research to find out about natural resources and interviewed parents, grandparents, and, in some cases, even great-grandparents to learn what life was like in earlier years. Children wrote biographies of their relatives' lives that included their memories about their own school days, important historical events, and generally what it was like in the past. These stories of "living history" were displayed during the Open House.

Even the kindergarten classes participated in the Heritage Fair. They had been learning about space and had no trouble displaying what the space program had contributed to our emerging heritage in the way of freezed-dried food, materials, and tales of extraterrestrial life.

To bring all of the various classroom activities together and to encourage families to visit all rooms, the school published a "passport" in which each grade had a page advertising its exhibit. Children were placed at each door to stamp the passports as families entered, and parents were encouraged by their children to get all pages stamped. The passports were sold at the main door for $2 per family to help defray the cost of the fair.

The Heritage Fair was very well-attended, mostly due to the children's enthusiasm. This enthusiasm was catching and caused families to stay and visit each classroom exhibit. Central office personnel and members of the community also visited the school that evening. Many of them had been involved during the study as guest speakers and in various classroom projects, so they had gained an insight into how much children learn when they are actively involved in the research process. Their comments were positive and centered around what our true goals are for elementary school children.

PARENT PROGRAMS

Sometimes families of children in one particular grade or classroom may be invited to attend a meeting for purposes of sharing school programs and curriculum. In these situations the classroom has generally been involved in a theme study that is winding down. A part of all theme study involves discussion as to how the knowledge gained will be shared with others. A natural culminating event for a study involves inviting parents and others into the classroom to "show off" projects and stages through which children progressed to learn about and develop the projects. Sheila Shearer, a second-grade teacher in Macomb, Illinois, enjoys sharing with the children her experiences of growing up in Hawaii. The children learn a great deal about Hawaiian history, geography, language, people, and culture. They learn from Sheila and also by reading books, writing, and by exchanging monthly letters with pen pals in Hawaii. In their letters they ask several questions about life in Hawaii and answer questions their pen pals asked of them in their last letters. They also learn a big repertoire of Hawaiian songs, stick dances, and hula dances—all of which come together in a marvelous program complete with handmade leis, "grass" skirts, and musical instruments. Throughout the program children pause in their singing and dancing to talk about the various facts they have learned about Hawaii. Elise Howard invites families to attend a "Night of the Notables." Her students study a famous historical figure and write a research paper. They then dress as the person they wrote about and make a presentation to family and friends.

Another program presented by kindergarten children at Oakwood School was a big hit among the parents. The children had researched and written or dictated reports about bears, cheetahs, and elephants. In conjunction with the P.E. teacher, they learned a number of animal games, songs, and dances. The children first presented their songs and dances, then read aloud their reports. The grand finale was an appearance by "little Tarzan!" The children were proud of their accomplishments, and the parents were quite impressed with how much their children had learned and could convey to others.

A final note about parent programs: No matter how hard you try to avoid scheduling conflicts, regardless of when parent programs take place, some parents simply cannot attend. Surveying parents to find out when they are most likely to be able to attend is a good idea. If there is no clear consensus, perhaps programs can be alternated between daytime and evening.

To further increase the probability that families will attend, consider sending invitations to special events. An invitation, unlike a flyer or announcement, conveys a more personal tone. Invitations can take many forms. Very nice invitations can be created with a desktop publishing program and then copied or printed for dissemination to large numbers of families. For smaller events, classroom teachers may want to fill out invitations purchased from greeting card companies. Students can also write their own invitations to their families. These are particularly effective in generating

For your consideration . . .

Following is a list of questions relating to Open Houses and parent meetings. Answering these questions may help you begin to assess your own feelings and experiences with respect to traditional Open Houses and parent meetings.

1. Information shared during Open Houses should be authentic for the curriculum and reflect what has been going on in the classroom.   **YES   NO**

2. At the start of the school year, parents should be encouraged to think and talk about their children's strengths and to set goals they believe their children need to pursue during the year.   **YES   NO**

3. Open Houses and parent meetings should be planned so as to achieve goals agreed on by the principal and faculty.   **YES   NO**

4. One of the goals of Open Houses and parent meetings should be to educate parents as to classroom curricular goals and strategies used to achieve those goals.   **YES   NO**

5. Open Houses, programs, and events should serve as an enhancement to instruction and not become an interruption or distraction.   **YES   NO**

6. Open Houses and parent meetings can serve as vehicles for children to share with family and community members what they have learned.   **YES   NO**

7. Schools should survey parents to find out when they are most likely to attend Open Houses and parent meetings.   **YES   NO**

attendance at events where students' work will be displayed, such as an author's tea or science fair. Many teachers find that they get a particularly good response when the family member's names are included on the invitation and when they request an RSVP. Regardless of the occasion, an invitation conveys more than an announcement. It conveys a sincere desire to have the family represented at a special event.

For parents who must miss a program, some schools have found that videotaping is a good alternative. Since most parents have access to a videoplayer—or are willing to rent one from a video store—most classroom programs are routinely videotaped for either checkout by parents, viewing by the children themselves, or for documenting student performance and growth over time. To help defray costs, a blank videocassette could be added to the supply list for each child. Parents have been very responsive to this medium for learning about what is happening in the classroom. Some teachers have even begun to videotape various in-classroom presentations and activities to which parents were not specially invited. These videos really help parents understand what goes on in the classroom—and as a result, parents are much more supportive.

SUMMARY

In this chapter the importance of goal setting and planning for Open Houses was demonstrated. Through examples, a number of ways that Open Houses have served to foster positive relationships with families and community members were shared. Although parents attending an Open House can sometimes learn strategies for helping their child at home, the primary purpose of an Open House is to communicate with others what children are doing and learning at school.

LOOKING AHEAD . . .

The next chapter includes a variety of strategies designed to help parents better fulfill their roles as parents and teachers. Particular emphasis will be placed on how to plan and deliver effective parent education workshops and meetings based on parents' interests and the needs of their children.

REFERENCE

First Day Foundation. *First Day Activity Guide*, Bennington, Vermont. *www.firstday.org* or call 1-877-First Day.

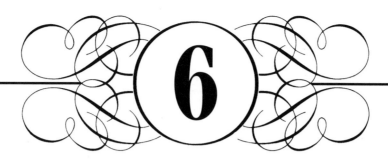

Planning and Delivering an Effective Parent Education Program

When well-meaning parents use strategies that are not only ineffective but also detrimental, children's confidence can be destroyed, particularly in the areas of reading and writing. Overzealous parents can drill a child endlessly on phonetic elements to the point where, when faced with an unknown word in print, the only strategy the child attempts is to "sound out" the word—without regard for word structure or comprehension. Similarly, children's writing may be reduced to only those words for which they have memorized the conventional spelling, especially when they are faced with a parent who is unwilling to appreciate the conventions of spelling the child is developing and the content the child is trying to express.

INTRODUCTION

The problem of ineffective parent help at home is one that must be addressed directly, with patience and care. Direct intervention must take place in the form of parent education, the goal of which is to teach parents strategies they can use at home to help their child. As you will recall from Chapter 1, research indicates that home-learning activities and gains in student achievement have a strong correlation. And, as discussed in Chapter 2, parents' lack of knowledge about how to help is a barrier to more effective parent involvement. In this chapter several strategies for helping parents gain the skills they need to help their children develop academically, as well as in other areas will be explored.

PARENT EDUCATION AND NO CHILD LEFT BEHIND

Schools receiving assistance from Title I, Part A must offer training and information to build parents' capacity for being more effectively involved in their children's education. According to USDE's document, *Parental Involvement Guidance* (2004):

> It is the responsibility of schools and LEAs to help parents understand topics that will help them become equal partners with educators in improving their children's academic achievement. Schools and LEAs must help parents understand such things as the State's academic content and academic achievement standards; state and local academic assessments, including alternative assessments; and how to monitor their child's progress and work with educators to improve the achievement of their child (p. 26).

> Schools must also offer family literacy services if a substantial number of parents have low literacy skills and/or do not have a high school diploma. Suggestions for parent training include "providing information about the essential components of reading instruction," "literacy programs that bond families around reading and using the public library," and "training parents in the use of the Internet to enable them to access their children's homework, communicate with teachers, and review information posted about schools . . . (p. 27).

CREATING PARENT SPACES AND PARENT EDUCATION CENTERS

A parent space or parent education center is a place within a school that parents can call their own. Though a whole room would be ideal, that kind of space is usually not available. A corner of a room, a space at the end of the hallway, or a special section of the library can become a place where parents can find information and materials especially for them. A bulletin board for displaying messages and parent education tips, a small table, a book rack, and a couple of chairs are all that is needed to establish this area. The space should be made as inviting as possible, and parents should know of its availability.

Some schools and districts have secured grant monies to enable the hiring of a parent coordinator. If such a person is available, her or his office is, ideally, located in the parent education center. If there are no funds to cover this position, some schools utilize a teacher aide or a school volunteer to work in the parent center a few hours a day. Schools might also consider giving a couple of interested teachers some release time from their classrooms to serve as co-coordinators of the parent center. These teachers could be responsible for coordinating the efforts of other teachers and volunteers.

In a parent space or parent education center, parents can receive general parenting tips and information, ideas for helping their children in home-learning activities, and assistance in contacting community and social service agencies, to name a few of the informational services provided by some parent centers. Parents might also find follow-up information such as materials, books, tapes, or videos that they can check out to learn more about a topic or to help them apply strategies discussed in a parent meeting. If the area is large enough, the parent space may become the gathering place for parent support groups, conferences, and meetings. A parent space can also function as an information center where notices and literature about policies, procedures, upcoming events, and other pertinent school and community information could be displayed. Appendix 4 includes a listing of organizations and other groups that sponsor Websites with excellent resources for parent education.

*P*ARENT EDUCATION: WHAT DO PARENTS NEED TO KNOW?

Perhaps the most logical place to start when considering parent education is with the parents themselves. Asking parents what their needs are *before* planning topics and educational opportunities is always a good idea. If the school has an active parent-teacher organization, a brainstorming session could be held for the purpose of listing topics and areas of need or interest. After a list is generated, groups of four or five adults can work to prioritize, and if necessary limit, the list to the top five or ten ideas. The groups could then share their ideas with each other, with one person serving as recorder to "tally" the number of groups wanting each topic. The topic with the most tallies would, for example, become priority number one. This list of topics could either be adopted for that year or could first be sent to all parents for their consideration and suggestions.

A survey might also be constructed for distribution to parents during registration or during the first Open House. For non-English-speaking parents, or for parents who have difficulty reading or writing, adult volunteers might be available to translate and to read the survey questions and record the individual's responses. In Figure 6.1 is a list of topics to which parents might respond by indicating whether they were *very, moderately,* or *not at all* interested. Space could be provided for parents to add other topics of interest.

In Figure 6.2 is a sample of a survey adapted from a Head Start Center. Parents are asked to check areas where they feel inadequate, as well as areas in which they would like training.

Surveys might include items for parents to indicate the most convenient time for attending parent meetings and workshops, whether or not childcare and/or transportation will be necessary, and whether any special accommodations need to be made. If many parents require language assistance, perhaps translators—parents who speak the same language and are willing to serve as "parent-mentors"—could be made available. There may also be a need to offer sessions in languages other than English. Finally, since some parents will not be available to attend meetings, or for whatever reason do not feel

Parent Education Interest Survey

For each topic, please indicate whether you are "V = very," "M = moderately," or "N = not at all" interested. This information will help us select parent education materials and plan workshops for the year.

_____ 1. Guiding children's behavior.

_____ 2. Is my child normal? What to expect as young children grow and develop.

_____ 3. Language Development: What's normal and what's not.

_____ 4. Nutrition: Tips for healthy eating.

_____ 5. Substance Abuse: Recognizing the signs.

_____ 6. Helping your child become a reader and a writer.

_____ 7. Supporting your child's math-learning and problem-solving skills.

_____ 8. Television: The good, the bad, and the ugly.

_____ 9. Helping your child develop good work habits.

_____ 10. Building self-esteem in children: Positive times together.

_____ 11. Resources in the community: Where to go for help.

_____ 12. Parent Effectiveness Training (PET).

_____ 13. Systematic Training for Effective Parenting (STEP).

_____ 14. Active Parenting.

_____ 15. Health Tips: When to call the doctor.

Figure 6.1

comfortable attending a group meeting, a variety of parent education options need to be presented. To help in determining preferred formats, the survey might include a list of options such as home visits, books, pamphlets and reading materials, parent education videos, and individual conferences with the teacher or other resource person.

When grandparents are serving as a primary caregiver for grandchildren, they need to be made aware of and involved in the school's parent education activities. AARP offers a number of resources to help grandparents care for and enhance the academic achievement of their grandchildren, including a monthly email newsletter, *Care and Family.* Many resources are available to members and non-members through their Website at *http://www.aarp.org.*

Parent Questionnaire

Name: _____   Date: _____

Address: _____   Phone: _____

Child(ren)'s name(s): _____

Directions: Please check in the appropriate column ("Very difficult," "Somewhat difficult," or "No problem") for each item below.

In my job as parent I have the hardest time in:

	VERY DIFFICULT	SOMEWHAT DIFFICULT	NO PROBLEM
1. Being an only parent	_____	_____	_____
2. Guiding my child's behavior	_____	_____	_____
3. Providing good nutrition	_____	_____	_____
4. Making time to listen and play with my child	_____	_____	_____
5. Having patience and understanding	_____	_____	_____
6. Understanding my child's growth	_____	_____	_____
7. Knowing what to do when my child is sick	_____	_____	_____
8. Other (please state)	_____	_____	_____

To do my job better as a parent I would like training in:

1. Child growth/development   _____
2. Child guidance   _____
3. Nutrition   _____
4. Health/First aid   _____
5. CPR   _____
6. Early learning strategies   _____
7. Working with special needs children   _____

Figure 6.2

*I*NVOLVING PARENTS IN CHILDREN'S LANGUAGE AND LITERACY DEVELOPMENT

Children of even the most disadvantaged circumstances are exposed to print early in their lives. Whether it be through grocery store specials, television, or mail delivered to the home, literacy events do occur—they are just not always recognized as such. According to Meisels (2001) a first step in involving parents in the literacy development of their children is to try to determine the "match" between the literacies of homes and those of the school. Dr. Patricia Edwards, a professor and researcher at the University of Michigan, is one researcher who has worked to discover ways in which the literacies and aspirations found in the homes of low-income parents can be integrated into beginning reading programs. As Edwards' points out: "Oftentimes the outsider does not recognize the everyday literacy practices and interactions that are embedded within the family cultures as literacy practices" (1991, p. 13).

Determining the Literacy Match: Family Stories

Working with both teachers and parents of children in prekindergarten through grade three, Edwards has developed separate programs for each group. Teachers in Edwards' study learn how to observe and interview parents in order to gather stories that illustrate the types of literacy practices taking place in the home. As discussed in her book with co-authors Heather Pleasants and Sara Franklin, *A Path to Follow: Learning to Listen to Parents* (1999), the questions teachers have typically asked parents center on the context of the school rather than the home. Citing Leichter's (1981) work, Edwards and her colleagues describe ways to gain information about the physical environment of the home, the interpersonal interaction between the child and others in the home, and the emotional and motivational climates in the home that condition a child for literacy and achievement. Teachers then use the knowledge they gain to help the parents become more effective supporters of their children's education.

To get started in gathering "family stories," these authors recommend that teachers spend time thinking about: (1) what they already know about a particular family; (2) questions they have that, if answered, might lead to an increased understanding about how to better help the child in reading; and (3) some places or opportunities that could provide a means for talking with these particular parents. In *A Path to Follow,* the authors provide a list of questions for teachers' use in selecting questions for parent interviews. The questions are divided into the following categories: (1) parent/child routines and activities; (2) child literacy history; (3) teachable moments; (4) home life; (5) educational experiences; (6) parents' beliefs about their child; (7) child's time with others; (8) parent/sibling/child relationship; (9) parents' hobbies, activities, and interest in books; (10) parent/teacher relationship; and (11) parents' school history—ideas about school.

The authors suggest that teachers might select just a few questions for the initial conversation, and then follow-up at a later time with additional questions. Although, tape recording these conversations is recommended, this is something teachers would want to first discuss with the parents, assuring them that the information will be kept strictly confidential and used only to benefit their child's literacy learning. Schools and teachers must be careful not to do what these authors call taking a "father-knows-best" approach with parents. Rather, they must realize that while teachers may have expertise on pedagogy, curriculum, and child development, they are not experts on individual families or children. Gathering parent stories is one way of validating the importance of the parents' perspectives on their children and their children's education.

Once information is gained through parent conversations, the teacher is to first list both positive and negative impressions gained during the conversation, and next to record the facts of the conversation using a "beginning," "middle," and "ending" format. Parent comments that really "stick out" in the teacher's mind should also be recorded. After considering this information, the teacher should pinpoint areas of confusion or puzzlement, missing information, and additional questions that might be asked. Finally, the teacher would make a list of instructional ideas that would benefit the student and involve the parent. The goal is to use the information from the family story to help the student in the classroom and support their learning at home.

For example, in one vignette shared by the authors, a teacher learns that a student is very interested in hockey but is afraid to take risks and so will not become involved in any team sports for fear of failure. The teacher wonders where the fear of failure comes from and plans to initiate a unit on sports with various cooperative groups researching different sports. As the student reads and writes about this topic of interest, the teacher hopes he will be able to demonstrate some of the fundamentals of hockey to his peers. She also plans a visit from some of the high school hockey players, after which she hopes to engage the student in an informal conversation about whether he has ever thought about being on a hockey team.

Edwards' (1991) study also included offering "Talking Your Way to Literacy" sessions designed to help parents acquire the language of schooling so that they would be able to successfully communicate with teachers and administrators. A similar type of program was developed in Illinois in 1995 entitled *Parents as Educational Partners (PEP) Curriculum: A School-Related Curriculum for Language Minority Parents*. The PEP curriculum consists of seven instructional units, which contain duplicable, classroom-ready materials appropriate for a wide range of English proficiency levels. The units, developed from needs assessments of language minority parents and school district teaching and administrative staff, may only be purchased in conjunction with PEP Curriculum training. For information contact the Adult Learning Resource Center in Des Plaines, Illinois (1-847-803-3535).

A language and literacy training program for parents of children age 0–3 is available through Baby TALK in Decatur, Illinois. Baby TALK is a non-profit organization serving families of very young children. Since 1986, hundreds of professionals from schools, libraries, and health-care and social service agencies have been trained in the Baby TALK method and the Touchpoints model based on the research and practice of Dr. T. Berry Brazelton in collaboration with Harvard Children's Hospital. Information about these programs can be obtained from their Website at *http://www.babytalk.org.*

Utilizing Print Resources for Parent Education

Some parents prefer to have access to books, pamphlets, and other printed materials for learning about particular topics or seeking answers to specific questions. The materials selected for use by parents should reflect up-to-date information, be written in a clear, readable manner in language appropriate for the parent audience, and be free from stereotypes and bias. Information on a wide variety of topics should be available, and parent input via surveys, questionnaires, and informal requests should be solicited on a regular basis to ensure that materials ordered and/or collected reflect parental needs. In Appendix 5 is a list of books and other print materials appropriate for inclusion in a parent library. If lack of space prohibits having a separate parent space or parent library, perhaps print materials might be housed on a special shelf of the school library—or even in the public library. If an arrangement is made with the public library, perhaps other schools in the system will want to be involved in contributing books and other print materials. In addition, the library staff may appreciate recommendations for titles of books in the area of parent education to be purchased with library funds.

Some teachers, including those at Oakwood School, have developed parent notebooks for lending to parents. A large three-ring binder contains a wide variety of journal articles, handouts, pamphlets, and brochures. Some teachers put each item in a plastic sleeve before inserting it into the notebook. Others use pocket dividers for containing items that cannot be hole-punched. Dividers with plastic tabs are used to categorize the items according to subject or interest area, with new categories frequently developed. For example, one first-grade teacher's notebook contains a section with information about beginning reading; another with information about stages of writing and invented spelling; another holds information about "hands-on" mathematics and the importance of manipulatives, patterning and problem-solving, and other sections contain information about social development, emotional development and childhood fears, motor development, and enhancing aesthetic, or artistic abilities. At the start of the school year, the teacher sends home a letter explaining the notebook and listing the types of articles included.

In addition to sending a letter and contents, the notebook is displayed during Open House, and parents are encouraged either to request information about a specific topic or simply to check out the entire notebook to browse for articles of interest. A parent response sheet accompanies the notebook each time it is checked out. This sheet provides regular feedback and helps the teacher learn about areas where parents would like to see more information.

*P*ARENT EDUCATION VIDEO LIBRARY

Since most parents have access to a video player, a collection of videos suitable for parent education can provide yet another option for some parents. In her book, *A Framework for Understanding Poverty,* Ruby Payne states, "Parent training and contact through video is invaluable, particularly in poor communities. One characteristic of poor communities is that virtually everyone has a VCR because of the value placed on entertainment" (p. 95). Payne describes a school in Illinois where each teacher made a 15-minute video containing a personal introduction, overview of the curriculum, and student expectations. Each teacher closed with an invitation to visit or call. Copies of the tape were rotated among the students in each class and were immensely successful in helping parents who were illiterate and/or without transportation gain an understanding of their child's teacher and classroom. The videos selected should be of good quality, contain important up-to-date information on a variety of topics of interest to parents, be appealing to the parents for whom they were selected, and be free from cultural or racial bias. In addition, the information should be presented in a clear, straightforward manner, using language suitable for the parent clientele.

Videotapes may be developed "in house" by schools or districts or purchased commercially. Videos ten to fifteen minutes in length can be effective in demonstrating single strategies for at-home-learning: for example, how to interact with a young child during the bedtime story routine or what to do when a child comes to a printed word he or she doesn't know. Videotaping parent workshops, particularly workshops with guest speakers, is another idea. Having these tapes is particularly helpful when parents have a strong interest in a topic but cannot attend the workshop.

Good commercial videos are widely available, many at very reasonable costs. Professional organizations are one good source to explore. For example, the International Reading Association has developed videos that are appropriate for parental viewing. A list of recommended videos is provided in Appendix 6, along with publisher information.

Some communities have become involved in supporting parent education video libraries. With donations from businesses and local members of the community, videotapes have been acquired and housed at a central location, such as a public library. This arrangement benefits both the schools and the community. Through a cooperative agreement with a local video store in Macomb, Illinois, parent education videos donated by various sources were bar-coded and housed in a special "family" section of the store. These videos were available for check out, free-of-charge, to the public. The video tapes in this collection covered a wide range of issues related to the care and education of young children, from how to cope with stress to knowing when to take a child to the doctor.

HOME-LEARNING ACTIVITIES

Research indicates that parents want teachers to tell them how they can help their child at home. Much emphasis is currently being placed on helping parents gain strategies for helping their children with academic learning at home. Homework is not a new idea; in fact, it has been a part of American education since formal schooling began (USDE 2002). According to *Helping Your Child with Homework,* a booklet published by the U.S. Department of Education, homework ". . . is important because it can improve children's thinking and memory. It can help them to develop positive study skills and habits that will serve them well throughout their lives. It can encourage them to use time well, to learn independently and to take responsibility for their work." There simply are not enough hours in the school day, and teacher time with individual children is limited. Parents who take an interest in the homework their children are bringing home can make a real difference in their children's achievement. There are other benefits for parents, however, helping children with homework enables parents to gain an understanding of what their children are learning in school and provides an opportunity for enhanced parent-child communication.

Many teachers provide a special "homework folder" and let parents know to check the folder each evening for work to be completed at home. Although helping with homework may sound like a relatively simple task, many parents find that it isn't an easy as it may seem. Parents often have questions about how much help they should be giving and how much their child should be expected to do on their own. They may also be concerned about the amount of time a particular task may take. Teachers can address these questions in parent meetings, or in videos or printed materials sent home. The USDE publication mentioned earlier, *Helping Your Child with Homework,* is an excellent resource for teachers to use to help parents understand the purpose of homework, ways to establish a homework routine and home study area, and ideas for monitoring homework. It is available at no cost online and in English and Spanish at *http://www.ed.gov/print/parents/academic/help/homework/ index.html* or by calling 1-877-433-7827 (1-877-4ED-PUBS). Bryan and Sullivan-Burstein (1997) offer a number of homework suggestions for teachers to use in developing homework: (1) note how long an assignment should take students to complete and then have the students write down how long they actually spent on the assignment; (2) add smiling, frowning and neutral faces on the corner of each assignment and ask students to circle the one that best describes their feeling about the assignment; (3) use games and fun activities as homework activities; (4) make assignments relevant to the students' lives outside the classroom; (5) suggest activities parents can do with their children; (6) ask parents to sign completed homework; and (7) reward homework completion.

The "Take Home Bags" created by Mandy Ricco were developed to foster parent/child interaction in literacy and math activities at home. Attached to each bag is a laminated notecard with a list of the contents of the bag and directions for the parent. Each bag contains all the materials needed for the family to do the activities together at home. Three of Mandy's Take Home Bags are described in Figure 6.3. Home learning activities are appropriate for students at all grade levels. Those shown in Figure 6.4 were developed by Jan Jacobus, a math teacher at Ingersoll Middle School.

Sheila Shearer, a second-grade teacher in Macomb, Illinois, has created twenty "author" bags for her students to check out for at-home use. Each bag contains a brief bibliography of the featured author, several books written by the author, and enrichment activities. A card listing the contents is attached to each bag. In addition to these bags, a special bear with its own bag of books and toys is rotated among the students with a journal for recording its experiences at each child's home. These take-home materials help foster a positive relationship between home and school and let parents know that parental involvement is a priority with this teacher.

Activities designed for parent and child interaction can be developed by the classroom teacher or purchased from a commercial publishing company. Activities should require no special equipment or supplies, should be written in a clear and easily understood manner, and should be relatively easy for the child to do with parental guidance. Most teachers prefer to review the activity directions before sending the sheet home, so that children will already be familiar with what they are to do. Whenever possible, the home-learning activity should relate to a study that is ongoing in the classroom. For example, a home-learning activity for children studying bugs might be to interview family members to find out how they feel about various types of bugs. In a study of seeds, children may be asked to take a walk with their parents to gather seeds to bring to school. Sometimes home-learning activities involve watching for current events on the news or watching the weather to record daily rainfall or temperatures. Family members assist by discussing the news and/or weather with the student. Most teachers find that having parents "sign off" verifying that the activity was completed is a good idea and one that increases the probability that parents will participate with their child. It is also a good idea to include at the bottom of each activity a place for parents to comment about whether their child could easily perform the task with adult guidance, the time required to complete the activity, and whether the task appeared to be beneficial. The addition of this comment section is especially important when using commercial materials that have not been developed expressly for your particular students and their families.

Alphabet Take Home Activity Bag

Willits Elementary School   **Mrs. Ricco's 1st Grade**

Dear Parents,
We have an exciting activity planned for you and your child. Take this opportunity to just relax and enjoy the time spent with your child. Please return the bag to school by this coming Friday. Thank you for your continued support.

Activities:
1. *Read Aloud Book*: Read the *Alphabet Mystery* story with your child. Instruct them to read the letters in the alphabet when they see them.
2. *Magnetic Letters:* Have your child arrange the letters in alphabetic order.
3. *Read Aloud:* Next, read together *Harold's ABC* by Crockett Johnson, with your child. Again, have them identify each of the letters and/or their sounds when you read.
4. *Purple Crayon Writing:* Have your child take the purple crayon and write each of the letters of the alphabet in alphabetic order on the provided writing paper. If they need help, have them look at the magnets.
5. *Purple Crayon Drawing:* Now encourage your child to turn their purple letter writings into drawings like Harold's in the book.

Objectives:
1. Letter recognition and sounds
2. Alphabetic order
3. Practice forming letters and handwriting
4. Print concepts

Materials Included in the Bag:
1. *Alphabet Mystery* book by Audrey Wood and Bruce Wood
2. *Harold's ABC* picture book by Crockett Johnson
3. Purple crayon
4. Writing paper
5. Magnetic alphabet letters

Parents: Please return all items on list to school. Thank you for your help!

Figure 6.3a

Gingerbread Take Home Activity Bag

Willits Elementary School   **Mrs. Ricco's 1st Grade**

Dear Parents,
We have an exciting activity planned for you and your child. Take this opportunity to just relax and enjoy the time spent with your child. Please return the bag by this Friday. Thank you for your continued support.

Activities:
1. *Read Aloud Book*: Read *Gingerbread Baby* by Jan Brett. Take the time to look closely at the pictures with your child. Discover all of the special touches that Jan Brett puts into her illustrations.
2. *Gingerbread Cookies*: Just add one cup of water and two tablespoons of butter to the box of mix. Cook and decorate cookies according to the directions on the box.
3. *Gingerbread Game*: Use your gingerbread cookies as placeholders for the game. Roll the die and move your gingerbread cookie according to the directions on the game board.

Objectives:
1. Engage in critical thinking and verbal activity
2. Appreciate illustrations
3. Counting and measuring
4. Purposeful reading
5. Small motor skills
6. One-on-one correspondence when counting
7. Following directions

Materials Included in the Bag:
1. *Gingerbread Baby* story book
2. 1 box of gingerbread mix
3. 1 cup measure
4. 1 tablespoon measure
5. 1 gingerbread man cookie cutter
6. Gingerbread Baby game board
7. 1 die

Parents: Please return all items on list to school. Thank you for your help!

Figure 6.3b

Bunny Take Home Activity Bag

Willits Elementary School   **Mrs. Ricco's 1st Grade**

Dear Parents,
We have an exciting activity planned for you and your child. Take this opportunity to just relax and enjoy the time spent with your child. Please return the bag by Friday. Thank you for your continued support.

Activities:
1. *Picture Walk and Read Aloud Book*: Before reading *Runaway Bunny* by Margaret Wise Brown, do a "picture walk" with your child. Ask him/her what they think the book is about from the picture on the cover. Glance through the pages of the book together, and without reading, talk about what it could be about. Next read the book aloud to your child and discuss if your picture predictions were correct.
2. *Second Read Aloud of Book*: Read the story aloud again. Give one puppet to your child. Have him/her act out the baby bunny part along with the story. Keep the second bunny for yourself and play the mother bunny part.
3. *Puppet Play*: Use bunny puppets to act out new things that the bunnies could become if the mom kept chasing her baby bunny. Be creative!!
4. *Writing*: On the Runaway Bunny paper, write down the different things that your bunnies become.
5. *Drawing*: Have your child draw a picture on the provided paper, of one of their ideas that the two bunnies became. Have them draw the baby bunny in the left column and the mommy bunny in the right column. At the bottom write what your bunnies have changed into.

Objectives:
1. Making predictions
2. Noticing and copying author's style
3. Motivation for engaged reading
4. Writing for a purpose
5. Extending a story line (sense of story)

Materials Included in the Bag:
1. *Runaway Bunny* story book
2. 2 stuffed bunny puppets
3. My Runaway Bunny story sheet
4. My Runaway Bunny drawing

Parents: Please check to make sure all of the materials on this list are returned and fill out the signature/response card. Thank you for your help.

Figure 6.3c

Area and Perimeter Home-Learning Activity

Choose a room in your house that you would like to redecorate and determine how much it would cost to paint the walls and ceiling, carpet the floor, and put trim on the walls. I would recommend choosing your child's bedroom. Before you begin, discuss what you think it would cost to redecorate a room if you did all of the work yourselves, except laying the carpet.

Cost for materials 1 gallon of paint covers **300** square feet and costs $20. Carpeting will cost $ 1.99 per square foot. Carpet padding will cost $ .39 per square foot. Carpet installation will cost $ .45 per square foot. (Figure this amount if you cannot lay carpet on your own.) Trim that is stained and varnished costs $ .75 per board foot.

Paint (Use a tape measure to determine the length and the width of the walls so you can figure the amount of paint you will need to purchase.)

	length		width
North wall	_____	X	_____ = _____
South wall	_____	X	_____ = _____
East wall	_____	X	_____ = _____
West wall	_____	X	_____ = _____
Ceiling	_____	X	_____ = _____
Total (add)			

Measure any cabinets, windows, or doors that do not need to be painted.

Window	_____ X _____ = _____
Window	_____ X _____ = _____
Door	_____ X _____ = _____
Door	_____ X _____ = _____
Cabinet	_____ X _____ = _____
Other	_____ X _____ = _____

Total (add the areas of windows, doors and cabinets) _____

What is the total area that needs to be painted? (subtract totals) _____

How many gallons of paint would you need? Cost of paint. $ _____

Figure 6.4a

Carpet (Find the **area** of the floor.)

North wall length_____ X South wall length_____ = _____

What is the total area that needs to be carpeted? (subtract) _____

How many square feet of carpeting would you need? _____

Cost of carpet. $_____

Cost of carpet padding. $_____

Cost of carpet installation. $_____

Trim (Measure only the places in the room that would require trim.)

North wall _____

South wall _____

East wall _____

West wall _____

Door (measure all around the door) _____

Door (measure all around the door) _____

Window _____

Window _____

Total feet of trim needed. (add) _____ ft.

Cost of trim. $_____

Total cost $_____

Now that you have finished figuring out how much it would cost to redecorate this room, compare this price to your estimated price. How much do you think it would cost to hire someone to do this same room in your house? In the future, would you hire someone or do it yourself?

Did you find this home-learning activity helpful in understanding the math required for this task?
　　a. very helpful　　　b. somewhat helpful　　　c. not very helpful

　　b. Comments:

Figure 6.4b

Data Collection and Integers Home-learning Activity

You and your parent have both been given $3,000 which must be invested in the stock market. Use the newspaper or the computer to research a variety of stocks that appeal to you. Once both of you have chosen a stock, assume that it was purchased the day you both made the decision. Unlike many day traders, you will not be allowed to pull your money out of the stock market until ten stock trading days have passed.

	Value
Stock name	
Parent's choice	$
Child's choice	$

Now that a stock has been chosen, you must figure out how many shares you were able to buy with the $3,000. (3,000 divided by the value of your stock)

Parent's number of shares_____ Child's number of shares _____

For the next few weeks, keep track of what your stock does on the chart below. Once you have recorded movement of the stock for ten days, determine if either of you would have made any money and discuss how you would have felt if you had used your own money.

Parent's stock

Increase/Decrease	X	# of shares	= The day's gain or loss (show with + or -)
Day 1_____	X	_____	= _____
Day 2_____	X	_____	= _____
Day 3_____	X	_____	= _____
Day 4_____	X	_____	= _____
Day 5_____	X	_____	= _____
Day 6_____	X	_____	= _____
Day 7_____	X	_____	= _____
Day 8_____	X	_____	= _____
Day 9_____	X	_____	= _____
Day 10_____	X	_____	= _____

Total loss or gain of money

(add the ten integers in the last column) $_____

Student's stock

Increase/Decrease	X	# of shares	= The day's gain or loss (show with + or -)
Day 1_____	X	_____	= _____
Day 2_____	X	_____	= _____
Day 3_____	X	_____	= _____
Day 4_____	X	_____	= _____
Day 5_____	X	_____	= _____
Day 6_____	X	_____	= _____
Day 7_____	X	_____	= _____
Day 8_____	X	_____	= _____
Day 9_____	X	_____	= _____
Day 10_____	X	_____	= _____

Figure 6.4c

Probability Home-learning Activity

Given below are the rules of a dice game called Chicago. Read the directions together first. It helps in this game to know just what you are up against in terms of the probability of rolling specific totals so before you begin playing this game figure the probability of rolling each total.

Chicago

Eleven possible scores can be made when two dice are rolled together and this game is based upon that fact. Any number of people can play it, so Chicago is a good family entertainment when there are lots of

Materials Needed: Two dice

Eleven rounds are played in all. The players are allowed only one roll of dice per round. In the first round all the players try to roll a total of 2. In the second round all the players try to roll a total of 3. The next round they all try for a total of 4; and so on until the eleven rounds have been completed. If you roll the correct number in the appropriate round you add this score to your personal total. For example, if you succeeded in rolling totals of 2,6, 9 and 10 when required, your total would be 27. The winner is the highest scorer after all the rounds have been completed.

Figuring out the odds
1. Write down all of the possible outcomes when two dice are rolled. You should have a total of 36 outcomes when you are finished. Example: 1 1,2 1,3 1 . . . .
2. Using the list of outcomes, determine the probability of rolling the eleven specific totals.

　　Against rolling a total of 2 =
　　Against rolling a total of 3 =
　　Against rolling a total of 4 =
　　Against rolling a total of 5 =
　　Against rolling a total of 6 =
　　Against rolling a total of 7 =
　　Against rolling a total of 8 =
　　Against rolling a total of 9 =
　　Against rolling a total of 10=
　　Against rolling a total of 11 =
　　Against rolling a total of 12=

3. As you can see from your table, the hardest shots are _____and _____while the easiest shot is___ .
4. Play this game and then discuss other games that also deal with probability.

Did you find this home-learning activity helpful in helping your child understand probability?
a. very useful　　b. somewhat useful　　　　c. not very useful

Comments:

Figure 6.4d

To solicit family involvement in home-learning activities, some prekindergarten teachers send home lists of items commonly found in the home that can be used as learning tools. Included in these lists are items such as empty boxes for nesting and for building; buttons for sorting by size, color, shape, and number of holes; and plastic glasses and cups for water play by which young children begin to acquire concepts of volume, measurement, and conservation. Reading through these lists helps parents begin to think of other items and new ways to help their child learn by manipulating common household objects.

Parent-child activities are also available commercially. One good example is Fast Start for Early Readers by Nancy Padak and Timothy Rasinski (Scholastic, 2005). This book contains 60 reproducible poems and companion activities, as well as parent letters in English and Spanish. Scholastic, Modern Curriculum Press, Creative Teaching Press, and other companies have developed take-home book bags containing a children's book, parent letter and suggested activities for reading and enjoying the book at home. Scholastic also has available an easy-to-use workshop series that uses over 70 children's books and take-home bags. The series is available in English and Spanish and includes presenter's guide and parent handouts.

*P*ARENT MEETINGS

Multipurpose parent meetings, such as those hosted by the parent-teacher organization, can serve a variety of purposes, including dissemination of information, socialization, parent advocacy, and parent education. Research shows that parents want to know more about the school program; therefore, curriculum sharing is an important function of the parent-teacher meetings scheduled at some schools. Each special program and subject area is highlighted at one meeting during the year, and, as often as possible, children are asked to participate in the program. For example, when the physical education program was highlighted at Oakwood School's parent-teacher meeting, the P.E. teacher talked to parents about the goals of the program and asked children to demonstrate various activities. Following the art teacher's talk at another meeting, family members were invited to view the children's art displayed throughout the building. Because these meetings are held in the evening and include children's participation, attendance is usually quite good.

Special guest speakers can also be invited to make a presentation. The topics chosen should have broad appeal to parents of all age groups, and the recommended presentation format includes a twenty- to thirty-minute lecture/demonstration followed by a question and answer period.

Follow-up of the information presented in the parent meeting is important, especially when time is limited, as is often the case at parent meetings where purposes other than parent education are being met. Having participants jot down two or three questions they have about the topic *at the close of the session* can help shape the follow-up opportunities offered. Handouts, a video, or perhaps a small-group discussion may be among the types of options offered. A brief synopsis of the presentation might be included in a future school newsletter to serve as a reminder to participants of information gained.

The website of the National Parent Teacher Organization (PTO) offers planning guides for four different parent nights: (1) Family Reading Night, (2) Family Movie Night, (3) Family Arts & Crafts Night, and (4) Family Game Night. Free kits are available to help teachers plan and publicize each night (*www. PTOtoday.com*).

*P*ARENT WORKSHOPS

A workshop can be a very effective strategy for helping parents gain the knowledge and skills they need to support their child's learning. By its very nature, the label *workshop* implies a session that affords hands-on involvement and a more intensive experience than can be gained through a parent meeting. Workshop topics can come from parent surveys and needs assessments, as well as from curricular issues that the faculty know need to be addressed. Whatever the topic, the emphasis should be on helping parents acquire strategies they can use at home with their children. Once the topic has been selected, consideration needs to be given to the logistics of scheduling, transportation, childcare, advertising, and planning the content of the workshop.

As far as a suggested length of time for a parent workshop, a 1½- to 2-hour workshop allows for ample time for presentation and for audience participation in small-group activities, question and discussion periods, and refreshments and informal conversation. Workshops should be scheduled at a time most convenient for the majority of the parents in your target audience. As discussed earlier, parents might be surveyed to determine "best" times for scheduling workshops and meetings. Also, you might consider having both a daytime and evening presentation time and/or videotaping the workshop to lend the tape to nonattending parents who are interested. Transportation is sometimes an issue for families, as is childcare. If these items are not covered in your school or program budget, perhaps a parent volunteer group or community service organization might agree to help.

While most parent workshops are held in school buildings, some consideration might be given to other locations, such as the public library or a local community center or church. Sometimes parents are more willing to attend a workshop held in a familiar place—one that feels comfortable and "safe." In one small community the meeting room of a local fast-food restaurant is a favored place for holding parent workshops. Regardless of where the workshop is held, availability of adequate parking, space, furnishings, audiovisual equipment, restroom facilities, and lighting and ventilation all need to be checked out before final scheduling arrangements are made.

Workshop format: parents only. Involvement is a key ingredient of effective workshops. Whether parents attend the workshop with their children or not, they need to be involved in activities related to the topic. In this section we discuss and give examples of "adults only" workshop sessions; then in the next section we describe characteristics of parent/child interaction workshops, giving examples of sessions that we have found to be particularly effective.

Workshops may be planned by one or two individuals or by an entire school staff. The more individuals who participate in the planning process, the greater chance you have for meeting the needs of more parents, since each individual brings different experiences and insights to the planning process. A good place to start is with *anticipated outcomes* or objectives for the workshop. What specifically do you hope parents will learn as a result of their involvement in this workshop? What do you want them to learn to do at home? Answers to these questions will help you form outcomes or objectives that can then serve as guideposts for the content and experiences you plan. Writing a *rationale* or purpose for the workshop, in language appropriate for the intended audience also serves to focus the content to be delivered. Although parents do want and need strategies to use at home with their children, they also need to understand why these strategies are important and how they will help their child. For this reason it is important that at least a portion of the workshop be devoted to helping parents realize the theory behind the practical strategies that will be shared. Having an understanding as to *why* the information is important also increases the chances that parents will actually *apply* the information at home. This part of the presentation should be carefully planned. Limiting the number of major points to be conveyed and providing a handout that reinforces them is recommended. Also, well-constructed visuals serve to focus the learner's attention and add interest and appeal to the presentation. Posters, overhead transparencies, and other visuals should be designed with the size of the room and audience in mind. Letters and words should be spaced well, in bold print or type that is clearly readable by everyone in the room.

Consideration as to how adults learn is also important. We know from theories of adult learning that information to be presented must be relevant to their needs, challenging, and interesting. We also know that recognition of what adults already know and bring to the learning task is important. Parents have a wide array of past experiences—some of which may contradict the information the school is attempting to impart. For this reason an opportunity to voice questions, concerns, and ideas related to the content presented must be provided. Since adults, like children, learn best through hands-on experiences, parents should be actively involved for at least a portion of the workshop. Arranging the room into learning centers where participants may engage in a variety of activities related to the topic has a number of advantages. Probably the most important advantage is that using centers reduces group size and promotes more interaction among parents and among parents and workshop leaders. Another benefit is that centers allow for participant choice based on areas of greatest interest and/or need. Finally, use of centers frequently results in reduced tension and anxiety of presenters, since the center format is more relaxed and informal.

Rotation to various centers can occur in many ways. Sometimes parents are miscellaneously grouped according to the color of their name tag or the table where they are sitting. Other times, parents select the group or center where they would like to begin. Having a group of four to eight parents in a center allows for adequate group interaction and hands-on participation. Also, encouraging parents to ask their questions during small-group center activities generally yields better results than if time for questions is provided only during whole-group times. If there aren't enough parents in attendance to allow for at least three parents in each center, closing centers temporarily and having parents move between a fewer number of centers is usually a good idea. Decide whether to have parents rotate with their group for a designated amount of time at each center or whether to allow parents to select only those centers that interest them most. You may decide to have parents choose to attend two or three centers from a total of four to six. Although parents may not get to attend all of the centers that interest them, this approach does allow for more time to be spent at each center. Having the handouts from each center available for all participants is one way to let everyone take home at least some of the ideas from each center.

Setting a time for participants to come together to discuss what they learned from the center activities is recommended. Workshop presenters may take a few minutes to redirect participants' attention to the rationale shared at the onset of the workshop. Handouts and other "make-it-take-it" materials serve as tangible reminders of the workshop and, again, increase the probability that parents will use the ideas presented with their own children. This is a good time to have participants evaluate the workshop. Finding out what worked well—and what didn't—as well as ideas for future workshops, is important. Informal evaluation can also take place throughout the workshop as presenters and/or other school staff members observe participants' reactions to and involvement in the various aspects of the workshop.

Part of planning a workshop should involve creating a written agenda. This agenda serves as the framework for more detailed planning of each segment of the workshop, from the first moment parents enter to the opening remarks and icebreaker or get-acquainted activity, to the closing statements and evaluation. Preparing a detailed, annotated agenda for use by workshop presenters is extremely helpful and serves to keep everyone focused and on schedule throughout the workshop. In Figure 6.5 is an example of an annotated agenda for a parent workshop

As most workshop presenters have learned, it is important to be an early bird. Some parents *always* arrive early! Workshop leaders or other school staff volunteers need to be on hand to greet parents; help them locate the coat rack, childcare area, and/or restrooms; fill out a name tag; and, in general, serve as host or hostess. Having coffee or juice already set up can help parents feel more at ease, since people tend to congregate around a refreshment table. Another good idea is to have displays of books and other materials related to the topic for the evening. In schools where there is a parent resource

Agenda
Messy Play is A-Okay

I. Welcome
   A. Welcome poster
   B. Area posters
II. Greeting
   A. Opening remarks
      1. Purpose of messy play
      2. Value of messy play to child's development
   B. Icebreaker
      1. Human bingo
      2. Relate to messy experiences recalled from parents' own childhood
   C. Introduction of presenters and their centers
      1. Lori Kies
      2. Lynn Kleine
      3. Dana Rees Rives
      4. Sharon Sample
      5. Martha Sprecher
   D. Break into groups by color of bingo card
III. Group Participation in Centers
   A. Painting activities
      1. Recipes for homemade paints
      2. Vegetable and fruit prints
      3. Use of various implements for painting
         a. fly swatter
         b. q-tips
         c. spray bottles
   B. Pudding is not just for eating
      1. Feely bags
      2. Finger painting
   C. Fun with paper and string
      1. Tissue paper and starch art
      2. Paper punch pictures
      3. Collage
   D. Fun with playdough
      1. Homemade playdough recipes
      2. Shaping, rolling, and cutting
IV. Conclusion
   A. Coming together as a large group
   B. Closing remarks
      1. Value of messy play
      2. Ideas gained in center activities
   C. Handouts, other ideas for messy play
   D. Evaluations

Figure 6.5

library, bringing to the room pertinent items on a cart and materials needed for checking them out is one good way to get some of the items into circulation. Finally, displays of children's work always draw parents' attention.

A get-acquainted activity helps "break the ice" and relax participants. If time permits, a "mixer" where participants circulate around the room chatting with each other works well. Activities such as "scrambled name tags," in which participants try to "decode" each other's first names, and the scavenger hunt activity described in Figure 6.6 are two icebreakers that have been used successfully in many workshop settings. If time or space is very limited, asking for a show of hands to such questions as "How many children do you have? One? Two? Three?" and "How many people live in the same town as the one in which you grew up?" can be directed to the entire group. This type of getting-to-know-you information could also be solicited in graph form on charts displayed prior to the start of the workshop. The information could be discussed at the workshop opening as a way to help everyone learn a little about the makeup of the group.

If possible, activities for the children in childcare can follow the same theme or topic of the parent workshop. For example, if the theme of the parent workshop is literacy development, the children in childcare might be reading stories, making bookmarks, and participating in various writing and bookmaking activities. In Figure 6.7 is a plan for activities that were conducted with children while parents attended a workshop on health and nutrition. In Figure 6.8 is the agenda given to parents attending this workshop.

Although a guest speaker may be invited to conduct a workshop or a portion of a workshop, the school staff should take responsibility for the planning and should convey to the guest speaker exactly what his or her role will be. Teachers and administrators certainly have many obligations and demands on their time; however, taking a leadership role in sharing helpful information with parents and demonstrating effective instructional strategies will reap many positive outcomes. Parents feel good knowing that teachers and administrators are experts and that they are willing to share their expertise with others. Workshop presenters inspire confidence in parents who have often had very limited opportunities to hear these individuals talk about their ideas and beliefs. Working with parents in a workshop situation enables teachers to demonstrate the exact strategies they want parents to use at home to support skills being acquired at school. Sharing this information with parents helps solidify the home-school partnership and is generally a very rewarding experience for teachers. Further, since teachers usually work together to plan and present a workshop, they often get many ideas from each other, and leave the workshop feeling as if they gained almost as much as they contributed. Workshop materials can be purchased commercially. There are many fine video series designed to be used in a workshop format. One such example is the STEP Program developed by American Guidance Services. In Appendix 6 are several other excellent examples.

Scavenger Hunt
Family Involvement

Find someone in the group who:

NAME

_____   1. Has only one child.

_____   2. Has both a boy and a girl.

_____   3. Is a single parent.

_____   4. Has three or more children.

_____   5. Was born the same year as you were.

_____   6. Has a child the same age as your child.

_____   7. Has lived in a household in which an older relative, e.g., a grandparent, is also living.

_____   8. Currently lives within fifty miles of his/her childhood home.

_____   9. Currently lives more than five-hundred miles from his/her childhood home.

_____ 10. As a child, lived in the same community as his/her grandparents.

_____ 11. As a child, lived in a state other than that which his/her grandparents lived.

_____ 12. Grew up in a family in which both parents worked outside of the home.

_____ 13. Was an only child.

_____ 14. As a child, lived on a farm.

_____ 15. As a child, lived in a city.

_____ 16. Is a full-time student.

_____ 17. Speaks more than one language.

Figure 6.6

Health and Nutrition Workshop: Childcare Activities

6:30–6:45 Introduction
1. Give every child a name tag depicting a picture of a food.
2. Free play in centers until everyone has arrived.
   - fruit/vegetable puzzles
   - housekeeping area with plastic foods and cooking utensils
   - food posters
   - playdough with food-shaped cutters and molds
   - book corner with various food-related books

6:45–7:15 Group Time
1. Divide children into groups according to age/grade level
2. Show display of foods and food pictures. Discuss each, asking children to tell about their favorite and least-favorite foods. Ask children to classify foods and food pictures into groups. Encourage as many different groupings as possible. These may include basic food groups, healthy/"junk" foods, sweet/salty, fresh/canned, or frozen foods.

7:15–7:30 Exercise
1. Show posters and talk about benefits of exercise. Point out that exercise can be fun.
2. Engage children in various fun types of exercise
   - Hokey Pokey
   - Ring around the Rosie
   - London Bridge

7:30–8:00 Preparation and Eating of Healthy Snack Foods
1. Show centers with foods to prepare for snacks.
2. Read through the picture recipe cards located at each center and demonstrate how to follow the pictures to make each snack.
3. Divide children into groups to rotate to each snack center.
   - Chicken feed: Measure amounts of cereal and dried fruits
   - Fruit kabobs: Make a pattern with various fruits
   - Fruitloop necklaces: String cereal on yarn to make an edible necklace.
   - Star sandwiches: Cut bread into star shape using a cookie cutter. Spread with pineapple/carrot sandwich filling or peanut butter/honey filling.

8:00–8:30 Storytime
1. Read big book version of Potluck by Anne Shelby.
2. Talk about a potluck. Give each child a paper plate on which to draw paste a magazine picture of a food they would like to bring to a potluck.
3. Let children share their potluck dishes with each other.

Figure 6.7

Agenda

Registration: 6:15–6:30
Horrabin Hall, Rm. 1, WIU campus
Welcome & Introductions: 6:30–6:40
Mini-Session One: 6:40–7:25
Dealing Effectively with Mealtime Hassles While Maintaining a Young Child's Health and Weight

Break: 7:25–7:40
Refreshment Centers. Make your own snack, featuring easy, nutritious recipes suitable for use with young children.
- Tropical sandwiches
- Crunchy carrot sandwiches
- Fruit kabobs
- Creepy crawlers
- Chicken feed
- Hot cocoa mix
- Hot spiced tea mix

Mini-Session Two: 7:40–8:25
Health Issues Young Children Face

Announcements of Future Workshops & Workshop Evaluation: 8:25
Please take a few moments to fill out the evaluation form and return it to the box on the registration table.

Figure 6.8

PARENT/CHILD INTERACTION WORKSHOPS

Another type of parent workshop is one where parents or other adults who play a significant role in the child's life attend the workshop with the child. Again, a 1½-hour time period works well, with the first 45 to 55 minutes devoted to activities participated in jointly by parents and children. As they enter the room, parents and children are greeted by a teacher who briefly explains how the room is set up, the activities that are available, and the purpose for this first part of the workshop: to give parents and children an opportunity to try out some effective learning strategies they can use at home. Parents and children are allowed to move to and from each activity at their own pace. In each activity area are signs with printed instructions. A school staff member is present to *facilitate*—not direct—each activity, with the parent being encouraged to let the child take the lead in the activity. An example from Lincoln Elementary School in Macomb, Illinois is shown in Figure 6.9. At some workshops, parents are asked to gather informally in a refreshment area as their children are taken to another room for their snack. At this time, parents are provided with pertinent handouts and other materials and have an opportunity to discuss with workshop leaders what the children experienced during the interaction, why the activities were chosen to enhance learning, and how the activities could be used at home.

The role of the facilitator at each activity area is key to the success of this type of workshop. The facilitator models behaviors for the parents and informally explains how the activity contributes to the child's learning and

---

SECOND GRADE FAMILY MATH NIGHT

Dear Family,

You and your second grade child are invited to a very special night of fun and learning on Monday, November 15 from 5:30 to 7:30 p.m. You and your second grader will have an opportunity to participate in three fun math activities in three different classrooms. These math games will enhance your child's learning. Beginning at 5:30, pizza and soda will be served to participating families. Math sessions will begin promptly at 6:00.

We hope that you and your second grader will be able to attend this event. Please decide with your child the four math activities in which you would like to participate. Mark your four choices on the form at the bottom of this page. Every effort will be made to honor three of your four choices.

Please tear off the bottom portion of this note and return it to school by **Friday, November 5**, to reserve your spot for Family Math Night.

Lincoln School Second Grade Teachers

_____

Yes, the family of _____ plans to attend the Second Grade Family Math Night on Monday, November 15.

_____ Number of adults who will attend

_____ Number of children who will attend

Math activities
Please mark the four activities in which you and your child would like to participate:

_____ Versa Tiles (solve math puzzles via tiles and patterns)

_____ Glyphs (a fun way to collect, display, and use data in the form of a picture)

_____ Number Cube Games

_____ Card Games

_____ Hundred Chart Activities

_____ Calculator Games

_____ Board Games

Figure 6.9

development. Without this, the activity centers may degenerate to the level of a "kiddie carnival" where the anticipated outcome is simply to provide a period of recreation and family fun. Parent/child interaction workshops also differ from a kiddie carnival in that they are most often designed with a special audience in mind—a particular group of children and their parents—and specific outcomes are anticipated. Other siblings are provided for in a child-care setting away from the workshop area to allow for undisturbed interaction between the child and one or more adults.

The topics for parent/child interaction workshops can, as discussed earlier, be drawn from parent interest surveys, needs assessments, or from the curriculum. Since these types of workshops are particularly suitable for parents and young children, topics may also come from information gained through home visits. For example, one teacher noticed that children were not often allowed to engage in activities that involved painting, cutting, or playdough. "Messy play" became the topic for a future parent/child interaction workshop where parents gained valuable experience and information about the importance of messy play to a young child's development. The parents and children made mud pies, played with playdough, painted with fingerpaints, and cut shapes from old magazines and glued them onto large pieces of newspaper. During the follow-up discussion period, parents discussed what they learned from this experience. Some described how hard it was for them to relax and play with their child; others talked about how nervous they were about making a mess. All agreed that clean-up was manageable and that the children had demonstrated wonderful creative abilities and language skills throughout the experience.

The planning for an interaction-type workshop needs to be done in as careful and thorough a manner as that for an "adults-only" workshop. It is not simply a matter of working up a few fun activities. For example, activities selected should be ones that will result in good interaction between parent and child. If an activity is too simplistic, too common, the parent will tend to draw back and observe—rather than participate with—their child. If the activity is too complex, requiring a great deal of adult assistance, the child's attention is likely to wander, and the adult may end up completing the task without sufficient involvement from the child. In addition, the activities selected should directly target the anticipated outcomes or goals for the workshop and serve to illustrate effective strategies for home use. Once children and parents have worked together to make a pinecone bird feeder, what are they to do at home? Teachers must consider the long-term benefits of the activities and carefully select those activities that will, hopefully, result in the most use at home.

Once activities have been selected, and directions for each have been written in language understandable to parents, key comments and suggested words of explanation for facilitators to share with parents should be planned. Without this conscious planning, it is simply too easy for a facilitator to get caught up in the moment and let parents get away without really understanding the purpose for a particular activity. Finally, a list of thought-provoking questions to trigger parent response in the second part of the workshop should be written out. These questions should be designed so as to lead the parent to some main ideas about the purpose and value of the activities presented. They might also serve to elicit parents' level of comfort in recreating the activities at home, as well as their ideas about extending the activities even further.

Sometimes special adult/child evenings are planned with the goal of promoting involvement of another individual in the child's life, such as an aunt, uncle, special friend, or grandparent. Alison Lewis hosts a Mother's Day Tea Party for children and their mothers, grandmothers, aunts, and special friends. Shelley Golden's prekindergarten program in Galesburg, Illinois, hosted a "Big Guy and Me" evening during which children and their male guests construct a bookshelf or other item to take home. While the anticipated outcomes for this type of workshop differ from the parent/child workshop described above, they do serve to promote interest in the program and some increased understanding of the importance of adult/child interaction at school and at home. As with the adults-only workshop, participants should be asked to evaluate the parent/child interaction session and give suggestions for future sessions. Facilitators can also assist in evaluating the workshop, noting whether parents and children are interacting freely, whether parents appear interested in the activities, and whether they have questions that indicate their intention to try out the activities at home.

The involvement of fathers is particularly important since research has shown that children do better in school when both mothers and fathers are involved (Child Trends 1998). Studies have also shown that specific efforts to involve fathers increases the likelihood that fathers will participate (Fagan 1999; Levine, Murphy & Wilson 1998).

*F*OLLOW-UP OF PARENT EDUCATION ACTIVITIES

Regardless of whether parent education is offered through books and printed materials, video tapes, or parent meetings and workshops, some planned follow-up should occur. Follow-up for written materials distributed on request from a parent might include a note or telephone call from the teacher asking if the parent's interests, concerns, or questions were accommodated or if assistance in locating additional material is desired. This serves as an invitation for the parent to talk to the teacher about what was gained from the materials. When written materials are sent to all parents, such as when a brief parent education article is attached to the school or classroom newsletter, a future newsletter may contain a note inviting parents to attend a brown-bag lunch discussion about the article. Parents who attended a particular meeting or workshop may also be invited to attend a small group follow-up session for purposes of describing how they used the strategies presented, asking questions, or sharing with others the difficulties they had in using the strategies. Follow-up may also be in the form of an additional handout of ideas related to the ones shared in a previous session. The point is that some follow-up be planned in an effort to assist parents in applying the strategies at home.

INCREASING ATTENDANCE AT PARENT MEETINGS AND WORKSHOPS

Why is it that some parent meetings and workshops are an absolute "sellout" while others draw only a handful of participants? Sometimes the answer can be found in the ways parents were notified about the meeting. Invitations need to appear well in advance of the scheduled meeting or workshop and need to come in a variety of forms. Including the date on the school monthly calendar, writing an enticing "advertisement" for school and classroom newsletters, sending fliers with information about the workshop, and having students write invitations are all examples of ways to send the message about an upcoming event. Some schools have found that attendance increases if parents have to preregister for the event and sign up in advance for childcare and transportation. Reminder notes can be sent to parents who preregistered.

Some teachers, despite efforts to plan excellent opportunities for parent education—scheduled at times convenient to parents—have been disappointed by very low attendance. If schools have followed the suggestions discussed earlier in this chapter, have surveyed parents to determine interests, needs, and preferred schedules, have arranged for transportation and childcare, and have invited parents far enough in advance and sent follow-up reminders, what else can they do? One strategy is to establish personal contact with parents. Having the parent coordinator, teachers, or parent volunteers call parents to tell them about the workshop and to extend a personal invitation is a very powerful motivator for some parents. One thing is for certain: Even when attendance is low, you can usually bet that the parents who did attend felt that the time was well-spent. And this will be reflected in the ways they interact with their children and in future home-learning opportunities they provide for their children. Finally, it is important for teachers and principals to keep in mind a point that was made in Chapter 1: we mustn't confuse *involvement* with *attendance*.

SUMMARY

"The parent is the child's most important teacher" has become a saying—a cliché—popular among educators who aspire to the creation of strong home-school partnerships. It is time for schools to recognize, not only through their words but also through their actions, that parents are *indeed* their child's most important teacher. In this chapter ways that schools can provide opportunities for parents to acquire skills and strategies they can use to help their children learn were described. Guidelines and suggestions for creating parent

spaces and centers, for utilizing print and video resources, for developing home-learning activities, and for planning and implementing parent meetings and workshops were also provided and the need for follow-up of parent education opportunities to assist parents in their efforts at applying newly gained strategies was stressed.

Parent education does make a difference! Even parents who were only marginally involved can begin to see that working with their child can be a very pleasant and productive experience. More importantly, teachers begin to see that there is a wealth of support and help available from parents—if we can find a way to tap into it. Before turning to the next chapter, you may want to take a few moments to consider the questions listed below. These questions are designed to help you think about your beliefs with respect to parent education.

*L*OOKING AHEAD . . .

The importance of two-way communication and parents as teachers will also be emphasized in the next chapter as we discuss home visiting. Criteria for establishing an effective home-visiting program and characteristics and responsibilities of home visitors will be examined.

For your consideration . . .

1. Parents are their children's first and most important teachers. **YES** **NO**

2. The school has a role in helping parents become better teachers of their children. **YES** **NO**

3. Some of the school's resources should go toward providing parent education opportunities. **YES** **NO**

4. Teachers should give parents strategies they can use to help their children learn. **YES** **NO**

5. A variety of parent education opportunities should exist. **YES** **NO**

6. Planned follow-up for parent education offerings should be provided to assist parents in applying strategies learned. **YES** **NO**

REFERENCES

Baby TALK (2004). *Baby TALK Dialogue, 10*(3). Decatur, IL: Baby TALK.

Bryan, T., & Sullivan-Burstein, K. (1997). Homework how-tos. *Teaching Exceptional Children, 29*(6), 32–37.

Child Trends, Inc. (1998). *What a different a dad makes! What research tells us about fathers: Child trends summarizes key findings.* Washington, DC: Child Trends, Inc.

Edwards, P. A. (1991). Fostering early literacy through parent coaching. In E. H. Hiebart (Ed.), *Literacy for a diverse society: Perspectives, practices, and policies* (pp. 199–212). New York: Teachers College Press.

Edwards, P. A., Pleasants, H. M., & Franklin, S. H. (1999). *A path to follow: Learning to listen to parents.* Portsmouth, NH: Heinemann.

Edwards, P. A., Danridge, J., & Pleasants, H. M. (2000, December). *Exploring administrators' and teachers' conceptions of "at-riskness" in an urban elementary school.* CIERA Report #2-010, Ann Arbor, MI: Center for the Improvement of Early Reading Achievement.

Fagan, J., & Iglesias, A. (1999). Father involvement program effects on fathers, father figures, and their Head Start children: A quasi-experimental study. *Early Childhood Research Quarterly, 14*(2), 243–269.

Goldsmith, E., & Terlin, A. M. (2003). *Reading starts with us.* New York: Scholastic.

Leichter, H. J. (1984). Families as environments for literacy. In H. Goelman, A. Oberg, & F. Smith (Eds.), *Awakening to Literacy* (pp. 38–50). Portsmouth, NH: Heinemann.

Levine, J., Murphy, D., & Wilson, S. (1998). *Getting men involved: Strategies for early childhood programs.* New York: Families and Work Institute.

Meisels, S. J. (2001). Assessing readiness. In R. C. Pianta, & M. M. Cox, (Eds.), *The transition to kindergarten.* Baltimore, MD: Paul H. Brookes. (Also available as CIERA Report #3-002. Ann Arbor: CIERA/University of Michigan.

Padak, N., & Rasinski, T. (2005) *Fast start for early readers.* New York: Scholastic.

Payne, R. (2001). *A framework for understanding poverty.* Sacramento, CA: Aha Process, Inc.

U.S. Department of Education (2004). *Parental involvement: Title I, Part A non-regulatory guidance.* Washington, DC: U.S. Department of Education.

The "Whys" and "Hows" of Home Visiting

A note from Kathy . . .

Many teachers—particularly those teaching in early childhood programs—are more nervous about home visiting than about any other aspect of their future teaching assignments. They are apprehensive about what might await them behind those closed doors, and they question their own ability to interact face-to-face with families—on their own "turf." In this chapter I hope to ease some of these fears and provide information that will help teachers and administrators feel confident in their abilities to accept the challenges that a home-visiting program brings.

INTRODUCTION

Home-visiting programs differ in goals, services offered, and in strategies used to achieve their goals and deliver services. They also vary as to the kinds of families served. Some programs, such as Head Start and most state-funded prekindergarten programs, have a number of mandatory home visits for all families of children enrolled, while other programs, such as Missouri's Parents as Teachers program, offer home visits on a voluntary basis to all families with children in a certain age group. Some programs are only available for families of children with special needs, some are designed for teenaged parents, while others only accept families with low socioeconomic status. Services offered through home-visiting programs include, but are not limited to, prevention of poor birth outcomes, prevention of child abuse and neglect, enhanced child development, and support to families of special-needs children. It is the last two of these services that fall into the realm of early childhood education; we will therefore limit our discussion of home-visiting to programs that seek to provide services related to promoting children's cognitive, social, and motor development.

Although differences exist, researchers have identified some common characteristics of successful home-visiting programs (Gomby et al. 2003; Olds and Kitzman 1993; Ramey and Ramey 1993). These include the provision of multiple services, use of professionals, and program duration of at least four visits. Further, families from higher-risk populations with multiple needs tend to benefit more from home-visiting programs than families who are able to help themselves without outside intervention. From this research, experts recommend that the following guidelines be applied to the planning and implementation of new home-visiting programs (Gomby et al. 2003). Home-visiting programs should

➤ Address the needs of both children and parents by direct service or by referral.

➤ Be flexible with regard to frequency, intensity, and duration of visits.

➤ Be sensitive to the unique needs and circumstances of the families served and should avoid rigid, formulaic strategies found in packaged child development and/or parenting programs.

➤ Utilize the services of well-trained, dedicated professionals.

➤ Engage in continuous evaluation.

➤ Set realistic goals and expectations.

DESIGNING HOME-VISITING PROGRAMS

The ultimate goal of most home-visiting programs is to involve and encourage parents in the development and education of their children. This is often accomplished through improved parenting competence. A key element in designing effective home-visiting programs is identifying desired goals and anticipated outcomes. Will the primary focus be on the child, the parent, or both? Is the primary goal to increase parental skill and confidence in working with their child or to provide direct service to the child? Answers to these and other questions will provide direction to the school or district seeking to establish a home-visiting program.

Another key element involves identification of the population to be served. Most programs associated with public and private elementary schools focus on children from birth to age five. Home visits, however, have been a successful part of the school experience for youngsters throughout the grades (Nielson 1991; Malanowski and Wene 1982; Hawthorne 1984). Home-visiting may also be offered to special populations within the school or district, such as to families of children enrolled in a prekindergarten, special-education, transition, or remedial program.

Once the goals and outcomes of the program and the target population have been identified, consideration can be given to services to be provided. While many programs provide a variety of services, most home-visiting programs associated with public and private elementary schools primarily offer services to enhance child development and/or parenting skills. At the same time, home visitors for these programs are generally well-informed as to organizations and agencies providing a wide range of services and can take advantage of opportunities to inform parents as to the availability of these services.

The services to be provided will generally dictate the staff qualifications needed and, sometimes, the schedule. If paraprofessionals are to be employed as home visitors, experts strongly recommend that they be given extensive training and that they work under the direction of a professional. Sometimes a parent coordinator with a degree in education, counseling, psychology, social work, or a closely related field is hired to oversee the home-visiting program. This individual may conduct home visits and/or train and support other teachers or paraprofessionals working with the program. In most of the Illinois prekindergarten programs, regularly scheduled home visits are conducted by each child's teacher. Some programs are designed with a classroom or center-based program that meets two or three days a week, with the remaining days devoted to home visits. Other programs are entirely home-based or classroom-based with periodic home visits scheduled during the year. The length of each home visit varies from program to program; however, the average visit ranges from thirty to ninety minutes.

Some home visits have as their primary purpose the establishment of relationships with people in the home. For these home visits, content is not an issue, since the visit is not one that includes goals related to child development and/or parent education. When the goals do include child development and/or parent education, the content and methods to be used in the home-visiting program should, ideally, be individualized to accommodate the needs and characteristics of the children and families served. In some programs a standard curriculum exists, and home visitors perform the same activities with all of the families. In other programs home visitors select from the standard curriculum activities that appear to address needs of each individual family. And in still other programs the parents, together with the home visitor, develop goals and select activities they feel will be of most benefit. The activities selected may or may not come from a standard curriculum. The latter strategy provides opportunity for the parent to help the teacher understand the family's goals, needs, and culture (Terdan 1992).

CHARACTERISTICS AND RESPONSIBILITIES OF THE HOME VISITOR

Ideally, the relationship between the home visitor and the parent will be one of collaboration and partnership, rather than one of expert and novice. J. Q. Adams, a professor of education specializing in cultural diversity at Western Illinois University, advises teachers to "assume a neighbor persona" when visiting with parents. He asks teachers to visualize a continuum with the "novice" at the far right end and "expert" at the left. In the middle is "neighbor." Adams suggests that the "neighbor" persona represents the best role for teachers and parents to assume. Approaching parents as an expert sometimes reinforces the old barriers and negative feelings that some parents still harbor about school. On the other hand the home visitor is a professional and should conduct herself or himself as such. The teacher serving as a home visitor is *not* a close friend nor is he or she a social worker or counselor. Assuming these roles often leads to problems that are counterproductive to the relationship. The home visitor is not there to "fix" the family. While they may benefit from some alternatives and ideas, families must choose their own solutions. Similarly, the home visitor should not be seen as a "babysitter" or a "confidant." Friendliness is important, but the home visitor is not the friend to turn to for free babysitting or marital advice. In Figure 7.1 is an annotated listing of other common pitfalls to avoid in working with families in a home-visiting program.

In a partnership relationship, both parent and home visitor are sometimes novices, sometimes experts. Both have equal status in shaping the goals and outcomes of the program as they manifest themselves in this particular situation.

Besides the obvious understanding of child development and early childhood education, the home visitor *must* have excellent interpersonal communication skills and the ability to relate to each family in light of its own culture, circumstances, and values. Coursework in counseling, psychology, and cultural diversity can greatly benefit a teacher who has not had an opportunity to gain some knowledge and skill in these areas. Personal characteristics such as warmth, friendliness, and a sincere desire to help others are also necessary. A nonjudgmental attitude is absolutely essential, as is a strict adherence to confidentiality. Home visitors are, by their very nature, visitors in another's home. A visitor maintains a pleasant demeanor, accepts hospitality as it is offered, and, in general, behaves as one would wish a guest to behave in one's own home.

Oftentimes trust has to be built before parents are willing or able to open their homes to program personnel. In some circumstances home visits occur in the yard outside the home or at a nearby fast-food restaurant. This is perfectly acceptable if a parent is hesitant or unwilling to have the teacher see the inside of the home. One way that home visitors build trust is by sharing their enthusiasm for working with the child and by recognizing the efforts that parents are making. It is important for the teacher to convey a sincere trust in the parents' desire and willingness to be a good parent. Comments such as "Larry looks so healthy! It's clear that you are meeting his nutritional needs" or "Miriam always looks so clean and neat!" offered in a sincere manner let parents know that you notice how they care for their child. Home visitors are also conscious of their own personal appearance when visiting with parents. Wearing informal attire, such as clean slacks and a pullover or shirt is generally preferred, since overdressing tends to project an image of a

Pitfalls to Avoid in Working with Families

Assuming Responsibility for the Family
It is important that you foster independence rather than dependence. Your role is to model developmentally appropriate practices and provide support to enable the family members to apply these practices in the future.

Imposing Personal Values on the Family
We must respect the right of each individual to have his or her own value system. If a family's values conflict with yours, try to talk honestly and openly about the differences without conveying disapproval for the values of the family. We can share our ideas as "another way," but the family must make its own choices, and we must respect its right to do so. It is important to convey the message that "It's okay to disagree. . . . We can still work together."

Becoming a "Friend" Rather than Simply Being "Friendly"
This is a professional relationship. Although friendliness is important to good relationship–building, being viewed as a "friend" can be counterproductive. Your role is not to babysit, loan money, provide transportation to social or non-school activities, etc.

Trying to "Fix" the Family
Family members may require your assistance in helping them assess their own needs and may benefit from your sharing alternatives and ideas. However, they must learn to determine their own needs and to seek their own solutions. It is counterproductive to tell the family what you see that's wrong—and how to fix it.

Stereotyping Families and Family Members
Families are unique and possess varying strengths and needs. We must seek to identify the individual characteristics that make up each family and attempt to meet each "where they are."

Trying to Be All-Knowing/All-Seeing
In other words, we cannot be all things to all people. We can be a support person, a resource person, and a link to other agencies and professionals in the community where other services can be obtained.

Failing to Deal with the Whole Family
Extended families, live-in relatives, and other individuals often play a critical role in the family. It is important to come to know the roles that these individuals play within the family.

Presenting a Narrow Range of Options
Although we can't be all-knowing, we can familiarize ourselves with a wide variety of agencies, services, and professionals available in the community.

Becoming Impatient
Changing attitudes and behaviors that have developed over many years takes time. Expecting change too quickly can lead to frustration for you, as well as for the family.

Figure 7.1

Inconsistency

The family must be able to trust that you will follow through on commitments and that you genuinely have their best interests at heart. Consistency is important to maintaining a good working relationship with the family.

Lack of Accurate Information

The information and assistance you provide must be accurate and complete. If you do not know the answer to a question, say that you don't know, find out, and get back to the family with the answer. Don't give inaccurate information. It is your responsibility to remain up-to-date on child development, parenting, and community resources.

Failure to Refer When Additional Help Is Needed

In very troubled or disturbed family situations, assistance intervention and treatment from professional, psychiatric, or protective services may be necessary. Get assistance from your supervisor before making these decisions and referrals. Educators are mandated reporters of child abuse or neglect, and under penalty of law must report any suspected cases of abuse or neglect.

Violating Confidentiality Rights

Any and all information about the family is strictly confidential and cannot be shared with your own family or friends. Information may be shared with others in your agency or system, if necessary for you to provide the best service for the family. It is a good practice to not promise a family that you will not tell anyone something they have revealed. It may be necessary to do so in order to help the family.

Figure 7.1 (cont.)

"teacher" or "expert" rather than of a "neighbor" and may make some parents self-conscious about their own dress.

PLANNING HOME VISITS

Planning for a home visit depends on the goals of the program. Home visits have been held to teach parents effective strategies for working with their children, for bringing educational toys and materials into the home, and simply for establishing a relationship between home and school. *Child-centered home visits* have as their purpose spending some time together with the child in the home environment and helping the parent and child feel good about themselves (Fox-Barnett and Meyer 1992). The teacher asks each parent for permission to visit the child, explaining that home visits afford an opportunity for parents, children, and teacher to get to know one another better. An exact schedule should be agreed upon, with five to ten minutes allowed for greetings and the next twenty or thirty minutes devoted to interaction with the child. The teacher is a "visitor" in the child's home, rather than a "parent educator," and as such encourages the child and parents to communicate more about themselves. Children may plan the visit, deciding where the teacher will sit and what the course of events will be. They often have a special toy or other favored object to share with the teacher during the home visit. There is usually follow-up in the classroom as teacher and child share the experience with the rest of the children. As described by Fox-Barnett and Meyer, the child-centered home visit is not a teaching time nor is it a time to help or counsel the family. If questions from the family do arise, a separate time can be arranged for getting back together, or the teacher can make the appropriate referral. The child-centered home visit is really a time for parents, teachers, and children to communicate without institutional barriers. As Fox-Barnett and Meyer state, "If the visit is not judgmental, instructional, or critical, but is open, informal, and characterized by careful listening on the teacher's part, the parents may feel that school is a more approachable place should they need help in the future" (48).

In a home-visiting program where child development and/or parent education is the purpose, the home visitor will probably begin with a child-centered visit in order to build a relationship with the family. Chatting with family members about their daily routine, interests, hobbies, and jobs is a good way to begin. You might ask parents what they like to do when they are "childfree." Informal conversation with the parent as to the family's expectations for the program and, sometimes, the use of a survey instrument or questionnaire are helpful next steps. Figure 7.2 is an example of a survey similar to one used in a Head Start center. The survey was adapted for use in a public school prekindergarten program.

Any information gained through assessments and screening devices should be taken into consideration as goals for the home visits are developed. Once expectations have been shared and a consensus has been reached as to the goals of the program, the home visitor might suggest a routine or format for the visits, soliciting input from the parent. The home visitor might also give examples of the types of materials and activities available to bring into the home. From there, the home visitor and parent can devise a schedule and a tentative agenda for the first few visits. Some programs do ask that parents sign a contract agreeing to be present at the agreed-upon times, to participate in the home visits, and to engage in follow-up activities with their child in between home visits. Other paperwork is sometimes a part of the program, but the home visitor should not let it get in the way of, or take precedence over, interaction with the parent and child. After the visit is over, the home visitor should take a few moments alone to write out an anecdotal record (an account of what took place during the visit—what was done and said). This record should focus on the progress made and include any strengths in evidence during the visit. It should also contain notes about any problems discussed or encountered, as well as requests that require follow-up. Finally, the anecdotal record should provide insight as to future planning for home visits.

Once the visits are underway, a typical visit might begin with the teacher chatting informally with the parent and child about the activities they have

Home Visiting Program Survey

What do you expect from this program? Please indicate whether each item below is "very important," "somewhat important," or "not important" for your child or for you as a parent.

1. What do you expect this program to do for your child?

	VERY IMPORTANT	SOMEWHAT IMPORTANT	NOT IMPORTANT
Develop social skills (learn to get along with others)	_____	_____	_____
Develop self-confidence	_____	_____	_____
Help prepare child for success in school	_____	_____	_____
Develop motor skills	_____	_____	_____
Develop language skills	_____	_____	_____

2. What do you expect this program to do for you, a parent?

Understand more about your child's development	_____	_____	_____
Understand what your child is doing at school	_____	_____	_____
Gain ideas for helping your child prepare for success in school	_____	_____	_____
Get acquainted with other parents and teachers	_____	_____	_____
Become aware of services available to you and your family	_____	_____	_____

Figure 7.2

been engaged in since the last visit. The teacher may want to provide a toy, book, or activity for the child while the parent and teacher briefly review the goals and plans set for this visit. Next, the teacher could introduce the new toys and materials, modeling with the child how to use each one, and explaining for the parent the value of each. Sometimes the parent may try out an activity with the child while the teacher observes and offers suggestions. After discussing any questions the parent may have, the teacher asks about other needs or goals and, with input from the parent, revises or establishes plans for the next visit. There may be a form for the parent and teacher to fill out together or one that the teacher leaves for the parent to fill out during the week. After goodbyes to the child and the parent, the teacher departs.

Barriers to Home Visits

In Chapter 2 we discussed barriers to effective parent involvement. Barriers included lack of communication, cultural and language differences, negative feelings that some parents harbor about schools, negative attitudes of some teachers and principals, and time constraints, to name a few. All of these barriers and more can stand in the way of effective home visits. Many teachers are understandably reluctant to conduct home visits. Reasons for their reluctance vary; they include lack of confidence in communicating with parents in their own homes, concern about cultural and language differences, concern about perceived conflicts in family values and childrearing practices, and concern over personal safety, to name a few of the major concerns stated by teachers. Some teachers need to conduct home visits with a "partner." The partner is typically a fellow teacher, though it may also be a parent educator, school counselor, or a volunteer parent mentor. The parent should understand in advance who will be visiting in the home with the teacher, and the role of the partner should be clarified. When language differences exist, having a fellow parent who speaks the home language can be especially advantageous. If such a person is not available, the teacher may try contacting someone in the community, perhaps the minister of a church in the area. This person would, ideally, be someone familiar to the family and who is well-respected in the community. Sharing the goals of the program with this individual and enlisting his or her support and assistance can often help school personnel gain entry into homes of parents who would otherwise be very reluctant, if not unwilling, to participate.

It is important that administrators and teachers understand the concerns that parents have about home-visiting (Hanhan 2003). The biggest concern that most parents have is that the teacher will *judge* them. They worry that the teacher will not approve of their housekeeping, their furniture, or the toys they have for their children. Some parents fear that the teacher will question their childrearing methods or try to tell them what to do. Others worry about the time that a home visit will take and about the expectations the teacher may have for the parent's involvement in educational activities. And still other parents are so concerned about such pressing problems as finances, health, job loss, or a family member's substance abuse that they fear they can't concentrate on child development or parenting issues at this point in their lives. All of these concerns are real, and in order for a home-visiting program to work, they must be addressed. The person most suitable for addressing these concerns is the home visitor. Establishing a relationship with each family is a must, and this can only be done if teachers are willing to reach out and meet families where they are.

For your consideration . . .

Following are several questions about home-visiting programs. Answering these questions should help you determine how closely your beliefs reflect the recommendations cited for effective home-visiting programs.

1. Home-visiting programs should address the needs of both children and parents by direct service or by referral.   **YES   NO**

2. Home-visiting programs should be flexible with regard to frequency, intensity, and duration of visits.   **YES   NO**

3. Home-visiting programs should be sensitive to the unique needs and circumstances of the families served and should avoid rigid, formulaic strategies found in packaged child development and/or parenting programs.   **YES   NO**

4. Home-visiting programs should utilize well-trained, dedicated professionals.   **YES   NO**

5. Home-visiting programs should set realistic goals and expectations.   **YES   NO**

6. Home-visiting programs should engage in continuous evaluation.   **YES   NO**

While some families reject the idea of a teacher coming into their home, they may agree to meet at a favorite place of interest to the child, such as a park or fast-food restaurant. The child can be asked to bring along a favorite toy. If parents refuse to participate at all in the program, you might try to provide options: biweekly rather than weekly visits, for example. Or perhaps another family member, such as an aunt or grandparent, might participate in the home visit until the parent feels able to do so. Another option might be to have the parent and child visit with the teacher in the classroom. Finally, the teacher might offer to drop off materials at the home, or at another agreed upon location, and spend just five or ten minutes explaining each. This option might lead to the parent's initiating longer sessions by asking questions or discussing the child's involvement in and reaction to the various materials and activities. In time, when a relationship is built and trust is formed, the parent may agree to a regular program of home-visiting.

SUMMARY

Home-visiting has the potential for dramatically improving communication between the home and school, particularly in situations that involve hard-to-reach parents. Benefits of home-visiting also include parents' increased use of educational strategies with their children, improved parent-child communication, and enhanced child development that impacts future school experiences. In this chapter you have been acquainted with information related to the design and implementation of home-visiting programs. Some of the concerns parents and teachers have about home-visiting were also explained. As stated by Terdan (1992): "Become an interested and appropriately involved friend of the family. This leads to a natural and positive interchange with parents" (2).

LOOKING AHEAD . . .

Helping parents understand their child's progress is a critical part of the communication process; however, there are many issues surrounding assessment, evaluation, grading, and the reporting of pupil progress. In the next chapter we examine ways to not only report progress to parents in an effective way, but also to involve parents and students in the assessment process.

REFERENCES

Delisio, E. R. (2004). Home visits forge school, family links. *Education World,* 2/10/2004. *http://www.education-world.com*

Fox-Barnett, M., & Meyer, T. (1992). The teacher's playing at my house this week! *Young Children 47*(5), 45–50.

Gomby, D. S. (2003). *Building school readiness through home visitation.* Sacramento, CA: First 5 California Children and Families Commission.

Hanhan, S. F. (2003). Parent-teacher communication: Who's talking? In G. Olsen, & M. L. Fuller (Eds.), *Home-school relations: Working successfully with parents and families* (pp. 111–133). Boston: Pearson.

Knapp, D. (1999). *Parents grateful that teachers make house calls. CNN.com,* September 7, 1999. *http://www.cnn.com/US/0090/07/teacher.home.visits/*

Olds, D. L., & Kitzman, H. Review of research on home-visiting for pregnant women and parents of young children. In R. E. Behrman (Ed.), *The future of children: Home visiting, 3* (winter 1993), 53–92.

Ramey, C. T., & Ramey, S. L. Home-visiting programs and the health and development of young children. In R. E. Behrman (Ed.), *The future of children: Home visiting, 3* (winter 1993), 129–139.

Steele-Carlin, S. (2001). Teacher visits hit-home. *Education World,* 10/09/2001. *http://www.education-world.com*

Terdan, S., & Freedman, J. (1992). The "parent-first" approach to home visits. *Extensions: Newsletter of the High/Scope Curriculum, 6*(4), 1–3.

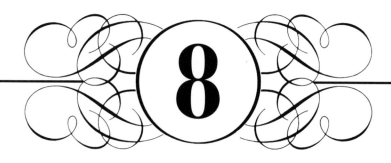

Assessment and the Reporting of Pupil Progress

Most schools face the grading dilemma. Pressure comes from some parents who say they want grades . . . and from teachers who feel that children won't be motivated to work hard if they are not given a grade. At the same time there are parents who complain that they don't get enough information about their child's progress, and teachers who feel that traditional grading procedures and report cards do not fit the way they instruct children in their classrooms. Do we keep giving children grades simply because "that's the way we've always done it?" Or do we begin to develop alternative reporting strategies that reflect the growth each child actually achieves and that give parents more information than simply A, B, C, D, or F?

ASSESSMENT AND EVALUATION MUST BE BASED ON THE CHILD'S PERFORMANCE

Evaluation of children must be *authentic* and *performance-based*. That is, evaluation must be based on what each child can do, rather than on an averaging of scores from tests and worksheets. In many schools, evaluation of pupil progress is based on a thorough analysis of performance samples collected over time. This collection of data, observation notes, and artifacts represents the knowledge and skills the child has acquired and can apply to his or her work. Teachers collect this information, record it, and share it with parents. To facilitate ongoing assessment and evaluation, some teachers keep monitoring books, a looseleaf notebook containing a section for each child. The teachers record observations of each child's oral and written language responses, as well as social behaviors exhibited.

In many schools children are asked to keep artifacts—samples of their work—in portfolios. Work placed in a student's portfolio may include a piece of art or a photograph of a piece of art completed by the student, a story or report written by the student, assessment sheets for theme projects showing scores—and, in some cases, grades—for spelling, grammar, punctuation, and content, as well as math quizzes, to name a few of the many artifacts. Students may also include narratives telling why a particular piece was included in the portfolio. Since most parents do not associate portfolios with assessment of progress in the elementary grades, teachers must educate parents as to the purpose of portfolios and how they serve as a strategy for learning. Parents need to know that a portfolio is more than a collection of student work (Freed 1993). Parents can be shown how the portfolio process assists their children in learning how to self-evaluate their own work, noting their own strengths and areas of need. Although parents do not need extensive training in portfolio assessment, they do need an awareness of the educational philosophy that supports the use of portfolios as a learning and assessment tool.

In many schools, teachers review all of the information and artifacts collected over a period of time, analyze each child's progress, and record the information on checklists shared with parents. The checklists reflect the curriculum, so that what is taught is assessed. Teachers indicate on the checklist whether children have "demonstrated" or "not demonstrated" a particular understanding or skill in their work. Written comments from teachers help to clarify and personalize the checklists. In this way ongoing assessment and periodic summative evaluation informs the curriculum and subsequent instruction. Most teachers ask the parents to sign, signifying their review of the checklist. A place for comments may also be included.

Other evaluative reports are usually sent home periodically. For example, teachers typically send home evaluation forms used to evaluate a final project. The skills to be evaluated through any given project vary, with all skills being checked periodically as students engage in authentic learning activities. Figures 8.1 and 8.2 include a project description and rubric used for one of the theme projects completed by students in Brian Lexyold's social studies classroom. Having this information can help parents be better teachers of their children. When parents are informed about what the teacher is looking for in terms of evaluation, they become aware of what to look for and where they can help. This teacher routinely posts all projects and rubrics on a class Website that is easily accessible by students and parents. After a project is evaluated, parents can use a password to log in to the gradebook to check their child's grade.

REGIONAL ASSESSMENT: AFRICA, ASIA, EUROPE, OR AUSTRALIA
(SELECTION MUST BE ON CURRENT UNIT)

<u>SOCIAL STUDIES STANDARD</u>
LOCATION AND PLACE –
  3.2   Knows how to read, use, and construct thematic and regional maps.
THE ASSIGNMENT:

1. **Making your map**:

    • You will carefully copy regions from a book or atlas to your map and add two make-believe cities
    For a proficient:
        • A proficient will have exactly two regions with one city in each.
        • Carefully copy two different regions from your book or atlas to your map (i.e. coniferous trees and desert scrub grasses).
        • Place one city in one region and the other city in the second region.
    For an advanced:
        • An advanced will have each of your two cities being in two different regions while also sharing a third overlapping region.
        • Carefully copy two different regions from your book or atlas to your map (i.e. 10-20 inches and 21-30 inches of annual precipitation). Color these different regions using differently colored stripes.
        • Next, using a different type of region (perhaps population density this time) find one that will overlap where you are going to place your cities so that both cities will share this third common region. Color the common region a solid light color.
        • Finally, place your two cities on your map so that each city will be in two different regions (the ones you colored with stripes) while also being part of the third overlapping region (the one you colored a solid light color).

    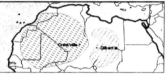

    • You may not use religions, languages, endangered species, or independence as your region(s).
    • Cities drawn on a regional border will be considered as occupying one of those regions, not both–no exceptions.

    • **ADD <u>MAP ESSENTIALS</u>: COMPLETE TITLE, MAJOR BODIES OF WATER, MOUNTAIN RANGE, RIVER, <u>ONE</u> LEGEND (INCLUDING REGIONS), SCALE, ONE LONGITUDE AND ONE LATITUDE LINE PLUS DEGREES, AND A FULLY-LABELED COMPASS. ALL THESE ITEMS MUST BE ON THE FRONT OF YOUR MAP OR IT/THEY WILL NOT BE INCLUDED IN THE GRADE.** You will not label countries.

2. **Writing about your regions:**

    • On a separate sheet of paper, identify the name of each of your cities and list the region(s) it belongs to.
    • Next, in separate paragraphs describe the strengths and weaknesses of each of your city's region(s).
    • **Strengths and weakness must refer to the region and not to nearby rivers, mountains, water, countries or you will be not proficient.**
    • Finally, in your last paragraph pick the best city and explain why it is better than the other.

3. **Rubric:**

    • The grading guide is how I will score you. Read it carefully as it contains additional information not mentioned here and self-evaluate your project by circling the individual bullets (dots) in each category on the rubric.

Figure 8.1

*E*VALUATION MUST INFORM PARENTS OF THE DEVELOPMENTAL LEVEL OF THE CHILD

Teachers provide work that fits each child's needs and abilities; they provide time and opportunity to grow. Children are then evaluated according to their individual abilities and levels of development. Because children are allowed to work at their level—a level that may be well below that of the typical child in the same grade—reporting progress can be very tricky. Parents, reflecting on their own school experiences and past report cards, can misunderstand when a teacher says that their child—a child functioning below grade level—is showing growth. Reporting procedures that indicate satisfactory progress in

Scoring Guide for Regions Project: Africa/Asia/Europe/Australia			

Location and Place Standard	PART	SCORE	PERFORMANCE
	PART 1	/30	IP P A
Checkpoint #2 — Knows how to read, use, and construct thematic and regional maps.	PART 2	/30	IP P A
	WORK HABITS		U C B A

Criterion	In Progress 2 pts.	Proficient 8 pts.	Advanced 10 pts.
Map PART 1 Checkpoint 3.2	• Regions are unclear, inaccurate and/or have several small or at least one major mistake. •Does not include or correctly use <u>ALL</u> map essentials. •Both cities are not clearly or completely placed in different regions or there are not exactly two cities.	•Regions are identifiable and accurate except for for one or two minor mistakes. •Includes and correctly uses <u>ALL</u> map essentials. •Both cities are clearly placed in different regions.	•Regions drawn on the map are precise and error-free. •Includes and correctly uses <u>ALL</u> map essentials and includes several extra. •Both cities are clearly placed in a different region while occupying a third region common to both cities.
Writing PART 2 Checkpoint 3.2	•Doesn't clearly describe each city's region(s) drawn on the map. •Incompletely describes a strength or weakness for each region that has a city in it or refers to other geographical information instead. •Explains why one city is better than the other without mentioning the regions it belongs to or <u>only</u> uses other geographical information.	•Identifies the name of each city and lists how each is placed in a different region. •Describes a strength and a weakness for each city's <u>region</u> drawn on the map. •Picks the best city and explains why it is better than the other using <u>only</u> the regions drawn on the map.	•Identifies the name of each city and describes how each is in a different region while at the same time sharing a third region common to both cities. •Describes one strength and one weakness for each city's <u>regions</u> drawn on the map and hypothesizes a future threat to one city's <u>region</u>. •Picks the best city and explains why it is better than the other using <u>both</u> the regions <u>and</u> other geographical information drawn on the map.

Figure 8.2

all areas, without clearly portraying the individual child's placement in the program, can be terribly misleading to parents, particularly if the child is later referred for special services or performs poorly on a state or district-mandated standardized test. Similarly, when these students go into middle and high schools where grades are still very much the norm, parents and students need to be prepared for a reporting process based on a comparison standard. To simply eliminate grades as a means of reporting student progress would cause tremendous turmoil among parents and educators—unless a system was already in place for showing growth in each child, while at the same time communicating levels and ranges of development.

Oftentimes a checklist or rubric can be designed in such a way as to help parents see the developmental progression of a particular concept or skill. Children's progress is noted under the stage evidenced most consistently at the time the report is sent. By reading about each stage, the parent can easily see where their child is with respect to progress toward the development of a specific element, such as conventional spelling ability.

Reports to parents need to address not only skills and concepts but also those areas of work habits and social/emotional development that play a large part in the child's reasons for success. Reports also need to include a place for narrative evaluations. When checklists are too detailed and lengthy, parents tend not to read them carefully; and sometimes what needs to be said cannot be conveyed in checklist format. Written comments are especially helpful in these circumstances. Teachers often indicate the level of development through written comments such as "While your child is making progress, he is not showing the amount of growth that is expected of students at this grade level." Although this information has been shared in face-to-face conferences, written documentation via the evaluation report is necessary.

Parents can also be helped to understand the range of development evidenced by students in a particular grade or class by viewing examples of student work. Displays set up during Open Houses and at parent meetings give parents a chance to see projects produced by other students. In addition, many teachers videotape student presentations and make the video available for parents to check out. Other teachers send home classroom "books" with entries by each child in the class. Parents have an opportunity to read each entry and to comment on the collection of writings. All of these are ways for teachers to help parents recognize the level at which their child is currently performing.

Parent education offerings and parent-teacher conferences represent other avenues for teachers to use to help parents understand what constitutes a "normal" range of growth and development, as well as understand the need to allow each child to progress at his or her individual pace. An understanding of developmental appropriateness as it relates to curriculum and to assessment and evaluation is also extremely important.

ASSESSMENT AND EVALUATION MUST INCLUDE INPUT FROM THE STUDENT

When children are asked to evaluate their own ability to apply the skills and concepts they are being taught, a conscious awareness develops, and they begin to take more responsibility for their own learning. For example, children can be asked to evaluate themselves on writing skills evidenced as they progress through each stage of the writing process: planning, drafting, revising, editing, and publishing/sharing. They also can be asked to evaluate their performance in a variety of settings: whole group, small cooperative group, literature study group, individual oral presentation, and so forth. Before an evaluation sheet goes home, teachers can ask children to write a letter to their parents explaining what the parents will see on the evaluation form. Students can also write letters to explain to their parents what they have included in their performance portfolios. Students evaluate what goes in their portfolios, explaining why they chose each item and what it showed they knew.

If students are keeping portfolios of their work, they need to be allowed to share their portfolio with parents. Students can take their portfolio home periodically and share its contents and their letter with their families. The teacher sends home a note to parents, telling them when the child will be bringing home the portfolio and asking that they go through it with their son or daughter, ask questions about the items included, and then fill out a written "Parent Response Form." In Figure 8.3 is a sample of a student portfolio feedback form that could be sent home for parents to fill out. Lynn West, an upper grade level teacher has had great success involving parents through

---

Student Portfolio Feedback Form

Date:_____

Student:_____

Did your child share the contents of the portfolio with you? _____

What part of the portfolio did you like best? _____

_____

_____

_____

_____

Was there any part that concerned you or that you had questions about? _____

_____

_____

_____

Did your child's progress come as a surprise to you? Why or why not? _____

_____

_____

_____

I have reviewed the portfolio and am returning it with this form.

_____
Parent

Figure 8.3

student portfolios. Some parents say they are surprised by what their child can do.

In Becky Oliver's first-grade classroom in Jacksonville, Illinois, children and their families are invited to a "portfolio party" at the end of the school year. One child brought almost his entire extended family! Parents, grandparents, and an aunt were present to examine the portfolio and to compare progress made by the child throughout the year. What a wonderful opportunity for building self-esteem and pride in one's accomplishments! Portfolio-sharing reaps many benefits, especially when children are actively involved in the process of evaluating and reporting their own progress.

ASSESSMENT AND EVALUATION MUST ALLOW FOR INPUT FROM THE PARENT

It is important that evaluation forms sent home by the teacher include a place for parents to comment on what they see happening with regard to goals set for their child. Strategies used to improve specific skills may also be part of the conversation. Sometimes parents have ideas that translate into very successful performance on the part of the student. Providing parents with ample opportunities to share their ideas promotes partnership and a clearer understanding of the evaluation process. In Figure 8.4 is a Midterm Report form developed by Susan Rusch, a teacher at Ingersoll Middle School.

Many teachers have a "homework folder" or "take-home folder" that children use to carry work samples and notes to and from home on a daily or weekly basis. Fran Schaller, a teacher in Springfield, Illinois, invites children to decorate a folder which is then laminated to increase durability. On the left inside cover of the folder, Fran staples several blank sheets of paper labeled "Parent/Teacher Notes." In a letter of introduction, she explains that parents may write notes to her in this space—and that she will write notes to them. Children take the folder home each day. At the beginning of the school year, Fran finds herself answering many questions from parents. This sets the stage for two-way communication throughout the year. Darla Hamilton has found that assignment notebooks are a valuable tool for involving parents in their child's daily activities. She has each student write the activities completed during the day under each subject heading. Homework assignments always go on the last line. Space is also provided for students to include a note about anything they need to bring to school, such as lunch money, a permission slip, or supplies. Parents are required to sign the notebook each night. Also, as a parent of a hearing-impaired child, Darla finds that she can easily ask her child questions about his day based on the information in his assignment notebook.

Barb Brinkman, a special education teacher, gives each student a spiral notebook that serves as a dialogue journal between home and school. The journal goes home one or more times a week, depending on need, with comments and/or questions from Barb. Parents are encouraged to add their comments and questions, carrying on a written conversation or dialogue with their child's teacher. Barb lets parents know that the journal is one option

Ingersoll Middle School Mid-term Report

(Date)

Dear Parents,

This mid-term letter is to alert you that your child is earning a low grade. The enclosed report tells the child's grade and a general comment from the teacher. Now we ask for your help. You know your child much better than the teachers do.

Please share with them any information which will help them understand the problem as you see it and that might help the teachers help your child. Please return this letter to school by (date). If we don't receive a response by then, we will contact you to be sure you have received it. Thank you.

Dear Teachers,

• I have received my child's mid-term report. Thank you for the information.

• I think that this would help my child do better: _____
_____
_____
_____
_____

• I think that you should know that: _____
_____
_____
_____
_____
_____

• I would like to discuss my child's progress with you on the phone.

• I will call the school during the teacher's available time this week.

• Please call me during this time period: _____

Signed_____ Date_____

Child's name_____

Figure 8.4

for communication. Some parents find this a very effective tool and write rather lengthy notes several times a week. Other parents report finding Barb's notes helpful, but they prefer to respond through telephone calls or face-to-face visits.

Holly Riggins has several parents she emails on a daily basis with behavior information and homework. Julie Arp calls parents when a child masters a difficult concept. This encourages families to celebrate learning at home. Email works well, too, for sharing positive information about students.

Some teachers ask parents to help in the design of an evaluation instrument for rating home assignments. The brief form would be attached to each homework assignment returned to school and would indicate the difficulty level, the child's understanding of the task, and comments and/or suggestions from the parent. These instruments provide helpful information to the teacher and also give the parent an opportunity to be involved in the assessment process. Other teachers ask parents to record their own observations about their child's progress on an evaluation chart sent home. In Figure 8.5 is an example of a parent observation form that could be sent to parents of

Child Development Observation Form: Four to Five Years

You are invited to take an active role in assessing your child's development by charting some of the following skills as they are first learned or used frequently by your child. Please use the following range of skills as a guide, keeping in mind that children acquire new skills at varying ages.

During This Year Your Child May Learn to . . .

DATE SKILL FIRST ATTEMPTED		DATE SKILL FREQUENTLY USED
_____	Talk with speech that is ninety percent understandable	_____
_____	Bounce and catch a large ball with both hands	_____
_____	Talk in sentences of four to six words or more	_____
_____	Count one to ten objects	_____
_____	Tell his/her name	_____
_____	Follow a two-step direction	_____
_____	Name six to eight colors	_____
_____	Name three shapes: triangle, square, rectangle	_____
_____	Ask for help when needed	_____
_____	Understand meaning of behind, in front of, under, and over	_____
_____	Dress himself/herself	_____
_____	Attend to toileting needs independently	_____
_____	Answer who, what, why, where, and what if questioned	_____
_____	Scribble/draw	_____
_____	Understand opposites: big/little, long/short, hard/soft	_____

Figure 8.5

children who will be enrolling in kindergarten in the fall. In Figure 8.6 is a parent survey for possible speech-language problems or concerns. The parent could be asked to return the form to school prior to the first day of school. In Figure 8.7 is an example of an observation form sent home to solicit parents' observations of their first-grade child's reading performance. A form that could be used during the year appears in Figure 8.8.

The conversation that is begun at the start of the school year can continue throughout the year as teachers offer parents the opportunity to be involved in the assessment process. Although not all parents will accept this

Student Handbook 2004-2005

Canton Union School District #66
Speech-Language Department

Dear Parent,
Good speech and language skills are important for your child's school success. Please check the list below for possible problems or concerns.

I. Articulation:

　　a. Difficult to understand the child's speech
　　b. Sound(s) are not correct. Some errors are acceptable for younger children.

II. Language:
　　a. Shows difficulty in organizing thoughts
　　b. Shows difficulty in remembering common words
　　c. Uses the wrong noun, verb, or pronoun such as "him" for "he"
　　d. Speaks only in single words, short phrases, or sentences
　　e. Has difficulty in understanding or following directions
　　f. Interrupts others and does not understand "turn taking"

III. Fluency:
　　a. Repeats sounds, syllables, words, or phrases
　　b. Cannot get some words out
　　c. Speech is not smooth and appears "choppy"; too fast or slow
　　d. Appears tense/uncomfortable or avoids speaking

IV. Voice:
　　a. Usually weak can hardly be heard
　　b. Sounds husky, hoarse, or has laryngitis often
　　c. Sounds like he/she has a cold or talks through his/her nose

V. Nonverbal
　　a. Poor listening skills
　　b. Frequently needs questions repeated directly to him/her

VI.　　Other Problems
　　a. Has cleft palate (repaired or unrepaired), cerebral palsy
　　b. Has difficulty hearing

Do you feel that your child often shows one or more of these concerns? If you do, please fill out the screening request below and return it to school. Your child will be checked and you will be contacted as quickly as possible. NO OTHER TESTING WILL BE DONE WITHOUT YOUR WRITTEN PERMISSION. If you have any questions or concerns, please contact the therapists for your child's school.

Beth Baker, Lincoln 647-7594
Teresa Falk, Westview 647-2111
Bridgette Kohler, 647-0136

Speech-Language Screening Request

Student's Name _____ Birthday _____

Teacher _____ Grade _____

What reasons do you have for feeling that your child may have a speech or language problem?

Figure 8.6

My Child as a Reader

Please indicate your observations of your child's reading during the past few weeks.

	USUALLY	SOMETIMES	RARELY	COMMENTS
1. My child enjoys listening to me read to him/her.	_____	_____	_____	_____
2. My child enjoys reading to others.	_____	_____	_____	_____
3. When my child reads, he/she knows most of the words.	_____	_____	_____	_____
4. When my child reads, he/she notices when something he/she says doesn't make sense.	_____	_____	_____	_____
5. When my child reads, he/she can figure out new words.	_____	_____	_____	_____
6. When my child reads, he/she sometimes guesses at words, but they usually make sense.	_____	_____	_____	_____
7. After my child reads, he/she can retell the story in his/her own words.	_____	_____	_____	_____

Figure 8.7

responsibility or approach it with the same seriousness of purpose that some parents will, chances are great that the partnership will be strengthened as a result of the offer having been made. Parents who do take an active role in assessment of their child's progress will, undoubtably, have a greater understanding of the information shared through the reporting process.

PARENTS MAKE A DIFFERENCE!

Child's name:_____

Date:_____

Parents are the first and most important teachers for their children. Please grade your child's growth in reading at home since the last reporting period.

A = Strongly Agree
B = Agree
C = Disagree
D = Strongly Disagree

My child: Comments
1. Understands more of what s/he reads   A   B   C   D
2. Enjoys being read to by family members   A   B   C   D
3. Finds time for quiet reading at home   A   B   C   D
4. Sometimes guesses at words, but
   the words usually make sense   A   B   C   D
5. Can tell the main parts of what was read A   B   C   D
6. Has a good attitude about reading   A   B   C   D
7. Enjoys reading to family members   A   B   C   D
8. Would like to get more books   A   B   C   D

Strengths that I see:_____

_____

Areas that need improvement:_____

_____

Concerns or questions:_____

_____

Parent's signature:_____

Figure 8.8

SUMMARY

Assessment and the reporting of pupil progress is a very challenging task. When schools attempt to involve parents in the process, they have found that parents come to understand more about the curriculum and their child's progress, have fewer questions, and are more supportive of both the teacher and the school.

The questions that follow relate to the guidelines we have shared in this chapter. Consideration of these questions may help you assess your beliefs about assessment and reporting of pupil progress.

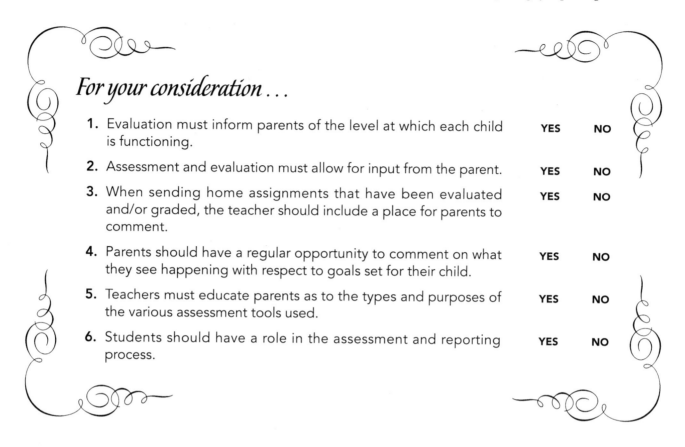

For your consideration . . .

1. Evaluation must inform parents of the level at which each child is functioning. **YES   NO**

2. Assessment and evaluation must allow for input from the parent. **YES   NO**

3. When sending home assignments that have been evaluated and/or graded, the teacher should include a place for parents to comment. **YES   NO**

4. Parents should have a regular opportunity to comment on what they see happening with respect to goals set for their child. **YES   NO**

5. Teachers must educate parents as to the types and purposes of the various assessment tools used. **YES   NO**

6. Students should have a role in the assessment and reporting process. **YES   NO**

*L*OOKING AHEAD . . .

In this chapter ways to involve parents in the assessment process were examined. This emphasis on two-way communication will continue, as guidelines and strategies for planning and implementing parent-teacher and student-parent-teacher conferences are shared in Chapter 9.

*R*EFERENCE

Freed, A. (1993). What should we tell parents about portfolios? *Illinois School Research and Development Journal, 31* (1): 18-19.

Planning and Implementing Effective Parent Conferences

Most teachers recognize the importance of regularly scheduled parent-teacher conferences, yet report being extremely frustrated with the way most districtwide conference days are scheduled. When parents are scheduled in ten- to fifteen-minute blocks of time, one right after the other, teachers are hard-pressed to report the students' progress or give the parents any time to express their views and questions.

*I*NTRODUCTION

All too often parents and teachers leave a conference feeling frustrated at not having had the time they needed to really communicate with one another. Ideally, conferences provide an opportunity to review goals and formulate plans and to facilitate a balanced look at all aspects of the child's development. Rather than a free-flowing exchange of questions and information, typical conferences often degenerate into a one-way reporting of pupil progress with hardly enough time left for parents to voice questions. And as discussed in earlier chapters, the parents of children who are experiencing difficulty in school often do not attend. Reasons for not attending were addressed in Chapter 2 as we discussed barriers to parent involvement. While that discussion will not be repeated here, it is understandable that parents who experienced difficulty during their own schooling would feel reluctant to attend a conference only to hear how their child is experiencing the same frustrations and difficulties. On the other hand, parents of children who are very successful in school often report feeling that conferences are a waste of time: "Why bother to attend if the teacher is just going to say 'Your child is doing fine?'"

different codes/lang

In *A Framework for Understanding Poverty,* Ruby Payne distinguishes between the formal-register discourse patterns used by teachers and the casual-register discourse patterns used by parents, especially those from poverty. She points out the problems use of these different discourse patterns cause, particularly during parent-teacher conferences: "Teachers want to get right to the point; parents, particularly those from poverty, need to beat around the bush first. When teachers cut to the conversation and get right to the point, parents view that as being rude and non-caring" (p. 45).

Regularly scheduled conferences with sufficient time allotted for each afford teachers and parents needed opportunities to get to know one another and to plan strategies for working toward shared goals and outcomes. In this chapter we will approach parent-teacher conferencing from the standpoint of what they *could* be: an excellent opportunity for teacher, parent, and even child to have uninterrupted time and privacy for productive conversation about the child's learning. Just how schools will go about finding ways to implement the strategies we suggest will depend, in large part, on each school's commitment to forging a strong partnership with *each* child's family.

convo about child's learning

*P*LANNING FOR PARENT-TEACHER CONFERENCES

Without the support of district level administrators and the school board, school personnel are limited in their abilities to plan and implement the kinds of parent-teacher conferences that are truly needed. Efforts must be made to help district leaders understand the problems associated with typical parent-teacher conferences and the gains to be realized from improving current conferencing routines and procedures. One way to garner support is to conduct a "satisfaction survey" with parents and teachers. Ask what they like about current conferencing procedures, what they would like to see changed, why they feel these changes are important, and the impact they believe the changes would have on student achievement and motivation. Gathering specific recommendations about the number of conferences to be scheduled each year and length of time for each also needs to take place. This will require decisions about alternatives for scheduling conferences. Many districts release children from school for a couple of days each year so that parent-teacher conferences can be scheduled districtwide. Other districts have "conference months" twice a year during which time they try to get all parents into the school for a conference. Substitute teachers are hired to "float" from one classroom to another when conferences are planned. Flexible conference times are scheduled, with the goal being one hundred percent attendance by parents at some time during the designated months.

Once a decision has been made to have parent-teacher conferences, a district or school level committee, or the faculty and staff from each school, needs to develop an action plan. Decisions concerning the scheduling of dates and times for conferences, advertising of conferences, provision of transportation, childcare, translators, and in-service training must be made.

To boost attendance and to take advantage of the large numbers of parents who do come into the school building for conferences, special activities and displays can be planned. Having coffee and juice available and someone on hand to greet parents as they arrive is a good idea. Very large schools sometimes enlist high school students to serve as "tour guides" to facilitate parents' movement around the building or to work as childcare assistants. Other schools host a book fair, often staffed by parent volunteers or older students, which takes place during the conferences. Book browsing gives parents and children something to do before and after their conference. Hallway displays of children's work also provide something of interest for parents who arrive early for their appointment. Finally, booths offering information from community service agencies, the parent-teacher organization, the school volunteer program, and so forth might be set up to reach parents coming into the school for conferences. Many schools let parents know that report cards will be distributed during the conferences. This serves as an incentive for some parents to attend.

Involvement of all school personnel and the parent-teacher organization during planning and implementation of conferences is important. Paraprofessionals, librarians, instructional leaders, home-school liaisons, visiting teachers, reading and math specialists, guidance counselors, secretaries, and *Get all involved* other personnel can all play a role in making parent-teacher conferences successful. These individuals can assist in scheduling and publicizing conferences, in preparing special hall displays or bulletin boards, in arranging for book fairs and other events to be coordinated with the conference day(s) and in arranging transportation and carpools for parents. On conference day they can serve as greeters and guides when parents enter the building, provide childcare, staff booths and other exhibits, and collect and tally parent conference evaluation forms. Teachers who are able to may serve as translators for non-English-speaking parents. Older students, parents, and community volunteers may also serve in this capacity.

Scheduling of conferences is a huge task, but making it as convenient as possible for parents to attend serves to improve attendance *and* foster good relationships. At the beginning of the school year, some schools ask parents to indicate preferred times for conferencing. These times are taken into consideration as conferences are set up. Flexible scheduling with both early morning and evening hours available for working parents is a must. Attention need also be given to the teachers who have children attending school in the system. As parents, they too need the opportunity to attend conferences with their children's teachers. Schools can also assist when parents have more than one child enrolled in the school. Teachers work with one another to schedule the conferences close together so that parents have to make only one trip. This coordination is facilitated by the principal or school secretary. Once tentative schedules are developed, a short teachers' meeting may be necessary to allow for negotiating conference times for families with more than one child enrolled. A letter of invitation is then sent home with the schedule of suggested times, and parents have an opportunity to respond and, if necessary, reschedule their appointment(s). In Figure 9.1 is an advance notice sent by Quincy, Illinois kindergarten teacher Alison Lewis.

When the letter of invitation goes home, some schools or individual teachers also send home tips for successful conferencing and suggested questions parents might want to ask the teacher. An example is shown in Figure 9.2. This information and a conference evaluation form for parents to fill out after each conference, needs to be prepared during the planning stage. Figure 9.3 is an example of a conference evaluation form.

Many teachers have children write a letter to tell their parents about an upcoming conference. Reminders about upcoming conferences can be placed in classroom and school newsletters and in the local newspapers. Schools might also consider sending letters to the businesses or industries employing a large number of parents of children enrolled in the school. Soliciting employer support can be advantageous, particularly if employees are willing to give parents release time to attend the conferences. The Chamber of Commerce sends out these letters in some cities, asking employers to release parents from work to attend conferences. Some schools put public service announcements about the conferences on the television and radio. In addition, students sometimes visit the radio station on a school field trip and tape messages that are broadcast the week of the conferences. These messages are usually written by the students and directed at parents. Messages include the name of the school and the dates of the upcoming parent conferences. Parents and community members tend to notice when children's voices are heard making a radio announcement, and the more children know about and are involved in the planning for parent-teacher conferences, the better the attendance. Teachers might also call parents who may need extra encouragement to attend.

Some attention to expectations for each conference may also be a part of this initial planning process. Teachers may be expected to (1) develop a plan, or work with each child to develop a plan, for each conference; (2) prepare a folder of each child's work, and/or (3) ask parents to fill out an evaluation form at the close of the conference. Teachers may also devise their own

Expectations of teachers

PARENT TEACHER CONFERENCES...Notes will be coming home on Friday informing you all about parent teacher conferences. A schedule is made with dates and times and please send it back next Monday (or as soon as possible) letting me know if that date and time will work for you! The 1st Quarter is over October 29! Can you believe it??? We will continue working hard and I will be assessing their progress thus far for their report cards. All this and more will be shared with you during your conference. I'm looking forward to meeting with all of you!☺

Figure 9.1

Getting the Most Out of Parent-Teacher Conferences

Conferences give parents and teachers a chance to work together to build the teamwork that helps children learn better. The five tips discussed below can help you, the parent, get the most out of each conference.

1. Think about what you want to discuss in the conference. You may wish to identify some issues and/or prepare some questions. For example:

   - How is my child doing in class?
   - Does my child use time well? Have good work habits?
   - Does my child turn assignments in on time?
   - Does my child get along with others?
   - What can I do at home to support what you are doing at school?

2. Talk with your child before the conference. Ask what your child thinks the teacher will say. Ask if your child has any concerns or problem areas in school. Talk about what your child likes most and least about school—and why.

3. Ask the teacher to explain anything you don't understand. If there are any terms or programs you do not know about ask. Sometimes programs are referred to by their initials. For example, TAG refers to the Talented and Gifted program.

4. Be prepared to talk and to listen. Tell the teacher what you observe at home. Talk about your child's interests, likes, and dislikes. Share any concerns your child has about school. Be sure to let the teacher know about anything that may affect your child's learning.

5. Follow-up. Work with the teacher to develop a plan for follow-up. If you think of a question you didn't ask, write a note or call.

— *Figure 9.2* —

Parent Evaluation of Parent-Teacher Conference

Please help us evaluate the effectiveness of our parent-teacher conferences by filling out this form and leaving it in the box provided. Thank you!

CIRCLE ONE

1. I feel the conference helped me better understand my child's abilities and needs.   **YES   NO**
   Comment:

2. I understand more about the instructional program.   **YES   NO**
   Comment:

3. I understand how my child's progress is determined.   **YES   NO**
   Comment:

4. I have some ideas I can use at home to help my child learn.   **YES   NO**
   Comment:

5. I was able to express my concerns and ask my questions.   **YES   NO**
   Comment:

6. I understood the teacher's explanations.   **YES   NO**
   Comment:

7. I have other concerns about my child's education that were not addressed.   **YES   NO**
   Comment:

8. I worked with the teacher to plan strategies for helping my child learn.   **YES   NO**
   Comment:

9. I felt welcomed by the teacher.   **YES   NO**
   Comment:

10. Overall, I am pleased with the conference.   **YES   NO**
    Comment:

Figure 9.3

personal reminder letters for the upcoming conference, including purposes and objectives for the conference and some means for gathering parent input and suggestions into the conference planning process. Asking parents to send back a form listing one or two issues, ideas, or questions they would like to discuss during the conference would provide the teacher with a little "lead time" for preparing to meet these individual needs and would convey to parents the desire to make this conference meaningful to them. In addition, having this information from the parents would assist the teacher in developing conference plans. A written plan with one or two objectives should be developed for each conference. Having such a plan helps focus a conference and ensures that the most critical issues will receive adequate attention. Figure 9.4 is an example of one conference plan. The form includes a place for recording the name of the child and of the parents, since last names are sometimes different. Also included is space for recording conference objectives and for writing some strengths and needs to be discussed during the conference. There is also space for writing down a few ideas or strategies to suggest for both the home and school setting.

Final planning for conferences includes setting up an area in the classroom where teacher and parents can comfortably talk. Adult-sized chairs are more appropriate than children's chairs or desks. Placement of the chairs is an important consideration. The teacher should refrain from sitting behind a desk, which conveys a formal "expert/novice" relationship rather than one in which parents and teacher come together as partners or as a team with the child. A small table for displaying the child's portfolio or folder of work is also needed.

DURING THE CONFERENCE: COMMUNICATING EFFECTIVELY WITH PARENTS

Most teachers have not had formal training in conducting parent-teacher conferences. Staff development opportunities designed to help teachers gain needed communication and conferencing skills can also result in an increase in teachers' self-confidence in working with parents. In addition to routines for conducting conferences, teachers need to develop active listening skills, strategies for facilitating problem solving and negotiation, and strategies for dealing with the angry—and possibly verbally abusive—parent. Teachers also need to be prepared to conduct conferences in which the child will attend with the parents. These parent-teacher-child conferences will be discussed in a separate section in this chapter.

Routines for Conducting Parent-Teacher Conferences

Conferences should begin on a positive note, with teachers greeting parents in a relaxed, friendly manner. Most teachers find that sharing a positive comment about the child and then asking the parent to share something positive

Conference Planning Sheets

CHILD'S NAME: _____ DATE: _____

PARENTS' NAMES: _____

CONFERENCE OBJECTIVES: (1) _____

_____

(2) _____

_____ .

STRENGTHS OBSERVED DURING THIS PERIOD _____

_____

_____

_____ .

NEEDS OBSERVED DURING THIS PERIOD _____

_____

_____

_____ .

SUGGESTED STRATEGIES TO TRY AT SCHOOL _____

_____

_____

_____ .

SUGGESTED STRATEGIES TO TRY AT HOME _____

_____

_____

_____ .

Figure 9.4

① Share positive(s)
    P + F
② Ask Open floor 4 parents

they've noticed about the child is a good way to start the conference. Before addressing the conference objectives, which would include relating information about the child's progress, the teacher should pause to ask the parents if they have something they would like to share and discuss first. If the parents have already given the teacher this information in advance of the conference, the teacher might point out how the stated conference objectives reflect the concerns and questions identified by the parents.

As pointed out in earlier chapters, teachers must use language appropriate for the parents, being careful to avoid use of technical terms and specialized vocabulary. Rather than assuming that parents know common acronyms used for various programs and tests, the teacher should simply explain that, for example, TAG stands for the Talented and Gifted program.

In reporting the child's progress, the teacher should share anecdotal information and concrete examples, relating the child's growth in light of the curricular goals, objectives, and expectations. In conferences where the child is not present, the child should have been involved in gathering together evidence of his or her progress. Examples may include lists of books read, written reports and stories, projects, and other assignments. Some teachers have children keep a scrapbook. One or two "best" examples are included on a weekly or biweekly basis, along with an explanation as to the growth the piece reflects and why it was included. Sometimes there are audio or video tapes of a child conducting a special classroom presentation or engaging in oral reading. While time does not allow for an extensive "showing" of the child's work over a six- or nine-week period, a sufficient number of items should be available to reveal a thorough look at the child's progress in all areas of the curriculum.

Parents should be given ample time to share their observations of the child's progress and to suggest their ideas for continued growth at school as well as at home. If the conversation goes too far astray, the teacher can tactfully refer again to the conference objectives. Strategies for follow-up of objectives and conference outgrowth should be jointly planned by teacher and parents; however, the teacher will need to initiate the discussion. Writing down the ideas suggested and eventually agreed upon is helpful as it not only keeps you "on task" but also serves as a reminder of what was said. Figure 9.5 is an example of a conference outgrowth form that could be used. At the end of the conference the teacher either gives parents a copy of the conference outgrowth plan or assures them that one will be mailed as soon as possible. Some teachers also give parents a set of home-learning materials or activities they can use to help their child at home. Finally, parents are asked to fill out an evaluation form designed to improve the overall conferencing strategy. If another parent is scheduled directly after the departure of one parent, the teacher could facilitate that parent's departure by putting away all conference notes in a folder and walking the parent to the classroom door. Material for the next conference should be in a closed folder to ensure that it cannot be seen by another parent but is still readily available.

After each conference teachers should follow up by continuing to communicate with the parents. The conference outgrowth form has a place for recording strategies and dates for follow-up. Some parents and teachers set a follow-up conference time. Others agree to make contact by telephone or to send written messages to share progress made. Oftentimes parents request information, or teachers offer to share information that is not readily available during the conference. These follow-up materials may be sent after the conference. Some teachers send individual letters thanking parents for attending the conference; others include a thank-you note in the next classroom

Conferences Outgrowth Sheet

CHILD'S NAME: _____ DATE: _____

STUDENT'S STRENGTHS: _____
_____
_____

STUDENT'S NEEDS: _____
_____
_____

STRATEGIES TO BE USED AT SCHOOL: _____
_____
_____

STRATEGIES TO BE USED AT HOME: _____
_____
_____

FOLLOW-UP PLAN/PROCEDURES/DATES: _____
_____
_____

_____   _____
Parent   Teacher

Figure 9.5

newsletter. All of these follow-up strategies serve as concrete reminders to parents about the strategies agreed on at the conference and increase the chances that parents will do their part at home.

Active Listening Skills

The quality of conferences depends largely upon the communication skills of both teachers and parents. Recognizing the potential impact of interpersonal and communication skills, some schools offer separate communication skills workshops for teachers and for parents. Parents who are recognized as good communicators may conduct or assist in conducting the parent workshop. Whether for parents or teachers, communication skills workshops should include strategies for active listening. Dialogue has been defined as "the process of successful relationship building" (Yankelovich 1999, p. 15). According to Shelton (1999), listening is the key to successful dialogue, however, the individuals involved must be willing to temporarily suspend their own judgments and opinions in order to be an effective listener.

Barrera and Corso (2003) have identified three qualities of successful dialogue: respect, reciprocity, and responsiveness. According to these authors, reciprocity and responsiveness must be based on respect. Reciprocity exists in a dialogue if each individual recognizes that the other person is equally capable: "Reciprocity requires acknowledging and trusting that every person involved has experience and perceptions of equal value. Reciprocity does not, however, require denying that one person has more expertise, knowledge, or authority than another person in particular areas . . ." (p. 45). Being responsive involves being open to new ideas and new solutions. Barrera and Corso point out that teachers must be willing to "stay with the tension of differing perspectives" in order to develop a collaborative solution that represents the varying opinions involved (p. 82).

Active listening is employed by a teacher when a parent indicates that he or she has a problem or an unmet need. Using active-listening strategies conveys an attempt on the part of the teacher to listen to and understand what is being said. Listening in a responsive manner involves listening "with focused attention, patience, and curiosity" (Freedman and Combs 1996, p. 44). Body posture is important. Adopting an "open" body position—with arms resting comfortably downward—and leaning slightly toward the speaker conveys a willingness to listen and to enter into a two-way exchange of information and ideas. In contrast, a listener who is leaning back with arms crossed over the chest is often seen as "closed"—disinterested, defensive, or even hostile toward the speaker. Maintaining direct eye contact, if appropriate to the speaker's culture, is recommended, as is responding with a nod or other facial movement that acknowledges listening.

Being aware of a parent's relaxed, open posture or of body tension, hesitation, or excitability can help the teacher better understand the message being conveyed. If a parent appears hesitant to share, the teacher might ask a leading question such as "Tell me what you see as your child's greatest strengths or interests." Getting the parent to talk about her child is a way to help her feel more relaxed and comfortable in discussing her concerns.

In addition to being a good observer, it is important to be a good listener. Rather than interrupting the speaker to share one's own views, the active listener listens. So often we only "listen with half an ear." Instead of really attempting to put ourselves in the place of the speaker, we spend most of the time the speaker is talking thinking of how we want to respond. As soon as the speaker pauses to collect his or her thoughts, we jump in with what we want to say. An active listener not only attends to the speaker's *words* but also notices the way the speaker shares the message. A respect for silence is helpful. If the speaker pauses, it may be because of an uncertainty as to how to put into words what he or she wants to say. If the listener senses this, a nod or a simple comment such as "Go on" or "I'd like to hear more" may encourage the speaker to continue. If the speaker is digressing too far from the main issue, the listener may redirect the speaker by saying "I was interested in the comment you made earlier about . . . Could you tell me more about that?" This conveys an openness to continuing the conversation, while at the same time helping the speaker get back on target. This strategy may also be used if the speaker is beginning to reveal too much. A parent who uses a conference situation to discuss personal problems may later regret having said too much and may withdraw from future contact with the teacher. While it is helpful for the teacher to know about changes in the home environment and problems that may interfere with the child's learning, the focus of the discussion should remain centered on the child and on strategies that may be used at the time. The teacher may, however, offer to refer the parent to other sources for help with the problem. Admitting that one is not equipped to handle a problem is not rude; offering to help locate someone who can is an acceptable way of conveying concern.

Briefly restating the main ideas conveyed by the speaker is a good active listening strategy. Since it is impossible to *really know* what another person is thinking and feeling, active listening responses should be offered in a tentative manner. That is, the listener shares the perceptions gained from the speaker in a way that invites confirmation. If the listener is relatively certain that he or she has understood the speaker, opening with phrases such as "So, from your point of view, . . ." or "What I hear you saying is, . . ." and "It seems to you . . ." lets the speaker know he or she was listened to and that the listener cares enough to check to see if he or she understood correctly.

In cases where the speaker has clearly and specifically stated the situation and/or the problem, restating the main points may be redundant and unnecessary. Silence or acknowledgement would be more appropriate, perhaps followed by a request for suggestions for solving the problem.

If the listener has experienced difficulty understanding the speaker's message, he or she might offer a tentative summary of the main points, beginning with phrases such as "Please correct me if I'm wrong, but as I understand you, . . ." or "Let me see if I understand you . . . ." and "This is what I think I hear you saying: . . ." If this is not possible due to a complete or almost complete lack of understanding on the part of the listener, a simple request for clarification is more in order.

Active listening is a skill that teachers need to develop to communicate more effectively with individuals who indicate the presence of a problem or unmet need. While active listening cannot ensure a successful conference, use of active listening facilitates conversation. Teachers who seek parents' opinions and ideas first find that a parent is more willing to work with the teacher on plans designed to have a positive impact on the child.

Facilitating Problem-Solving and Negotiation

Teachers who have a genuine desire to participate in a partnership with the family will approach conferences with an attitude of sharing and learning, as well as with a willingness to consider parents' perspectives. Starting off the conference on a positive note and giving parents the opportunity to first share their concerns (before addressing issues the teacher needs to discuss) demonstrate respect for the parents and the role they have in their children's education. When a team approach is used in problem-solving conferences, teachers are more likely to avoid many of the pitfalls that plague some teacher-parent interactions. It is a good idea to be cognizant of these pitfalls and the ways they manifest themselves within the conference situation.

As stated in earlier chapters, the teacher must avoid the role of the "expert." Use of technical terminology and labels to describe the program and the child's performance only serves to put the parent on the defensive. In a team approach there are no experts and novices—only partners. When describing a child's behavior or performance, the teacher should do precisely that—*describe*. Use of negative labels and terms, such as *behind, immature,* and *hyperactive,* are unsuitable in a parent-teacher exchange. Similarly, speaking in "absolutes" is rarely a good practice. For example, "Stan rarely chooses to read during free-choice time" is better than "Stan doesn't like to read." It's also important to speak in specific, rather than general, terms: "Linda is not doing well in math" is a general statement that is not nearly as informative or helpful as "Linda knows her times tables from one through four but has difficulty remembering the five through nine tables."

Another pitfall to avoid involves engaging in unprofessional conversation. Although usually meant to make the parent feel as if the teacher really understands a problem or situation, sharing personal information about oneself or about other children and/or parents is unprofessional and may even represent a breach of confidence. Parents do not need to know that the teacher was also divorced or suffered from a previous illness. And divulging information about other families, however insignificant it may seem, is strictly unacceptable. A teacher may say, for instance, "Many parents find that preadolescents are quite a handful!" but should *not* say "Well, you are not alone. You know, the Smiths have been having quite a time with Shelly this year."

Sometimes the teacher ends up, quite by accident, in the middle of a family squabble. For example, a parent may say to the teacher: "My husband says 'spare the rod and spoil the child.' What do you think about spanking children?" The teacher has to be very diplomatic in answering this question. A response that recognizes the existence of a broad range of guidance and discipline techniques and includes an offer to share some of the strategies used in the classroom is less likely to result in the teacher's getting "caught in the middle" than a direct yes or no answer would be.

Finally, in a team approach, the teacher does not assume ownership of problems and all responsibility for solving problems but rather shares in problem-solving situations with parents—and child, whenever appropriate. Assuming ownership of a problem conveys a variety of messages, most of which are negative. To start with, taking all of the responsibility for solving a problem suggests that the parents lack the ability to contribute in a meaningful way. It also reinforces the stereotypical picture of the teacher as expert.

Also, whether the teacher has initiated the problem-solving conference or whether one or both of the parents have asked for assistance, ownership of the problem also means ownership of the solution. That is, if the solution fails to yield the desired results, the teacher will most likely be blamed.

Sometimes parents ask for advice. When this happens, it's usually a good idea to keep in mind that people who ask for advice have probably already gotten a great deal of it from relatives, friends, and neighbors. They may be seeking confirmation of a decision they have already made, in which case conflicting advice from the teacher will not necessarily be welcomed. They may be confused, and rather than actually wanting the advice they ask for, they may actually be seeking additional information and alternatives from which to make their own decisions. It is probably human nature for us to want to offer advice and help others solve problems; however, offering several speculative suggestions and letting parents choose their own solution is much preferred. When teacher and parents are working together to solve a problem that involves the child, they all should contribute to the discussion. Whenever possible, the teacher should refrain from sharing an idea that the parents may be able to offer on their own. Having parents' ideas become part of the solution is highly desirable and helps promote ownership of both problem and solution.

Strategies for Dealing with Angry and/or Verbally Abusive Parents

Regardless of how teachers may try to maintain a pleasant team approach with all parents, most teachers at one time or another have an unpleasant encounter with a parent. Being the receiver of an angry outburst is a frustrating experience, particularly when the outburst gives rise to feelings that range from fear or helplessness to anger (Hirschhorn and Barnette 1993). When a teacher feels he or she may be abused by a parent who has scheduled a conference, that teacher would probably be wise to ask the principal or another school staff member to sit in on the conference. If this is not determined to be the best course of action, the teacher may meet with the parent in an area that allows for privacy but is not secluded from other school personnel. If an angry parent drops in for a conference—unannounced—the teacher may quickly need to excuse himself or herself to let the office know that a "visitor" is in the building. The principal or other staff member could then wait in the hall near the teacher's room for the duration of the conference.

Although there are a small percentage of teachers who face physical danger from an angry, abusive parent, most teachers do not. Unfortunately, there are many teachers who are approached by angry parents who become verbally abusive. Whether an explosive situation can be defused depends largely on the teacher's reaction. Following are several techniques for dealing with angry, verbally abusive parents. The five steps described below should be used, as needed, in the order listed.

1. *Try to remain as calm and unemotional as possible.* While it is only human nature to feel anger when confronted with an angry, verbal

tirade, we need to make every effort not to show our emotions. Mentally counting to ten while looking directly at the parent and maintaining an expressionless face will make us appear calmer than we actually feel. Since behavior is contagious, some parents will stop short when no response is made to their outburst.

2. *Acknowledge the parent's anger.* Responding to a parent's outburst by issuing a calm acknowledgement of his or her anger often results in an end to the tirade. Saying "My goodness! I can certainly tell that you are very angry" or "I see that you are angry. Let's sit down and talk" lets the parent know that he or she has your attention and that you are willing to converse. If it is clear that the parent is angry because of an error made by the teacher or the school, it is generally best for the teacher to acknowledge the error and apologize, then offer to talk about plans for either remedying the situation or making amends. If the parent is angry because of a policy situation that would require political action to bring about change, the teacher may suggest that the parent issue a complaint with the building principal, the district superintendent, or the school board.

3. *Make a list of the parent's complaints.* When the teacher is listening carefully enough to record each complaint, sometimes the parent slows down and makes an effort to convey main points in a clearer, more appropriate manner. The teacher should convey an earnest attempt to write down every complaint and should ask parents to clarify complaints that are too general before engaging in problem-solving activities. If the parent stops, the teacher can request that he or she look over the list to check for completeness and accuracy. Then, the parent can be asked to share suggestions or solutions for remedying the situation. The teacher would again write down any suggestions offered by the parent. Writing down complaints and possible solutions helps to clarify the problem and leads to more effective problem solving. It also helps prevent later misunderstandings about what was said.

4. *Tell the parent how his or her angry words are making you feel.* If unsuccessful in attempts to employ the first three techniques, the teacher may then try to interrupt the parent's flow of anger. For example, while still trying to portray a calm and unemotional demeanor, the teacher may say "Your raising your voice does not help me understand the situation" or "I am extremely uncomfortable with the tone of voice you are using."

5. *Stop the conference.* When the teacher has tried, unsuccessfully, to defuse the situation by remaining calm, acknowledging the parents anger, and stating discomfort with the parent's behavior, it is time to call an end to the conference. No one benefits from an extended angry outburst: not the teacher, not the child, not even the parent.

To accept abuse will not remedy the situation, and it is emotionally draining on the teacher! The teacher should make a simple statement like "It's not going to be helpful for us to continue this conference today. We can make another appointment to meet when we are both calm." Chances are, if the parent is really angry, the teacher may have to repeat the statement and then physically remove himself or herself from the room. Walking toward the office while calmly repeating the statement for a third time usually manages to achieve the desired result. The parent may leave angry, but the teacher is relieved, at least temporarily, of the situation. Also, while efforts to defuse the situation failed, the teacher did not do anything to impact negatively on future communications.

Use of one or more of these techniques for dealing with angry, verbally abusive parents is a way for teachers to maintain professionalism, while at the same time refusing to be the target of a parent's anger. While the situation will be no less unpleasant, most teachers will feel some sense of satisfaction knowing that they were able to employ a sound strategy for attempting to resolve the situation.

UNSCHEDULED CONFERENCES

While the majority of conferences are scheduled, occasionally a parent will drop in unannounced to chat with the teacher. Except for the occasional thirty-second encounter in the hallway to exchange small bits of information, conferences should be scheduled. Certainly teachers should not be expected to conduct a conference without planning nor should administrators have to find someone to cover the teacher's class. An "appointment-only" policy for conferences benefits everyone, and parents should be well-informed of the policy and of the reasons why schools must adhere to it. In an effort to be accommodating to parents who failed to schedule a conference and who feel they have a pressing issue to discuss, schools sometimes create problems by going ahead with the conference. In such a case, the teacher is not adequately prepared and in all likelihood cannot give the parent the attention he or she deserves. In addition, the teacher does not have the time to raise issues he or she knows need to be addressed. Spur-of-the-moment conferences only serve to shortchange the parent, the teacher, and, most of all, the student.

While parents should know of and adhere to the appointment-only policy for conferences, school personnel should know how to respond graciously to the parent who does drop in unannounced. Everyone coming into the school, unexpected or not, should receive a warm smile and a pleasant greeting. For the parent who inquires about chatting with a particular teacher, the response might be routine, but sincere: "Oh, I'm sure . . . would want to meet with you, but all conferences are by appointment only. We want to ensure that each conference is well-planned and conducted in privacy to ensure a satisfying outcome for both teacher and parent. I'll be happy to have . . . contact you as soon as possible to set up a time that is convenient for both of you." Parents who persist should receive the same pleasant but firm message. Consistency in dealing with parents who drop in unexpectedly will result in fewer requests for unscheduled conferences.

*P*ARENT-TEACHER-CHILD CONFERENCES

Although most schools still exclude the student from the parent-teacher conference, students increasingly are being invited to take an active part in conferences for which the goal is to share progress, discuss particular strengths and needs, and form plans for continued growth. Children need to contribute to their parents' understanding of the child's progress, and structured involvement of the child in the conference can be an excellent vehicle for doing so. Inclusion of children in the parent-teacher conference is not really a new idea; educators have for years advocated letting children play an active role in evaluating and setting goals for learning (Readdick, Golbeck, Klein, and Cartwright 1984; Tanner 1978; Mathias 1967). Teachers have reported that young children are more likely to develop increasing skill in self-evaluation and decision making when permitted an early and continued role in conferences (Readdick et al. 1984). Furthermore, Mathias (1967) indicated that both parents and teachers were more likely to have positive discussions when children were present. Readdick et al. (1984) devised a four-step conference sequence for parent-teacher-child conferences. In Step 1, the teacher elicits assessment of the child's progress from the child and the parents. The teacher joins in the assessment and an effort is made to "construct a total picture of the child as a growing and learning person" (154). Setting goals and objectives based on the assessment is achieved in Step 2. Oftentimes, the teacher suggests several tentative goals and objectives and asks the child and parents to indicate their preferences. As the child and parents gain experience in this type of conference procedure, the teacher may look first to the child to formulate goals and objectives. In Step 3, learning activities are specified. The intent is for child and parents to participate with the teacher in generating a list of ideas for meeting goals and objectives. In early conferences the teacher may need to identify for the child and parents feasible alternatives, with the child and parents expressing their preferences. Once activities have been selected by the child, with input from the parents and teacher, Step 4, identification of evaluation procedures, commences. Again, in early conferences the teacher may need to identify how the child's progress will be evaluated by each (child, parent, teacher). As the child and parents gain skill and comfort in the conferencing process, the teacher may share available evaluation techniques with the child and parent, selecting from among alternatives presented by the teacher. If feasible, the teacher would, in Step 4, first ask the child how his or her learning should be evaluated.

As mentioned in Chapter 8, student portfolios can play a major role in these conferences. In fact, letting children know they are going to share their portfolios at periodic conferences with both teacher and parents present often produces a year-long increase in effort and accountability.

Preparation for parent-teacher-child conferences is much the same as for traditional conferences. The teachers gather observation notes and checklists, as well as grades, and the information that went into the determination of each grade. If available, a copy of the goals that were set at the beginning of the year by the parent and child are also included. When the student is to be involved in the conference, that student is also involved in the planning. Many teachers ask the child to review what is in his portfolio and plan a presentation for his parents. In preparation for the conference presentation, the student may share his "presentation" with a peer or be videotaped during a "trial run" of his or her presentation. This gives the student an opportunity to view himself as a presenter and to critique and make any changes prior to the conference. Children can also be given responsibility for gathering other items to be shared. These may include a list of all books they have read, and a list of written reports, including planning notes, rough drafts, and revising and editing notes. In addition, all children take an active part in setting up displays and projects that will be viewed by their parents. Finally, teachers generally ask each student to write a letter to preview for parents what they will find out at the conference. In Figure 9.6 is a letter sent to parents to explain the upcoming student-led conferences at Cresthill Middle School. This letter was developed by the "Cougar 8" team teachers: Ann Kitchin, Holly Krull, Brian Lexvold, and Randi Lornell. Their evaluation survey appears in Figure 9.7.

After the teacher has greeted the parents and exchanged pleasantries, the child takes the lead in sharing what is in the portfolio. The teacher supports the very young child in making this presentation, but as the child gains experience, it is amazing how much insight can be gained by the parent and teacher when the child puts his or her ideas and rationales into words.

When teacher and child collaborate on reporting what they know about the child's progress, the benefits far outweigh the information that is shared. The awareness of everyone involved—parent, teacher, and even child—improves. There are many benefits of student-led conferences. Not only are students actively involved in the conference, they take greater responsibility for their schoolwork and learning. They also build self-esteem, confidence, and communication skills, and learn to evaluate their own learning. As the channels of communication are opened, parents tend to receive more information about their child and his or her work and have an opportunity to assist in developing future learning goals. Finally, teachers report feeling less stressed and more positive (Hackmann, et.al., 1998). Sometimes the work shared by the child does not meet with expectations held by the parents and/or the teacher. The teacher can monitor the parents' reaction to the child's presentation and either defend or agree with their analysis. It may be that little progress has been made toward the goals set early in the year by parents and

COUGAR PARK 8 CONFERENCES

January 20, 2005

Dear Parents,

We are well into the third quarter and it's now time to plan for winter conferences. We invite you to visit Cresthill with your student the afternoon and evening of February 16 and 17. S/He will share with you portfolios that provide evidence of progress in each class and detailed personal goals for the rest of the year.

To promote student ownership and accountability, these conferences will be **led by your student,** as they were in October. Since student-led conferences may be new to you, here is what you can expect. As you and your student enter the room, you will be greeted by one of your student's teachers, who will guide you to a conferencing area; the student will retrieve his or her portfolio. The portfolio is a collection of work that is representative of what your student has done so far in the third quarter. Using a prepared script, your student will share and reflect upon his/her work habits/content grades and goals contained within his/her portfolio. At most, ten other conferences will be going on at the same time, and the teachers (Mrs. Krull - Science, Mrs. Kitchin - Language Arts, Mr. Lexvold - Social Studies, and Ms. Lornell - Math) will **try** to visit each group for a few moments to clarify questions, provide direction, or observe the conferencing. **Due to the number of conferences and their format, it is unlikely that all four teachers will visit you.** Parents with additional questions or concerns will need to fill out a "contact" card, and the appropriate teacher(s) will get back to you via phone or e-mail. Once you have finished conferencing, you may be asked to fill out a brief survey before you leave to conference with your child's elective teachers.

To help the conferences run smoothly, we have divided our team in half according to your student's last name. We ask that you **try** to attend on the appropriate night. **Please number your top three time choices beneath the appropriate day** and have your student return this paper to Mr. Lexvold, and he will *star* your scheduled conference time. Your child will be responsible for returning this form back to

you. All conference times will be assigned on a first come, first served basis.

Thank you for your support in providing the best learning experience for your child.

Cougar Park 8 Teachers

Student's Last Name A-K
Wednesday, February 16

Time	Top Three Preferences
3:30 - 3:50	_____
3:50 - 4:10	_____
4:10 - 4:30	_____
4:30 - 4:50	_____
4:50 - 5:10	_____
5:10 - 5:30	_____
5:30 - 5:50	_____
5:50 - 6:10	_____
6:10 - 6:30	_____
6:30 - 6:50	_____

Student's Last Name L-Z
Thursday, February 17

Time	Top Three Preferences
3:30 - 3:50	_____
3:50 - 4:10	_____
4:10 - 4:30	_____
4:30 - 4:50	_____
4:50 - 5:10	_____
5:10 - 5:30	_____
5:30 - 5:50	_____
5:50 - 6:10	_____
6:10 - 6:30	_____
6:30 - 6:50	_____

Figure 9.6

child. Reviewing these goals *with the child present* is more beneficial than when parents and teacher review goals in the child's absence. Children need to take an active part in evaluating progress toward goals. They also need to be intricately involved in developing action plans that will impact on their future growth. Following each parent-teacher-child conference at Amanda Arnold Elementary School, a written narrative summarizing the agreements made in the conference is prepared. After each party reads this narrative, it is placed in the child's portfolio along with the child's current goal-setting sheet and learning profile.

Cougar Park 8 Survey

Thanks so much for taking the time to fill out this survey for our team. We value your thoughts/comments on the following questions:

(Most responses can just be circled.)

1. Cougar Park 8 has informed us throughout the year in an effective manner about my student's grades.

      Strongly agree   Agree No Opinion Disagree   Strongly disagree

Are you signed up for online grading through Mr. Lexvold's Website?

                                Yes   No

How often do you check your student's grades on the Website?

    Comments, if any:

2. Both the **fall and winter** student-led conferences were helpful in showing my student's ownership in his/her progress.

      Strongly agree   Agree No Opinion Disagree   Strongly disagree

    Comments, if any:

3. The school administration did an effective job communicating the new grading system.

      Strongly agree   Agree No Opinion Disagree   Strongly disagree

    Comments, if any:

Thank you for your time: Cougar Park 8 Teachers

— Figure 9.7 —

SPECIAL CONFERENCES

The progress of special needs children is reviewed on an annual basis before the writing of a new Individualized Education Program (IEP) occurs. This process should be viewed as a cooperative venture aimed at student growth—with parents and whenever appropriate, with children, as key players. Many parents are intimidated in IEP conferences, which typically involve a number of school personnel and specialists. Helping parents feel as comfortable as possible should be a major objective of conference planning by school personnel. Schools that let parents know their input and suggestions are expected and valued can generally anticipate smoother, more productive conferences. One way to share with parents the important role they have is to send home tips for preparing for the IEP meeting. Including information as to who will be present at the meeting and the role and responsibility of each individual helps parents prepare, particularly those who are new to the process. Suggestions for parents include jotting down notes about out-of-school observations of the child's progress, reviewing the previous year's IEP and school records, reviewing homework assignments attempted and/or completed by the child, observing the child in the classroom and in therapy sessions, and talking with the child about his or her perceptions and possible concerns.

Parents may also be encouraged to develop a list of questions to ask at the conference. Some suggested questions to be covered in every conference may be sent home in advance. These may include: "When will the related services begin and end?"; "How much time will my child be receiving at these services each week?"; "How much time or how many classes will my child have with nondisabled peers?"; "Is my child eligible to receive extended school year services?"; "How will my child receive services (in the classroom, resource room, through consultation, etc.)?"; and "What modifications will my child have in the regular classroom setting?" Parents may also be encouraged to ask questions that are not answered by the information on the IEP, such as: "How well does my child get along with others?"; "How is my child progressing?" "What is my child's classroom behavior like?"; "What types of rules or procedures is my child expected to follow?"; "What are the consequences when my child fails to follow stated rules or procedures?"; and "How can I support my child's learning at home?"

As with traditional parent-teacher conferences and parent-teacher-child conferences, conferences for parents of children with special needs must be well-prepared, well-organized, and project a team approach. When all of the key players are prepared, the conference becomes more focused and objectives are more readily accomplished.

ALTERNATIVES FOR NONATTENDING PARENTS

Despite efforts to schedule a conference with each and every child's parents, some parents still may not acknowledge the school's invitation or request for a conference. Although lack of interest may be the reason, there are probably other circumstances that result in the lack of attendance. Barriers discussed in Chapter 2 become most evident when it comes to the scheduling of parent-teacher conferences. An important part of the evaluation process for schoolwide or districtwide conferences is to ascertain which parents did not attend and, if at all possible, to ascertain the reasons why.

A plan should already be in place for reaching nonattending parents or, if necessary, a parental substitute (grandparent, uncle, aunt, etc.). The plan might include alternative conferencing strategies such as home visits for parents who are only comfortable on "their own turf." Teams of teachers may consider holding conferences in local neighborhoods or housing projects if children are bused to the school from other areas of the city. Conferences might also be held in other neutral locations. Perhaps conferences could be held in the coffee room of a local job site, such as a factory or large business, where a number of parents are employed. Arrangements would, of course, be made in advance with employers. Other neutral locations include local community centers, churches, libraries, and even fast-food restaurants. One teacher brought in conference folders and let parents and children know that he would be at a local fast food restaurant from 6 to 9 P.M. one evening. The restaurant served free coffee to the parents and mini ice-cream cones to the children.

Sometimes parents who do not speak English need to know that a translator will be available during the conference. If a parent volunteer is serving as the translator, having that person make personal contact with the parent before the conference may make a difference. Having another individual, such as a fellow parent or a member of the local neighborhood clergy, agree to contact any nonattending parent on behalf of the school and perhaps offer to sit in during the conference, might also result in more parent conferences.

As an alternative for family members who simply cannot arrange their schedules to attend a conference at the school building, some teachers offer to send home a videotape of a student-teacher conference. This works especially well at the middle school level. The conference is taped, just as if the parent were in attendance. Before the conference, the student and teachers outline what the conference will cover—student participation in school activities, achievements, strengths, and areas of need. While the tape rolls, the students review samples of their work and discuss their individual progress with the teachers. When necessary, teachers do discuss learning difficulties or problem behaviors on the video. In these cases in particular, teachers make follow-up phone calls after the parents have had an opportunity to view the videotape.

TELEPHONE CONFERENCES

Another alternative to the face-to-face conference is the telephone conference. Though not nearly as effective for sharing student progress and working together to develop plans and strategies for future progress, the telephone conference is better than having no contact at all. Problems associated with telephone conferencing include finding a convenient time for the call and, when necessary, establishing a time limit for the call. In addition, since establishing a close rapport is hard to do without face-to-face contact, sharing information that is delicate is difficult, such as when a student is performing poorly or needs to be referred for special services.

Despite shortcomings associated with telephone conferencing, such calls can be made more effective if teachers follow a few simple guidelines. First of all, teachers need to prepare for the telephone call. Using the conference planning sheet described earlier in the chapter is a good idea. Also, having samples of the student's work available during the conversation is helpful when describing specific examples that are indicative of progress made, strengths, and/or needs. A conference outgrowth form should also be used during the telephone conference for recording shared views and expectations as well as strategies for helping the child in his or her future progress. This form would be mailed to parents as a follow-up to the telephone conference.

If at all possible, the telephone conference should be scheduled. Calls that come during the dinner hour, or when parents are busy putting little ones to bed, are generally not appreciated. Also, calling a parents' workplace is considered inappropriate in most instances. A note may be sent home asking the parent to indicate a convenient time for the teacher to call. Attached to the note should be a brief description of what the teacher hopes to accomplish through the conference and suggested questions that the parent may want to ask the teacher. If the parent does not respond, the teacher may call to set up an appointment for the telephone conference. The teacher should be prepared to proceed with the conference if the parent is willing to do so.

When the parent answers the telephone, the teacher should identify himself or herself, using a tone of voice that conveys warmth and friendliness. It's usually a good idea to ask if this is still a good time to talk and to thank the parent for accepting your call. Rather than asking the parent to engage in an exchange of pleasantries, the teacher would probably be wise to proceed from the first greeting to making a brief comment or interesting anecdote about something good the child did or was involved in at school. This comment would be followed by a question to the parent about his or her perceptions of the child's progress and what the parents have observed at home. The conference would proceed as would a traditional face-to-face conference, except for the inability of the parent to see the child's work. The teacher, in describing the work, could invite the parent(s) in to see the work and/or could offer to have the child take the work home for an evening. A telephone conference does have drawbacks, but when successfully accomplished, it may serve to increase the chances of having the parent attend a future conference.

A telephone conference may also be used as a strategy for getting to know parents. Some teachers routinely call each parent to introduce themselves and convey the need for working together closely during the upcoming year. This personal touch is appreciated by most parents who are impressed with the teacher's willingness to involve them in their child's education. The teacher can tell the parent that future calls may be made to share the child's progress and that regularly scheduled conferences will provide a time for all parties to work together in developing a plan for future growth.

Telephone conferences may also be used to provide follow-up for face-to-face conferences. Sometimes the teacher needs to relate progress or lack of progress toward an agreed-upon goal. If an issue has already been discussed in a face-to-face conference, sharing updated information by telephone is both personal and efficient.

Notes about all telephone conferences should be recorded and placed in each parent-teacher conference folder. These records should reflect the date and time of call, objectives, outcomes, and teacher's perceptions. As with any other conference, information gained through a telephone conference is confidential and should be treated as such.

For your consideration . . .

Following are several questions about parent conferencing. Answering these questions should help you determine how closely your beliefs reflect the recommendatons cited for effective parent conferencing.

1. Conferences should provide an opportunity to review goals and formulate plans. **YES** **NO**

2. Conferences should be designed so as to facilitate a balanced look at all aspects of the child's development. **YES** **NO**

3. Once administrative support has been secured, a district- or school-level committee, or the faculty and staff from each school, should develop an action plan for parent-teacher conferencing. **YES** **NO**

4. Schools should employ full- or part-time staff who speak the major languages spoken at home and utilize such staff, if needed, to assist with conferences. **YES** **NO**

5. Teachers should start off conferences on a positive note, first giving parents the opportunity to share their concerns. **YES** **NO**

6. Children need to contribute to their parents' understanding of the their progress, and structured involvement of the child in the conference can be an excellent vehicle for doing so. **YES** **NO**

7. When children are to participate in the conference, they can review their work samples and plan a presentation for their parents. **YES** **NO**

8. Teachers should have an understanding of strategies for dealing with angry, verbally abusive parents. **YES** **NO**

9. School leaders should protect the rights of parents and children by working to establish guidelines for the sharing of information within the school and with individuals or agencies outside of the school. **YES** **NO**

10. A plan should be in place for reaching nonattending parents or, if necessary, a parental substitute. **YES** **NO**

11. Schools should make every effort to reach one hundred percent of thefamilies. **YES** **NO**

CONFIDENTIALITY

We would probably be remiss if we did not emphasize the necessity for confidentiality in a chapter on parent-teacher conferencing. Although principals are usually very aware of the need for confidentiality and of the terrible consequences that can occur when confidentiality is not maintained, reminding teachers of confidentiality issues prior to conference time is probably a good idea. The principal must be the number-one advocate for the parent and for the child. Information shared in a parent-teacher conference cannot be shared in the teacher's lounge, with other parents, or with members of the community. The trust that parents place in teachers must be treated with respect and care. In conversing with a friend, one sometimes assumes that what is shared is *not confidential unless* the friend says that it is and asks that it not be repeated. In dealings with parents, *all* information shared should be treated as *strictly confidential.*

School leaders can protect the rights of parents and children by working to establish guidelines for the sharing of information within the school and with individuals or agencies outside of the school (Lawrence and Hunter 1978). Such guidelines may include permission to share information with other professionals who may be able to increase the teacher's effectiveness in working with the family and to increase the ability of other school personnel who will work with the same family. Sharing information with outside agencies should occur only after written permission from the parents or legal guardians has been obtained. Asking for parental consent to share information that would be helpful to another professional is always a good idea. It conveys respect for the parent's privacy and for the trust they have placed in the teacher. Especially when decisions are made concerning information to be forwarded to the next year's teacher and/or to another school building, the parent should be consulted before information gained through a parent-teacher conference is shared. The teacher might say to a parent, "This information would be helpful for Stacy's next teacher to have. How would you feel about my sharing it with him/her?" Finally, only the minimum information needed to help the child should be shared. Lengthy details are generally not necessary and should remain confidential, as should any notes the teacher took during the conference.

SUMMARY

Working with parents is a *process* that takes time. Teachers must work hard to develop rapport and trust. Developing effective communication skills and conferencing strategies takes organization, time, and practice. Teachers often reveal anxiety at "doing or saying the wrong thing" when conferencing with parents. Yet, teachers who are well-prepared and who help parents feel prepared and comfortable are most likely to report conference satisfaction.

The professional confidence that comes with training and practice is a key element in effective conferencing. Not all conferences are successful—and a few are downright unpleasant! In this chapter strategies for planning and implementing a variety of parent-teacher and parent-teacher-child conferences were shared along with ideas for communication skills training for teachers and for parents. Open and honest communication about a child's progress has great potential for helping each child achieve maximum growth. And, more so than any other parent involvement tool, the parent conference has the potential for building lasting partnerships between home and school.

*L*ᴏᴏKING AHEAD . . .

There are many ways to involve parents and community members in the education of children. Opportunities for volunteer assistance and support can be found in every classroom and program in the school. In the next chapter, ways to establish a successful volunteer program for your school or classroom will be shared.

*R*EFERENCES

Barrera, I., & Corso, R. M. (2003). *Skilled dialogue: Strategies for responding to cultural diversity in early childhood.* Baltimore: Paul H. Brookes Publishing Company.

Freedman, J., & Combs, G. (1996). *Narrative therapy. The social construction of preferred realities.* New York: W.W. Norton.

Hackman, D. G., Kenworthy, J., & Nibbelink, S. (1998). Student empowerment through student-led conferences. *Middle School Journal, 30*(1), 35–39.

Hirschhorn, L., & Barnett, C. (1993). *The psychodynamics of organizations.* Philadelphia: Temple University Press.

Mathias, D. (1967). Parent-teacher conferences: There is a better way. *Grade Teacher, 85,* 86–87

Payne, R. (2001). *A framework for understanding poverty.* Sacramento, CA: Aha Process, Inc.

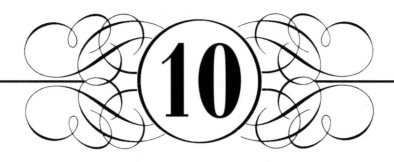

Getting Parents and Community Members Involved: Keys to an Effective Volunteer Program

I will never forget my oldest daughter's outcry which occurred in the grocery store late one afternoon. She was questioning whether I would accompany her class on a trip to the fire station. When I said I couldn't because I would be teaching a class at that time, she began wailing, very loudly, saying "But everyone's mother is going. You have to go!" I felt so guilty. The next week, when the teacher asked for a volunteer to send in sprinkles for the cookies the class would bake, I was so pleased to have something I could contribute!

*I*NTRODUCTION

Good volunteer programs must be carefully planned, and the planning must begin with a look at the goals and objectives. Teachers must understand that the goal isn't to have parents duplicating papers or cutting out figures. While the positive attitude developed by parents and the services they render are *benefits*, the *primary* goal is for parents to become knowledgeable advocates in their child's education. Through their close association, volunteers gain a better understanding of the school and its programs and are more likely to assist their children in learning at home and show their support within the community.

In this chapter a broader definition of the traditional school volunteer, looking at ways that parents and community members "volunteer" their services inside as well as outside of the school building and the school day will be promoted. Characteristics and examples of a variety of effective school volunteer programs will be shared and the role that parents play as "volunteer teachers" supporting their children's education through home-learning activities and experiences will be emphasized.

WHO ARE VOLUNTEERS?

Traditionally, school volunteers are parents who assist in the classroom, the library, the lunchroom, and on the playground. They make copies, collate and staple papers, put up bulletin boards, and cut out game pieces. They serve as "room mothers," host class parties, accompany students on field trips, and organize fund-raising activities. In a nutshell, they are an extra pair of hands ready to help out with a variety of school activities.

With increasingly large numbers of mothers in the workforce, traditional school volunteer programs have all but dissolved in many schools. The demise of the volunteer program not only forces teachers to assume even more tasks without assistance but also creates a gap in the home-school relationship. The fact is, *most elementary school children like to have their parents involved at school.* Every child wants his or her mother to help with the class party, or to chaperon the class on the field trip. With mothers holding down full-time jobs, not only are the children disappointed but also working mothers report feeling extremely *guilty* at not being involved in ways their own mothers were. If parent involvement is the school's goal, we must find ways to allow *all* parents to contribute, regardless of whether or not they are free to come into the building during the school day.

A *volunteer* might be defined as anyone who contributes services without receiving payment. Defined in this way, parents and other members of the community who perform a service or contribute in some way to the school—and who are not paid to do so—are volunteers. All too often schools fail to look beyond the parents of the children enrolled in the school, and beyond the school day, when they consider potential volunteers. This limited thinking results in lowered expectations for a volunteer program. Rather than looking for parents who are "free" between the hours of 8:00 A.M. and 3:30 P.M., teachers and administrators should take stock of specific tasks that need to be accomplished and then consider who among the parents or community might be able to perform each task. While some of the tasks, such as those mentioned above, require being physically present at the school during the school day, any number of tasks can be completed outside of the building during nonschool hours. The principal of one school approached a local office supply company about photocopying the programs for the school play. The company agreed and even reduced samples of the children's writing and artwork to decorate the program. Parents volunteered to take stacks of programs home to collate, fold, and staple, since the programs were of a size that required doing these tasks by hand. Lynn Traser, a teacher in Macomb, Illinois, showed parents how to cover pieces of cardboard with wallpaper samples to make "blank books" for the students to write in. After the demonstration, parents made a book for their own child and then took home supplies needed for making additional blank books for classroom use. Parents of children enrolled in Camille Breheny's kindergarten class at St. Paul School in Macomb are asked to sign up to bring the homemade playdough at least once during the year. She provides the recipe. Parents also collect empty containers and "junk materials" used in various art projects throughout the year. Since the kindergartners engage in frequent cooking projects, parents are often asked to send in a cup of flour, sugar, cookie sprinkles, food coloring, or other ingredients. These donations save the school money and reduce the amount of out-of-pocket spending that Camille incurs. Most importantly, they provide an easy way for the parents—the majority of whom all work outside the home—to contribute.

In addition to parents of the children enrolled in the school, some schools involve older students. Structured programs, such as those administered by some high school home-living classes and Future Teachers of America groups, have made a wonderful contribution by providing classroom helpers and volunteer tutors who can work in the school during or after school hours. Schools that are in close proximity to a college or university often have interns or student teachers who work in the classrooms without receiving pay for their services. More informal arrangements, such as the use of "sixth-grade buddies" in Camille's kindergarten class, also provide the "extra hands, eyes, and ears" that early childhood teachers need and appreciate. Senior citizens also serve as volunteers for many school systems. "Adopt-a-grandchild" programs, in which senior citizens "adopt" individual children or classrooms within a school, provide both children and adults with an enriching experience. Some "grandparents" offer to bake cookies, assist with classroom cooking or craft projects, sew "book bags" for the backs of chairs or desks, read to children, or listen to children read, to name a few of the many ways these individuals assist in classrooms. In Figure 10.1 is an excerpt from the Lincoln Elementary School Newsletter published by principal Ed Fulkerson. Mrs. Thorpe is a member of the school's "Grandma Readers" program. Note that students and parents were invited to hear this special "Grandma Reader." Mrs. Thorpe and other grandmas—and even some grandpas—volunteer their time to read with individual students 20 minutes each week. In addition to a holiday party, they hosted an end-of-the year ice cream party for readers and children.

Involving retired citizens serves as a wonderful community relations program and also helps to meet the needs of children who need the loving care of an older person. According to a report by Civic Ventures (2004), "The 55+ population will almost double between now and 2030, while the number of Americans 65 and older will more than double" (p. 5). In their national survey of older adults "working with children and youth" was the number one choice of volunteer options. Free from the stresses of full-time employment and child-rearing, over 27 million senior citizens volunteer almost 7.5 billion hours annually (Independent Sector 2003).

February 2005
A message from Mr. Fulkerson . . .

It's hard to believe but only 4 months remain in the school year. January is behind us, the days are getting longer, and the sun is finally rising a little earlier. Several new pictures are now available on our Lincoln School homepage. Feel free to log onto http://district185.macomb.com/~lincoln/ at anytime.

We are excited to announce that Ms. Ardith Thorpe, the grandmother of a Lincoln School student, will be sharing the story *If A Bus Could Talk* with our students on Friday, February 4th in the library. The oral presentation will follow the Civil Rights Movement and Rosie Parks. The 20-minute program will be presented to Kindergarteners at 9:30, 1st grade at 11:20, 2nd grade at 10:40, and 3rd grade at 2:10. Please feel free to join your child's class if you are available.

Have a great month of February, remember to hug your kids, and keep our troops in your prayers!

Figure 10.1

Individuals representing business and professional groups can assist schools in a variety of ways, from providing guest speakers to hosting field trips and donating supplies and materials. For example, during the last few years some discount stores have built collection boxes and started community-wide campaigns to gather school supplies for schools to give to children who cannot afford them. Some of the companies that manufacture school supplies have also made direct donations to the schools. Fast-food restaurants, working in conjunction with local soft-drink companies, have been known to donate to the schools a percentage of each drink purchased. Some schools participate in adopt-a-school programs and partnership arrangements with various businesses. These represent a form of volunteerism, to be discussed in more depth in the next chapter, which deals with fostering positive community relations.

Members of civic, service, and church groups are often quite active in helping the local schools. Organizing after-school tutoring and/or enrichment programs, coordinating programs such as Reading Is Fundamental, hosting fund raisers, and donating used clothing, materials, and supplies are among the many ways these groups volunteer their services to the schools.

In many communities the majority of the voters no longer have public-school-age children. In the next chapter we will discuss the importance of involving these individuals, as well as a variety of strategies for doing so. Securing volunteer services from this group is often difficult; however, efforts should be made to solicit their service. Community members who have special expertise in a particular area may be invited to share their knowledge with classes. Similarly, individuals who have traveled to other states and to foreign countries are often pleased to be asked to share their photographs and experiences with students who are studying that geographic area. Schools need to be creative in finding ways to involve parents of formerly enrolled children.

INVOLVING PARENTS IN THE CLASSROOM AND SCHOOL

Whether or not a formal volunteer program exists, parents and community members should be encouraged to visit the school and the classrooms. Parents and other adults can serve as casual visitors, participating in and lending assistance with classroom activities, meals, or celebrations. They can provide resources to extend and enrich opportunities for the children. They can also visit the classroom as observers to extend their knowledge of children's functioning in the classroom.

In Figure 10.2 is a sample volunteer information sheet distributed by Eastview School in Canton, Illinios. Development of a few simple guidelines for parents usually prevents problems anticipated by the teacher. For example, parents who come into the classroom to observe may be given a list of behaviors to look for. This might include children's abilities to work independently as well as cooperatively, work habits children exhibit, and strategies children use to solve problems and negotiate differences. Visitors coming in to share resources or lead an enrichment activity usually welcome receiving some direction from the teacher. Tips such as "Whenever possible include concrete objects and visuals in a presentation," "When sharing a visual give the children plenty of time to look and ask questions," "Speak in language

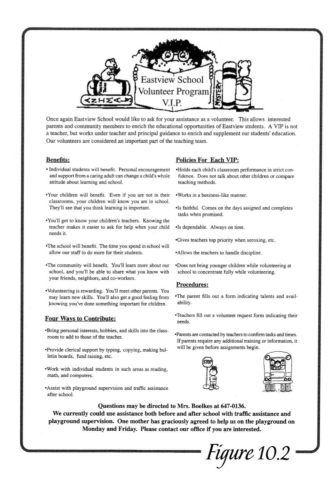

Figure 10.2

the children will understand," and "Plan on speaking no more than ten minutes before stopping for discussion" are examples of guidelines the teacher might set for guest speakers.

Some schools have established teacher assistance centers where parent volunteers can work one evening a week copying, laminating, and cutting and pasting game pieces and other materials for teachers. Other schools are starting "publishing centers," where students' texts can be typed and bound in book form. Children work in their classrooms to plan, develop a rough draft, revise, and edit their pieces. Their work is then submitted to the publishing center, where it is typed by a parent volunteer. Spaces for illustrations are defined, and the pages are bound into a book. This task can be performed at the publishing center, or the parent can take the materials home. This is a very beneficial activity for parents, as it helps them understand how children become writers; and, through work with younger students, they gain an understanding of developmental spelling.

Many teachers conduct their own survey of parents' interests, hobbies, and areas of expertise. Figure 10.3 shows the survey used by Eastview Elementary School to solicit volunteers. This information can be recorded on file cards or in a computer database. Use of the computer for storing and organizing volunteer information makes it easy to change, add, or omit information in the future.

Application for Joining Eastview's VIP Program Volunteers

Please consider becomming a school volunteer this year. The school will benefit from your help, and you will find your contributions personally rewarding. Please complete the information below and return this form to your child's teacher as soon as possible. Thank you.

Name:_____ Phone _____

Street/Address:_____

City:_____ Zip:_____

Please list your profession and/or any special abilities/hobbies you feel you could bring to the students at Eastview School.
_____

In order to match teacher requests with VIP interests and skills, please check the categories that you would be willing to do.

_____ Computer   Volunteers assist small groups of children with educational software.

_____ Tutoring   Volunteers work one-to-one or with a small group of children.

_____ Reading   Volunteers listen to children read orally.

_____ Library   Volunteers help the library categorize and shelve books.

_____ Typist   Volunteers type or use word-processing for staff. This could be done at home.

_____ Copies   Volunteers help with copying, collating, etc.

_____ Filing   Volunteers cut educational articles from magazines and do filing.

_____ Errands   Volunteers run errands for the school.

_____ Laminator   Volunteers laminate educational materials using the school's machine.

_____ Traffic   Volunteers will assist directing traffic before or after school.

_____ Special Day Helper Examples: Vision and hearing helper, picture day helper, etc.

Figure 10.3a

PLEASE COMPLETE BOTH SIDES

We need you!

Please indicate the times you would most likely be available to help.

_____ Mon. morning	_____ Wed. afternoon	_____ Any morning
_____ Mon. afternoon	_____ Thurs. morning	_____ Any afternoon
_____ Tues. morning	_____ Thurs. afternoon	
_____ Tues. afternoon	_____ Fri. morning	
_____ Wed. morning	_____ Fri. afternoon	

_____ I prefer short-term projects.

_____ I can only work at home.

_____ I have volunteered at Eastview School before.

Comments and suggestions:

Children attending Eastview School:

_____   Teacher_____
_____   Teacher_____
_____   Teacher_____

Comments and questions can be directed to Mrs. Boelkes (647-0136). We appreciate your willingness to help!

Date_____Signature_____

Figure 10.3b

Having a file of volunteer service information is especially helpful when there is a specific task that needs to be done. For example, if fabric scraps are needed for a class project or if a cloth pocket chart needs to be replaced, a teacher might look in the file for a parent who listed sewing as an interest. It is important that all parents who respond to the survey indicating tasks they would be willing to perform *are asked* to volunteer. The teacher would work to involve all parents in some way, at some time during the year.

Interested parent volunteers and a dedicated teacher helped Ingersoll Middle School solve their problem of caring for students whose parents had to drop them off at school very early each morning. Students can get a pass to go to a morning activity room to study, read, listen to music, or play games (see Figure 10.4). Sandra Kennedy, the school counselor at Ingersoll involves parents and community members as resource persons and guest speakers for the school's career awareness program. Volunteers can interact with the classes in person or through the Internet.

Parents know they are performing a valuable service when they work as facilitators at the learning centers in Alison Lewis's kindergarten classroom at Madison School in Quincy, Illinois. While Alison is involved in shared reading and/or writing experiences with a small group of students, parents

MORNING ACTIVITY ROOMS

With help and support of several volunteers and one energetic teacher, Ingersoll is providing a variety of opportunities for students who must arrive early to school each day. Students can get passes in the cafeteria before school to go to the media center to work on academics or to classrooms where they can play games, listen to music, or read quietly. The morning room project, organized by Mrs. Franciskovich, allows students to get a pass in the cafeteria before school to attend one of the "theme" rooms being supervised by volunteer parents. The number of passes is limited; and once a student reports to a room, he must stay until the first period bell rings.

The morning room project was created to give more options to the large number of students who ride the bus and arrive at Ingersoll very early. Unless receiving additional help from a teacher, students who do not ride the bus are still encouraged to arrive at Ingersoll no sooner than 8 AM, the official start time of Canton teachers.

Figure 10.4

help at the art center, the science center, or the math center. These volunteers sign up by the month, usually for one day each week. Alison makes sure they know the objective and directions for each center. Children are very comfortable working with the parents, and parents know their help is extremely important (see Figure 10.5). In addition to these regular parent volunteers, Alison invites many parents and community members into the classroom during a community helpers unit (see Figure 10.6).

THE ROLE OF A VOLUNTEER COORDINATOR

During the last few years many districts have hired parent coordinators. Paid through parent involvement grant monies and state or district funds, these highly trained individuals work to coordinate the program in a district or school. When there is a parent coordinator, this person generally serves as volunteer coordinator also. Responsibilities include identifying the need for volunteers and the potential jobs that volunteers can do, organizing recruitment efforts, arranging training for teachers and orientation and training for volunteers, working with others to develop a volunteer handbook, maintaining records to document volunteer contributions, coordinating any special recognition and awards programs, and participating in on-going evaluation of the volunteer program. Where there is no one individual paid to fulfill these responsibilities, the building principal must provide the necessary leadership in seeing that these activities are carried out by various individuals on the school staff. Having a volunteer coordinator who is a parent volunteer may be a workable arrangement in some schools. In such cases, having one or two teachers serve as "volunteer liaisons" is helpful.

CHARACTERISTICS OF EFFECTIVE VOLUNTEER PROGRAMS

Although individual classroom teachers and individual schools within districts *can* maintain effective volunteer programs, the most successful programs are those in which there exists not only a school-level administrative

PARENT VOLUNTEERS...
Parent volunteers have started for this month and I want to thank those for helping in writing groups! It makes a huge difference to have helpers so all 22 kids can write everyday (and read of course)! I look forward to seeing the rest of the volunteers as the month goes on...☺

Figure 10.5

OUR COMMUNITY UNIT IS GOING GREAT!!!!

WOW!!!! Thank you so much to all the families for helping make our unit about the Quincy community so much more fun and interesting!!!! All of you have helped by sending back the mommy and daddy job sheets- we are displaying them on a bulletin board so people can read about your great careers!!!

Also, our community visitors have been great so far!!!

On Tuesday.....My friend, Chad Tuzzo came to talk about being a police officer...

On Wednesday....Jacob's dad came to talk about being a pharmacist AND Wyatt's dad shared about his job as a doctor. Thank you so much! They were great and the kids learned a lot!!!!

Upcoming visitors...Today......at 12:30 Eric's mom will talk about being a hair stylist.☺

On Friday...At 12:00 Ashlynn's mom will talk about being a nurse and at 12:30 Hunter G. parents will talk about working at Vatterott College.

On Tuesday....At 12:00 Wyatt's aunt will come and share about being a florist and event planner.

On Wednesday...At 12:00 Wyatt's uncle will come- a DVD rep AND Caleb's dad will come and talk about being a State Police Officer at 12:30.

On Thursday... We have Hunter S.'s dad coming to share about his job that travels around the world as an attorney. If you could come at 12:30, that would be great because we have gym at 12:00.☺

Then lastly, on Friday....The mayor comes in the morning at 9:00 a.m. to read a story. And in the afternoon, we have 12:00 Kara and Kendra's dad coming, who is a design specialist. Afterwards, at 12:30 Olivia's dad is coming to share about being a developer.

Figure 10.6

commitment to volunteerism but also a district-level commitment. Involvement of all schools within the district is strongly supported by the district superintendent, central office staff, school board, and building principals. A unified effort results in a marked increase in the number of parents who get involved and stay involved throughout their children's school careers. Civic, service, and religious organizations, as well as businesses and professional groups, are also more likely to be active supporters of the schools when the expectation for volunteerism is held districtwide.

While some districtwide planning for volunteerism may exist, each individual school's staff is actively involved in the planning of the volunteer program at their school (see Figure 10.7). Brainstorming a list of tasks that volunteers could perform, identifying potential volunteer groups as well as individual volunteers, conducting surveys as to potential volunteers' willingness to support the school through out-of-school or in-school activities, generating guidelines for classroom and school volunteers, developing a volunteer handbook and training program, and planning for ongoing appreciation of volunteers are among the planning activities in which school staff members may participate.

Planning for Volunteers: Sample Guidelines for Getting Started

- Meet with school personnel to develop a common understanding of the benefits, goals, and objectives of a volunteer program.
- Appoint volunteer coordinator(s) and/or liaisons.
- Survey needs, considering activities that can be conducted both in the school and out of school.
- Identify potential volunteers.
- Write job descriptions for various volunteer jobs.
- Plan and implement a variety of recruitment activities.
- Identify interests/skills of potential volunteers.
- Determine training/orientation needs of teachers.
- Determine training/orientation needs of volunteers.
- Develop training/orientation programs.
- Develop volunteer handbooks for volunteers and teachers.
- Conduct training and orientation programs for volunteers and teachers.
- Develop record-keeping devices/forms.
- Plan ways to recognize and reward volunteer contributions.
- Plan ways to evaluate the effectiveness of the program.

Figure 10.7

Schools with the most successful volunteer programs have active and continuous recruitment designed to bring new volunteers into the school throughout the year. This necessitates ongoing placement, orientation, and training of volunteers. Although these activities take time, so does building and maintaining a quality volunteer program that yields consistent benefits in terms of parent and community involvement and support. A frequent flaw among volunteer programs is the once-a-year recruitment and placement of volunteers. Not only does this result in fewer volunteers, it also contributes to volunteer "burn out." Not many individuals want to be stuck in the same job for a long period of time; most prefer some variety and change. Schools that provide a vehicle for volunteers to switch activities periodically, if desired, have a better track record when it comes to retention of volunteers.

Orientation activities should be designed to help the volunteers get to know the program, learn "who's who" and "what's where," and become acquainted with the expectations held for the job they will assume. For in-school volunteers, the orientation would include getting to know the facility, including where they will work, where supplies are kept, where they can store a sack lunch, location of vending machines, where they can eat, and so forth. A volunteer handbook can be immensely helpful and should include policies and procedures of the volunteer program, such as attendance, childcare, transportation, sign-in, confidentiality, and general responsibilities. In addition, the handbook should include the school philosophy and mission statements, name/job title/position and room or office number for all school personnel, school calendar and daily schedules, a map of the school, and school policies and procedures that impact on the volunteer program. Figure 10.8 is a list of sample policies to be included in a volunteer handbook.

A written job description is recommended for each position. This job description will help volunteers understand how their position fits into the larger picture and will also give them an idea of other positions they may like to fill. The training planned would depend on the requirements for each job and may include observation of live or videotaped demonstrations of tasks to be performed, role-playing, and/or supervised practice. In planning training opportunities, staff members need to consider not only the tasks associated with each job but also the special terms or "jargon" used. For example, *duty roster, lunch count, collating, time-out* are terms used daily in most schools. They may not, however, be familiar to new volunteers. Identification of a supervisor for each volunteer is also important and may be linked to the training program. A classroom volunteer would most likely be trained and supervised by an individual classroom teacher, whereas clerical volunteers may be trained and supervised by the school secretary. In systems where there is a paid parent coordinator, this person is often responsible for placing, training, and supervising volunteers. For example, training for volunteers with classroom responsibilities typically includes how to work with children, the importance of talking with and listening to children, tips for reading aloud to children, how to help children solve problems, and positive guidance techniques. The training for volunteers not working in classrooms generally

Volunteer Program Policies and Procedures

1. *Attendance:* This information would include the importance of regular attendance, as well as whom to call if the volunteer will be absent. Procedures for signing-in on arrival and signing-out on departure could also be included.

2. *Childcare:* If childcare is to be provided, the name of the person to talk with about arrangements would be included in this section. If no childcare is to be arranged, a statement as to whether or not younger siblings will be permitted in the building could be included.

3. *Transportation:* Carpooling arrangements, busing, and other sources of transportation would be included, along with the names of individuals to contact about transportation needs and services.

4. *Record-keeping logs:* Procedures for keeping track of volunteer hours and service would be explained in this section.

5. *Confidentiality:* A discussion of confidentiality would include what information is considered confidential and potential consequences if confidentiality is not kept. A form for volunteers to sign promising to maintain confidentiality would be included.

6. *Emergency situations:* What to do in the case of emergencies would be included in this section. Procedures to follow in the event of natural disasters, fires, playground or school building accidents involving a child, parent, staff member or other volunteer would be specified.

Figure 10.8

includes how to perform specific tasks and where to get materials, supplies, and assistance. In the "Lasting Impressions" parent program in the Quincy, Illinois, public school system, former coordinator Peg Simon asked teachers to contribute to a "teachers' job box," those tasks volunteers could perform in the volunteer workroom or at home. When a volunteer had a few moments, Peg would pull something out of the job box and demonstrate the task. Parents who had been made aware of the job box often stopped by to see if there was anything they can take home to complete.

Another characteristic of successful volunteer efforts is program evaluation. In schools where there is a regular and thorough evaluation of the volunteer program and where changes are made as indicated by the evaluation results, the program is, understandably, more successful. Ongoing evaluation occurs throughout the year as data are kept regarding number of volunteers, including retention rate, services rendered, hours contributed (both in and outside of the school building), and dollar amount donated (both in direct donations and in labor and services). Periodic analysis of these data enables the school leaders to make changes as needed before the program is unduly affected. At least once a year, a more in-depth and comprehensive evaluation takes place, with surveys conducted to ascertain teacher and volunteer satisfaction and to determine future direction of the volunteer program. At this time recruitment procedures, methods for orienting and training volunteers, information in the volunteer handbook, and means of showing appreciation for volunteers would also be reviewed and revised as warranted before the next academic year.

Finally, in schools where teachers and school leaders engage in frequent volunteer appreciation activities, more volunteer satisfaction and higher rates of retention exist. The ways schools show appreciation for volunteers include personal on-the-spot expressions; highlighting volunteers and volunteer activities on a school bulletin board or in the school or classroom newsletter; sending photographs and articles about the volunteer program to the local newspapers; including volunteers in staff/faculty events, as appropriate; hosting special luncheons, teas, potlucks or coffees; writing letters of appreciation; and giving out end-of-the-year certificates and awards, such as caps, T-shirts, or coffee mugs with the school logo. In Figure 10.9 is an excerpt

Thanks

SUPER JOB!

BOOK FAIR SUCCESS

The Ingersoll Book Fair held from October 21-28 was another success. The funds earned from the book fair will be used to expand our Accelerated Reader program. Ingersoll earned more than $850 in vouchers and cash to purchase books and educational supplies from Scholastic Book Company and to purchase additional computerized quizzes for the AR program.

A special thanks goes to Mrs. Lynne Waldrop and Mrs. Kim Standard, book fair co-chairpersons, and all the parents who volunteered their time to make this book fair a success. Our volunteers were truly responsible for the success of our book fair.

The success of the book fair is a reminder that middle school students still love books. Please don't forget the importance that reading has for all students in all subjects. With the new link to Ingersoll's Accelerated Reader quizzes on our home page, you can even select books for your child that are AR books and are at their reading level.

Figure 10.9

from the Ingersoll Middle School newsletter thanking parents for their help with the school book fair. Regardless of the type of appreciation activities planned, volunteers should know that their services are needed and useful. The best appreciation activities are those that are sincere and personal and that do not consume large amounts of time for school personnel or for volunteers. For example, knowing each volunteers' name and recognizing each volunteer with a smile and a personal greeting is one important way to show ongoing appreciation. Some schools have special name tags with the name of the school, the volunteer's name, and the word *volunteer* written underneath. This simple gesture helps give volunteers a feeling of importance and belonging and lets them know that school personnel recognize and appreciate their presence.

RECRUITMENT OF VOLUNTEERS

The best recruitment strategy is personal contact. Principals and teachers who reach out to parents and community members and who take the time to explain school and/or classroom goals are more likely to be successful in their efforts to solicit volunteer services. One-to-one contact with parents and parents of former students, as well as group contact through presentations to civic, service, professional, and religious groups, result in increased school support. For example, school leaders at Washington School in Quincy, Illinois, prepared a fifteen- to twenty-minute presentation that includes showing a video filmed at the school. The presentation was delivered at the meetings of numerous organizations, along with a brief brochure about the school and ways the community could be involved and supportive. The school succeeded in garnering the support of various individuals and organizations that signed up as "guest readers" and which supplied various needed materials, supplies, and services throughout the year. Among the many services and programs the school offers is a "beauty parlor" and a "clothing store" staffed by volunteers. Children in need can get assistance in washing their bodies and hair and in finding clean, good used clothing. This service results in more children who feel good about themselves and who are learning to care for and take pride in their physical appearance.

Other recruitment strategies involve writing articles for school and classroom newsletters; arranging for feature articles in the local newspaper; placing brochures and recruitment information in the offices of local health departments, doctors, dentists, and attorneys; asking banks and department stores to put information in bank statements and bills; and sharing information at booths set up at local malls, shopping centers, and stores, as well as during school events, fairs, and trade shows.

Recruitment of parents should include reasons why they should volunteer their services to their child's school. Reasons cited may include: (1) teachers and children need their help, (2) parents are already experienced in working with at least their own child, and (3) their child will be proud of their involvement and will benefit from their contributions. Recruitment of community members, as well as parents, should include a note about the opportunity for volunteers to work in areas where they feel comfortable and productive and the fact that volunteers can contribute services and goods both in and outside of the school building and the regular school day. A list of potential jobs that volunteers might contribute should be included in the recruitment information. This list could include school projects such as building, repairing, or installing playground equipment; planting trees and shrubs; building bookshelves, reading lofts, and other classroom furnishings; repairing equipment; and organizing toy/book/clothing exchanges. Other jobs could be categorized according to classroom-related tasks, such as tutoring, reading to children, listening to children read, showing videos and filmstrips, playing games, supervising learning centers, supervising computer and bookmaking activities, talking about their country of origin, and sharing music, art, or games of their culture, to name a few of the many potential jobs for in-classroom volunteers. Tasks listed under a category for out-of-school contributions might include furnishing refreshments, writing/typing newsletters, coordinating volunteers, furnishing dress-up clothes and/or costumes, collecting recycled materials for use in classroom projects, providing childcare for another volunteer's children, serving on a telephone committee, washing art shirts, and cleaning and repairing toys and dolls used in the prekindergarten and kindergarten programs.

Whenever possible, recruitment activities should be personal and should be geared to a specific task or tasks—for example, soliciting volunteers to build or install new playground equipment, getting someone to clean and repair toys and dolls, or asking a service organization to organize the Reading Is Fundamental program or a book fair. Individuals will often agree to a "task-specific" job rather than sign up for what they may view as a long-term commitment. Once individuals make a positive contribution to the school and are appreciated for their contribution, they are more likely to volunteer their services in the future.

*T*EACHERS' RESPONSIBILITIES FOR CLASSROOM VOLUNTEERS

Before volunteers arrive the teachers need to have a plan for what they will do. Starting with simple but meaningful tasks, such as listening to children read, is usually a good idea. The experiences planned should give the volunteers a sense of accomplishment and reward and be neither too challenging nor too simplistic. Finding out special interests or talents of each volunteer is helpful. A parent with musical or artistic ability may really enjoy working with the children in those areas, whereas someone without skill or interest in these areas may be very uncomfortable being asked to do so. Whatever the task, the instructions need to be very clearly stated, orally and in writing, and all materials and supplies need to be readily available. The teacher should also talk with the children about the volunteer and his or her role in the classroom.

Ideally, each teacher and volunteer should have an opportunity to meet to discuss the tasks as well as discuss classroom procedures and rules when children are not in the room. In addition to explaining specific tasks and gaining the volunteer's input and suggestions, the teacher should reassure the volunteer that the teacher will step in if necessary to remind a child of classroom rules. When the volunteer arrives for the first day with the children present, the teacher should introduce the volunteer to the children, making the volunteer feel as welcome as possible. Showing where to put personal belongings and giving reminders as to the location of the restroom, workroom, and vending machines is also helpful. If possible, the teacher and volunteer should have some time together after this first experience to discuss how everything went and any questions the volunteer might have. Keeping in touch through personal contact and message boards is important, though not always easy. Teachers have to really make an effort to find time meet with the volunteer to discuss plans and evaluate activities. Although this adds yet another task to the teacher's busy week, the time spent will pay off in terms of the increased contributions the volunteer will be able to make. In time, most teachers wonder how they ever got along without these wonderful classroom volunteers!

*I*N-SERVICE FOR TEACHERS

When teachers have an opportunity to participate in a training session on effective use of volunteers, fewer initial problems are encountered. Similarly, if problems are mounting in an existing program, this may be an indication of the need for a refresher training session. The training program for teachers needs to be separate from the planning sessions held to organize the program and should include information about planning for and using volunteers, both in and out of the classroom. Communicating with volunteers is a topic that bears ample discussion. How to clearly explain tasks and expectations and how to convey constructive criticism are two common topics needing attention. For teachers who are expected to train volunteers to perform task-specific classroom jobs, some assistance in developing training materials and handouts might be needed.

*P*ARENTS' IN-HOME "VOLUNTEER" CONTRIBUTIONS

Parents need to know that their efforts to stay informed and involved in their child's learning activities at home represent some of the most significant volunteer contributions that can possibly be made. Parents frequently ask, "How can I help my child at home?" *All* parents should be involved in reading to their child, listening to their child talk and read, helping their child with homework, and providing out-of-school experiences that enrich the child's learning. Parents can also volunteer their time to work with their child on home-learning activities that require adult-child interaction, such as those described in Chapter 6. The research cited in Chapter 1 regarding the effectiveness of home-learning activities in boosting student achievement has triggered an increase in use of what Joyce Epstein at the Center on Families, Communities, Schools, and Children's Learning at Johns Hopkins University calls *interactive homework assignments*. Teachers are sometimes paid to work together to develop assignments matched to their own curricula and learning objectives. The assignments are used throughout the year with students and their families and are then revised based on feedback and evaluation from students, parents, and teachers. Teachers who devise home-learning activities that require adult and child interaction find that most parents readily volunteer to participate in these activities with their children. Parents also report feeling good about their ability to help with the academic development of their children.

For your consideration . . .

Following is a list of questions that may serve to help you clarify your beliefs about the role of volunteers in the school program. In addition, these questions may serve as a starting point for a school staff to begin to examine the development of a volunteer program.

1. There are a number of tasks that volunteers could undertake to help our school.   **YES   NO**

2. The teachers and the children would benefit from assistance from classroom volunteers.   **YES   NO**

3. The school would benefit from increased involvement of community members.   **YES   NO**

4. Parents should be asked to contribute service to the school.   **YES   NO**

5. Community members should be asked to contribute service to the school.   **YES   NO**

6. A variety of options for service should be provided for parents and community members.   **YES   NO**

7. Parental involvement in completing interactive homework assignments with their child should be viewed as an important volunteer service.   **YES   NO**

SUMMARY

Involving parents and community members in volunteer activities reaps many benefits. These individuals can actively support the school by volunteering goods and services to be performed either in or outside of the school building. According to research, having volunteers visible in the school building shows that the school is open to them and that teachers are willing to work with parents and community members to provide the best possible education for all children.

LOOKING AHEAD . . .

In this chapter the importance of involving parents and community members as volunteers was emphasized. Building positive relationships with community organizations, agencies, and businesses will be explored in the chapter that follows.

REFERENCES

Civic Ventures (2004). *Experience after school: Engaging older adults in after-school programs, An Experience Corps Tool Kit.* Available online at *http://www.experience corps.org/images/pdf/toolkit.pdf*

Independent Sector (2003). *Experience at work: volunteering and giving among Americans 50 and over.* Available online at *http://www.independentsector.org*

School-Community Partnerships: Utilizing Community Resources and Fostering Positive Public Relations

Our work as a taskforce has led us to conclude that it is unfair to expect school districts as we know them to support the ambitious goals we are advocating for schools and for school children. In order to achieve both high academic results and equity for all a system's schools, we envision a new kind of school district— what we call a local education support system—that marshals all a city's resources to fulfill three functions: (1) provide schools, students, and teachers with needed support and timely interventions; (2) ensure the schools have the power and resources to make good decisions; and (3) make decisions and hold people throughout the system accountable with indicators of school and district performance and practices (p. 1).

—*School Communities That Work: A National Task Force on the Future of Urban Districts.*

INTRODUCTION

Education is a cooperative enterprise that is most successful when everyone accepts and exercises personal responsibility. In the preceding chapters the schools' role in involving parents in their children's education was emphasized. Attention has been given to communicating with parents and providing parent education opportunities. In the previous chapter strategies for involving parents and community members in ways that directly benefit the school, the teachers, and the children were offered. In this chapter you will examine the positive benefits schools are afforded when they enjoy the reputation of being a "good school." Strategies for enhancing public relations and fostering community involvement through a variety of classroom and school projects and procedures will be shared.

BUILDING PUBLIC RELATIONS: PLANNING FOR ACTION

Schools that make regular use of the media and do everything they can to let their public know how "good" they are usually do not have a public relations problem. Unfortunately, much of the good news about education is only shared among educators. Studies show that there are now more adults with no school age children than ever before. Since most of the information about the schools is shared through word-of-mouth and the newspaper, educators need to be certain that the good news gets at least as much coverage as the bad news. Public relations can be defined as the methods and/or activities employed to promote a favorable relationship with the public. Business and industry have the right idea when they hire public relations experts to promote their products and services. Schools would do well to employ some of the same strategies used by not only business and industry but also by institutions of higher education in promoting their mission to the public. While few if any school districts can afford to hire full-time public relations experts, school leaders do need to ensure that certain tasks associated with public relations are getting done. Consistency in maintaining close, regular contact with the public is a key to good public relations—and to support at the polls!

Development of a plan for public relations facilitates action and progress toward an improved school-community relationship. Such a plan includes specific objectives that, when accomplished, lead to enhanced public relations. For each objective, the tasks or activities to be completed and a time line for doing so are listed along with names of individuals responsible for accomplishing each. One activity might be to make a videotape of the school to be shown at meetings of civic, service, and professional organizations. A copy of the video could be sent to "feeder" schools and daycare centers, as well as to city officials and legislators. Brochures and other printed information, and a brief presentation by the principal and key teachers, could accompany the video showings.

As the old saying goes, "a picture is worth a thousand words." There's just nothing like getting individuals into the school for garnering support and increasing community awareness. Some schools host various groups of individuals for school tours and coffee. Family day, senior citizens' day, grandparents' day, retired educators' day, bankers' day, real estate agents' day—the possibilities are endless! A thirty- to forty-five-minute tour by the principal or another staff member is generally sufficient for giving these individuals a glimpse of the school, its programs, teachers, and students. Each visit should conclude with information as to how these individuals could support the school, including a description of the volunteer program and any particular needs facing the school at that time.

The Chaska, Minnesota middle schools host principal luncheons each month for approximately ten parents. The luncheons promote two-way communication and enable parents to learn more about the school and to voice concerns. Area business leaders in Macomb, Illinois serve as "Principal for a Day." Sponsored by the Chamber of Commerce and the local district, five representatives shadow each principal from 7 A.M. to 2 P.M. and then attend a reception with school board members, superintendent, principals, and Chamber Board chair. The program serves to strengthen relationships by enhancing communication and building an awareness of the schools and their programs.

Schools should also remember to take advantage of existing publications for disseminating information about the school. There should be routine sharing of the newsletter with representatives of community organizations. In addition, these and other appropriate school publications should be placed in the offices of doctors, dentists, attorneys, and real estate agents, as well as at public health centers and other locations in the community.

Working with the Media

A media representative who is interested in the school and who recognizes the importance of portraying a positive public image for the school is one of the best friends a school can have. Getting to know the local media staff members is important, and establishing a relationship with these individuals is sometimes more readily accomplished when fewer school personnel are responsible for communicating directly with the media. Generally, the principal or principal designee and a central office administrator serve as media contact persons. The school media contact person should determine which media representatives are responsible for covering school events and should issue frequent invitations for these individuals to visit the school. Every effort should be made to determine their special interests and ideas for keeping the community informed about the educational system. Having a good relationship with the media representatives is helpful for schools in determining priority "news." Schools have many interesting programs and activities; however, not all are appealing to the general public. Stories that feature new methods or techniques, such as use of technology, and stories that illustrate other, more complex issues such as accountability and curriculum reform, are likely to pique the public's interest. Special events and programs involving the children are covered by the media when time and space allow. In larger cities with many more schools, gaining media coverage is often more difficult. Maintaining a strong relationship with the media representative—and carefully selecting news to be shared—becomes even more important.

The school media contact person would be responsible for sending news releases to the various media representatives. Sometimes one medium works better than another to publicize a particular story or event. For example, since television is a visual medium, a story conveyed through an interesting scene is more likely to attract the interest of a television reporter. "Talking heads" in a television interview and "grip and grin" photographs of two individuals shaking hands or exchanging a check or certificate do not command the most interest.

It's also a good idea to consider whom the school wants to reach with each message—and, when necessary, to tailor messages to fit the intended audience. For example, which radio station, television station, and print media are likely to reach senior citizens? professionals? members of business and church groups? New residents? Depending on the location of the school, print resources might include daily newspapers, weekly shoppers' guides, local TV guides, local magazines, and inserts in billing statements. Church bulletins, company newsletters, and college newspapers may also be an appropriate avenue in some communities for sharing school-related news.

Since most media representatives prefer to write their own copy, school personnel can assist by giving the necessary facts as early as possible so as to allow for media representatives to call for additional information, schedule photographers, and write their own story. Newspaper reporters work from an "inverted pyramid" format when they develop a story. This format is recommended for school personnel who write news stories for submission to local papers. The most important information should be first, in case the article gets cut short due to space constraints. When enlisting the media's assistance in publicizing an upcoming event, the recommendation is to follow a "who, what, when, where" format and include a contact person and phone number where that person can be reached. All news releases should be typed double-spaced, with a heading that reads "For Immediate Release" or "For Release after . . ." and the appropriate date. Get information about the amount of "lead time" media representatives need when covering stories and deadlines for regular submissions. A good rule of thumb is to make the initial contact two to three weeks in advance. A follow-up telephone call placed the morning of the event can serve as a reminder for the photographer.

The South St. Paul, Minnesota school district's high school principal solicited community assistance in solving an attendance problem. He first wrote an article which was published in the newspaper. Then, he shared attendance information on the school Website. Finally, he received district support to fund signs which read "If you're skipping school, skip this place." The signs were distributed to area businesses for display on doors and in store windows.

Since most schools are at one time or another faced with a negative situation where news media and the public want information, it is important that all school personnel know who is to issue such information. In most cases the district superintendent, the school board president, or the school principal deal with the media. Sometimes, however, a reporter may contact a teacher directly. It is important that everyone knows the procedure for handling requests for information—whether the information requested is positive or negative. First of all, the school person should ask for the reporter's name and affiliation. If the school person receiving the call is the best person to respond to the question or request, a face-to-face meeting should be arranged whenever possible. If a telephone interview is to be conducted and the reporter has called without prior notice, it is generally most appropriate for the school representative to ask the reporter to call back at a specified time. This allows the school person time to gather thoughts and support materials. If the reporter represents a radio station, the school representative should ask if the conversation is being taped for broadcast and should plan accordingly. When speaking with radio and television reporters, the school representative should be as brief as possible. As when conversing with parents, the school representative should use language that is free of educational jargon and clearly understandable to the general public. Finally, school personnel should understand that everything they say to a reporter—even in a social setting—may end up in print. It has been said that educators are their own worst enemies, for many are all too quick to complain to neighbors, friends, and acquaintances about what they see wrong with the school or school system. If we want to portray a positive image to our public, if we want to instill confidence in others insofar as the school's ability to provide children with a good education, if we want to build a strong relationship with our community, then we must refrain from being bearers of bad news. Instead, we must learn to toot our own horns—and toot them loudly, clearly, boldly, and often.

COMMUNITY INVOLVEMENT: WORKING TO OVERCOME OBSTACLES

Researchers such as Shirley Brice Heath and Milbrey McLaughlin (1991) have questioned the adequacy of the schools as social institutions "because they are built on outmoded assumptions about family and community" (623). Many children are no longer raised in stable communities where neighbors, parents, and teachers all know one another and share similar views. Dramatic changes in family structures, as discussed in Chapters 1 and 2, have made a strong impact on the school as a social institution. Similarly, the changing faces of neighborhoods—many of which have seen the closing of small businesses, a decrease in the impact of social institutions, and loss of the neighborhood school—have contributed to marked changes in what were once regarded as "our schools." School leaders, in collaboration with teachers and parent representatives, must think carefully about what schools expect from communities. Mobilizing resources within the community to enhance the learning experience for children is critical today. Historically, schools did not "do it alone." They had the support of close-knit neighborhoods, extended families of children, and local small businesses. In recent years, however, the changes that have taken place in homes, communities, and in schools and school districts have placed incredible responsibilities on school personnel who have been asked to perform an increasing number of nonteaching-related tasks. While tending to the social, emotional, physical, and psychological needs of students cannot be overlooked, schools must have substantial support from not only the parents but also the community-at-large.

As stated by Kowalski (2000), "Whether American's schools meet the challenge of the twenty-first century depends on both the nation's political and educational leaders. Both groups must envision and pursue reform that addresses multiculturalism and poverty, and they must do so in a manner that integrates the community and school" (p. 33). Many educators and policymakers favor a community schools approach. As defined by the Coalition for Community schools, "A community school is a place as well as a set of partnerships between the school and other community resources. It's integrated focus on academics, services, supports, and opportunities leads to improved academic learning, stronger families, and healthier communities. By sharing expertise and resources, schools and communities act in concert to educate children. Schools are not left to work alone" (p. 1).

Maintaining a "presence" in the community can go a long way toward helping schools build a positive public image. School leaders who encourage faculty, staff, and student involvement in the community and who expect maximum use of community resources in the curriculum are more successful in promoting school-community partnerships. Sharing with all school personnel the need for and value of an effective school-community relations program is an important first step. When staff members have an understanding of the short-term as well as long-term benefits of forging a strong school-community relationship, they are more likely to take an active role in accomplishing goals and objectives. Determining the annual percentage of public participation in the school and the impact that such participation has had on the school's programs and activities is strongly encouraged. This information helps school leaders recognize areas of strength, as well as needs to be addressed in a plan for community involvement.

In districts where children are bussed from one community to attend school in another community, schools must first determine what they mean when they say "community." Is reference being made to the immediate area surrounding the school? Or is reference being made to the neighborhoods represented by the student body? The best answer is probably "both," since excluding either from the definition would be cutting off an important potential partner with a preexisting vested interest in the school. Also, when one considers the impact a school's image has on the voting public, it is easy to see why schools need to reach beyond their immediate neighborhood in fostering good relations.

UTILIZING COMMUNITY AGENCIES, ORGANIZATIONS, AND RESOURCES

Every community has service agencies and organizations available to assist families with a variety of needs. Effective schools recognize needs and work to link families with appropriate resources. Although services differ somewhat from community to community, similar services can be found in most communities. Police and fire departments, public health and assistance agencies, libraries, and more have a long history of providing services to families and resources and support to classrooms and schools. In larger communities, additional resources such as zoos, museums, organized park district programs, transportation services and a wider array of businesses, social, professional and community organizations can be found. All of these are fertile ground for teachers to gain resources and information for classroom use.

Identification of resources in the extended community and the creation of a school database and printed materials facilitate use of community agencies and outreach to various organizations, businesses, and groups. In Figure 11.1 is a brochure prepared by Mandy Ricco who developed this list of family resources for the school district.

Forms of Community Involvement

Community involvement has been defined as the "actions that organizations and individuals (e.g., parents, businesses, universities, social service agencies, and the media) take to promote student development" (Nettles 1991, 380).

Adopt-a-School programs have spread throughout the country since the early eighties. Adopt-a-School is a partnership between a business and one school. Businesses share numerous resources with schools. In exchange, the schools gratefully acknowledge each company's support by publicly recognizing its contributions.

Partnership arrangements require careful planning and monitoring. Successful programs are characterized by defined goals, a planning committee comprised of company and school representatives, stated objectives, needs assessment, and orientation for school personnel. The Peoria Area Chamber of Commerce funds an Adopt-A-School Program Website for the Peoria, Illinois public schools. The site lists program goals, benefits for businesses and for schools, and the latest Adopt-A-School news. In the Springfield (Illinois) Public Schools, the Adopt-a-School program is cosponsored by the Chamber of Commerce. The Adopt-a-School concept was originally presented to the chief executive officers of twelve leading firms in face-to-face meetings conducted by a representative of the chamber of commerce and the district superintendent. Approximately two weeks later, the corporate officers were contacted to ascertain whether they were interested in participating in the program. Nearly all agreed to join. As word spread, other companies began to call to inquire about participation in the program. Each business and each

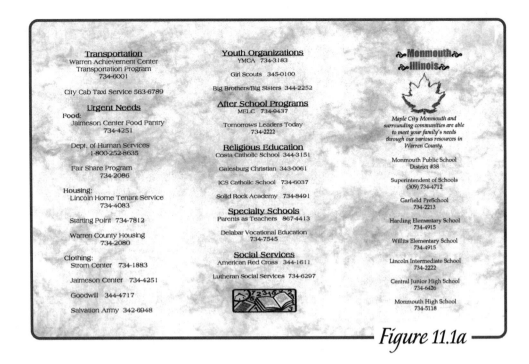

Figure 11.1a

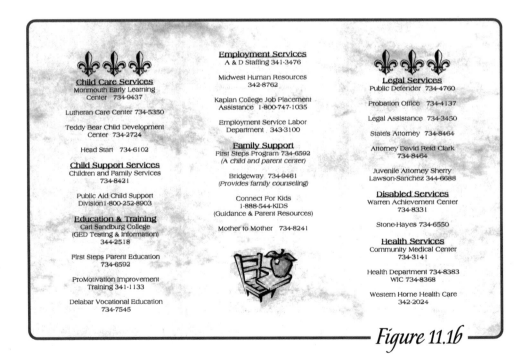

Figure 11.1b

school put together a team of interested employees to serve as liaisons to coordinate the partnership activities, with the primary purpose of making citizens more knowledgeable about what was happening in their schools. The program in the Springfield Public School System has grown with each school having between three and eight partners, depending on enrollment. Partnership activities have included collaborative fund-raising events to benefit the schools, recognition of honor students and students with perfect attendance, penpal activities between students and employees, company assistance in planting trees at the school, the development of a "Kids Beat" news broadcast prepared and presented by students and used as a part of a television station's newscast, and collaborative community service projects such as filling and delivering Christmas baskets for the needy. Individuals directly involved in the partnership program in Springfield feel that the program has helped change public attitudes about the schools by fostering a spirit of cooperation between the private and public sectors of the community. One of their partners is the Southern Illinois University Medical School who adopted Enos Elementary School over 17 years ago. Enos serves just under 300 students, 98 percent of whom come from low-income homes. An SIU committee organizes activities and hundreds of SIU staff members donate time, talents, supplies, and money each year.

Professional sports teams are also active in the Adopt-A-School Program. The Chicago Bulls take advantage of their unique position to influence youth by adopting one Chicago public school each year and supporting several others. In addition, each year they donate approximately 4000 books to Chicagoland children, host "Reading Time-Outs" for children and players, and also assist with numerous other reading initiatives through their Chicago Bulls All-Star Reading Team comprised of players, former players, and their families. Reading is also kept in the limelight through book exchanges between fans and players before each home game.

While structured programs such as the ones listed above do exist, they are not available to all schools. Individual school personnel must take the lead in initiating efforts designed to bring the community and the school closer together. In some communities, African-American business leaders have initiated programs to tutor or mentor African-American students—particularly male students. Providing multiple opportunities for community members to have personal contact with school children served to enrich the curriculum for children and strengthen the school-community relationship. This kind of community connection can, however, only be initiated when the administration sees the value and provides active support.

The school principal gave her full support when first-grade teacher Amy Morris in Macomb, Illinois, proposed an Adopt-a-Classroom program (see Figure 11.2). To promote a positive relationship between the business community and the Lincoln School students, and also to increase students' reading, writing, and communication skills, area businesses volunteer to "adopt" primary-grade classrooms. The children keep in contact with the business by writing monthly letters to the employer and/or employees. The business reciprocates by sending a minimum of one employee monthly to the classroom to serve as a guest reader. During the twenty- to thirty-minute visits, these visitors also shared specific information about their jobs. Some businesses also make cash donations, which are used to purchase books and supplies for the classroom. At the end of the school year, a field trip to the business is scheduled with transportation often being supplied by the business. A variety of

Macomb Schools

Lincoln Elementary School
MACOMB COMMUNITY UNIT SCHOOL DISTRICT #185
315 N. BONHAM • MACOMB, ILLINOIS 61455
PHONE: 309/833-2095

#1
Preparing Students for Success

Ed Fulkerson
Principal

What:	Adopt A Classroom Program
Who:	A Macomb Business Organization and a Lincoln School Classroom
When:	September - May (or as determined by classroom teacher and business)
Why:	To promote a positive relationship between the business community and Lincoln School students.
	To provide positive role models for Lincoln School students from the Macomb business community.
	To increase the reading, writing, and communication skills of the students.
How:	Through the Adopt A Classroom Program, the business employee(s) or organization member(s) and the classroom students will be encouraged to jointly participate in the following activities:

1. Each month* a minimum of one employee or organization member will come in and read, share an activity, or discuss a hobby to their adopted class. (*The business and classroom teacher may increase or decrease the number of visits to the classroom as needed.)

2. The class will keep in contact with their adopted business by writing to them each month.

3. If possible, upon completion of the Adopt A Classroom Program, the classroom will take a field trip to and tour of the business, if appropriate.

Figure 11.2

businesses participate in the program, including several local restaurants, a pet store, a beauty/barber shop, a record store, a bank and the local branch of a large factory, to name a few of the many participants. Local newspaper coverage for the program is excellent, with photographs and accompanying stories that feature each participating business at least once during the year. In Ed Fulkerson's school newsletter he thanks the many businesses who helped their school during the year (see Figure 11.3).

Teachers can incorporate community involvement into their collaborative planning activities conducted with the children. As teacher and children discuss plans for a unit of study, they can consider ways to inform and involve the community. By doing this the children begin to think of themselves as

December 2004
A message from Mr. Fulkerson . . .

A very busy month of December is upon us. The students are getting ready for the Santa's Breakfast program Saturday the 4th, singing each day in music class with Ms. Kurasz and Ms. Ramos (who is substituting while Ms. Johnson is on maternity leave). At the same time, Ms. Sanner's art classes are preparing at a frantic pace for the yearly event held at MHS. Please plan on attending the programs that day and seeing all of the neat things going on at Lincoln School! Also, remember a pancake breakfast graciously prepared by the Kiwanis Club will be served at the same time.

I have made a decision this year that we will no longer be having classroom gift exchanges. Instead, individual classes will have the option of participating in service projects to assist those in our community that are less fortunate. As an example, our 2nd and 3rd grade classes are working out details for a food drive throughout the month of December, complete with a student bell-ringer who goes door-to-door each morning collecting non-perishable goods for the Salvation Army and other area food pantries.

In keeping with the spirit of the season, it's appropriate to thank some individuals and businesses who help out at Lincoln School. First, a thank you to Rick Fox at Timberhill Nursery who has donated labor towards our flower beds this coming spring. Second, a big thank-you goes out to Citizen's National Bank for underwriting a major portion of our monthly PBS reading visits (including books) in our kindergarten classrooms. Third, thanks to optometrists Dr. Botts and Dr. Culver who've helped out with some of our students needing eye exams and glasses. Finally, thanks to many individuals and all the area business and community groups that are helping our school with Santa's Breakfast. These include: Cathy Early State Farm, Burger King, Cameraland, Aramark, Monet's Garden, MDH Day Health Services, Hardees, Hy-Vee, Jazzy Jingles, Karen Martin's Suzuki Violins, Kiwanis, McDonald's West, Niemann's, Tranquil Gardens, Walmart, Wendy's, Western Distributing, MHS Student Council, MHS Drama, MJH Holiday Band, MJH Holiday Singers, Town & Country Clover 4-H, and YMCA Dance & Tumble Center.

Parents, in an effort to meet the Illinois State Learning Standards, we have developed "curriculum maps" for each of your child's classes. These "maps" list the topics that are covered during the school year on a month-by-month basis and follow the state guidelines. Please take an opportunity the next time you are on-line to look over the maps associated with each class. The directions shown below here can easily be accessed by going to the district Web page at http://district185.macomb.com/ and clicking on the link labeled Curriculum Maps found on the left hand column.

Regardless of religious beliefs, at this time of the year take time to reflect on the blessings each one of us possesses. I am thankful for my family, friends, and colleagues. I hope that each of you is just as blessed. Also, continue to keep our troops and their families in your thoughts and prayers. The sacrifices our military personnel make to keep the freedoms we enjoy are truly a treasure. Have a super month of December!

Figure 11.3

part of the community outside of the school and, at the same time, of the community as their audience. For example, local restaurants can be asked to print children's original poems and stories on their placemats. The placemats then will serve to draw customers from the school who want to see the children's writings; and members of the general public see that the school is teaching the children to write. Children at one school decorated grocery sacks with an advertisement for their favorite book. Parents shopped at the participating stores because their children wanted them to see the sacks, and the public became more aware of how the school was promoting literacy.

Education Foundation Partnerships

An education foundation is a form of school/business partnership that involves financial contributions from either corporations or private citizens. Although foundations have a reputation for being philanthropic, many school districts have developed their own foundations. Contributions are deposited in a nonprofit account governed by a local board of trustees that functions separately from the school board. Foundations are generally organized by a committee comprised of school leaders, parent representatives, and key community and business leaders that drafts a statement of purpose and operational guidelines. A board of trustees is appointed, articles of incorporation and bylaws are adopted, and tax-exempt status is obtained. In addition, regulations regarding membership, meetings, officers, committees, and other matters are decided (O'Connell 1985). The funds are earmarked for special projects, such as mini-grants for classroom projects, sabbaticals for teachers and administrators to engage in advanced study, and so forth. In addition to soliciting donations, fund-raising activities are generally conducted. For example, the Macomb Education Foundation in Macomb, Illinois, worked with three local grocery stores to develop a coupon booklet. The booklet, which sold in the community for $25, contained coupons for $5 off of grocery bills of $50 or more. The total value of the booklet to the purchaser was $45. Since its formation, the Macomb Educational Foundation has provided many books, science equipment, and other classroom resources, thus enriching the educational program for students. In Carlsbad, California business leaders developed one of the first educational foundations in 1983. Since then they have donated over 2 million dollars to the Carlsbad Unified School District.

Community Service

Becoming aware of specific community needs is also important as schools seek to establish a two-way partnership where both schools and communities benefit. In some communities school facilities are open to organizations such as the Scouts and 4-H clubs that meet during after-school hours. Sometimes the gym is available in the evenings for community basketball games, joggers, and walkers. Polls are often set up in schools during elections. The school library is kept open for community use during the summer at Bridgeview Elementary in Leclaire, Iowa. Whatever the activities, supporting worthwhile community activities through provision of facilities helps build a feeling of ownership among community members who may not otherwise have reason to enter the school building.

Many schools are beginning to realize the benefits of involving students in performing acts of community service. In Canton, Illinois students recycle cans, collect can goods and coats for the needy and assist in other recycling drives. Lincoln School primary-grade students choose to participate in a community service project rather than in a holiday gift exchange. The second- and third-grade students rang bells and collected food for the Salvation Army

For your consideration . . .

1. A school's reputation in the community is important.   YES   NO

2. Community members should know about and be involved with their local schools.   YES   NO

3. Schools should portray a positive image to the public.   YES   NO

4. Community agencies, organizations, and individuals have much to offer the school curriculum.   YES   NO

5. The school has a responsibility to serve the community through various projects and activities. YES   NO

6. The school should have a regular plan for sharing with their public the good things that are happening. YES   NO

7. Fostering public relations should be a continuous, ongoing activity.   YES   NO

8. Whenever possible, the school should open its doors to the community.   YES   NO

and for a local food pantry. These kinds of activities help children understand the organization and interdependence of their community and how community service impacts upon residents.

SUMMARY

Different types of community involvement are likely to have different effects and meet with different results in different communities. Recognizing various community characteristics and their effects on involvement is important for school leaders who, at the same time, recognize the need for a three-way partnership of school, parents, and community. As stated by Edwards and Young (1992), "Boundaries separating the responsibilities of home, school, and community are blurring, calling into question the traditional conceptions of parent involvement as one-to-one relationship between parent and teacher" (78). If schools are to continue to accept the challenge of "education for all," they will need broader support from society-at-large. However, garnering this support is difficult in the face of critics who disregard current social milieu and equate the poor school performance of some students with poor schools. School leaders must work to develop and implement strong plans for fostering public relations and building community ties before the support that is so badly needed can be realized.

The questions on page 205 are designed to help you think about your school's position with respect to community involvement and the need for increased public relations.

Looking Ahead . . .

Having community members and parents become more involved in schools through volunteer efforts is important. Also important is having parents as decision-makers and advocates for their children's education. In the next chapter opportunities for involving parents in these kinds of leadership roles will be explored.

References

Annenberg Institute for School Reform (2002). *School communities that work: A national task force on the future of urban districts,* Providence, RI: Brown University.

Coalition for Community Schools (2003). *Making the difference: Research and practice in community schools.* Washington, DC: Coalition for Community Schools.

Heath, S. B., & McLaughlin, M. W. (1991). Community organizations as family: Endeavors that engage and support adolescents. *Phi Delta Kappan, 73*(8), 623–627.

Kowalski, T. J. (2000). *Public relations in schools.* Upper Saddle River, NJ: Merrill Prentice Hall.

Nettles, S. M. (1991). Community involvement and disadvantaged students: A review. *Review of Educational Research, 61*(3), 379–406.

Empowering Parents to Serve as Advocates for the Education of Their Children

Parents in many schools are invited each year to be part of an advisory team that talks and plans with the principal and superintendent. Issues ranging from curriculum to traffic safety, to building and playground maintenance, to a vision for the future, have all been discussed at these school advisory meetings. Parents appreciate the opportunity to be involved and know their input is valued, especially when they can see actions taking place that they recommended.

INTRODUCTION

Parents must participate actively in their children's education by encouraging good study habits, monitoring homework, and exhibiting a commitment to continued learning in their own lives. Additionally, parents must be active participants in the work of the school.

Throughout this book you have encountered strategies for inviting parents to be active participants in their children's education. Strategies for involving parents in setting goals for their children's learning and in the assessment of that learning, maintaining consistent communication between home and school, providing opportunities for parents to volunteer their services, and helping parents to become better teachers of their children have been shared. In this chapter the involvement of parents in decision-making activities that impact on their children's education will be discussed. Extending the partnership arrangement to include participation in a range of decision-making issues requires that the relationship be built on cooperation, trust, and mutual respect. In schools where such a relationship does not yet exist, school leaders would be wise first to work to enhance the partnership relationship through strategies designed to increase two-way communication. Through a shared exchange of feelings, information, and ideas, both parents and school personnel will, undoubtedly, identify issues that need to be addressed. Then, by bringing together members of each group to work collaboratively in the development of recommendations for improvement, the school will have begun to empower parents as decision makers and as advocates.

DEVELOPING "FAMILY-LIKE SCHOOLS"

Although parents and teachers share the responsibility for educating children, each performs some functions independently of the other. Decision making has traditionally been within the purview of the schools, and parents' attempts to participate or influence the outcome has been viewed as "interference." The exclusion of parents from decision-making activities is representative of a model that Epstein (1990) calls "a division of labor that pulls the spheres of school and family influences and responsibilities apart, decreasing overlap and restricting interactions between parents and teachers" (104). In contrast, Epstein advocates a "combination of labor that pushes the spheres of family and school influence together," resulting in what she calls "school-like families" and "family-like schools" (104). Employing the strategies presented in previous chapters results in the creation of school-like families as teachers enlist parents as partners in their children's education. Family-like schools result from attention being paid to each student's family life, self-concept, aspirations, social skills, and talents. Schools can empower parents to assist them in making decisions that further a family-like school model. Having parent advisory teams meet with the principal, district superintendent, and school staff is an example of one way to further this model. In Figures 12.1 and 12.2 are excerpts from two school newsletters encouraging parent participation in these meetings.

ACCEPTING PARENTS AS PART OF THE DECISION-MAKING TEAM

In virtually every school there are parents who are well-equipped to participate in making decisions that will affect the educational experience for all children. Developing a forum for parents and teachers to ask questions and share concerns about the school and to take part in the solution-finding process is one way of tapping the expertise that is sure to exist. As the reform efforts occurring in schools all across the country grow, so do the number of "stories" about the support—or lack of support—from parents. School districts are beginning to learn that parents can thwart or slow down the whole process if what the school is doing is not clearly understood.

Volume 3   *Ingersoll Middle School*   Number 3

Third Quarter Newsletter

Byron L. Sondgeroth   **February 2003**   Patrick M. Twomey
Principal   *www.cantonusd.org/ingersoll*   Assistant Principal

SPRING PICTURE DAY

Ingersoll's spring picture day is scheduled for Tuesday, March 4, 2003. This is also a district school improvement day with students being released at 11:37 AM. For spring pictures, all students will have their pictures taken using a unique background. The pictures will be developed and given to students later that month. Students who choose not to purchase any of the pictures will need to return their complete package with all the pictures. Parents who wish to purchase pictures can choose from a variety of package options, keeping those pictures they purchase and returning those they do not want.

SCHOOL BREAKFAST

The American School Food Service Association announces National School Breakfast Week from March 3-7. The theme is "Make Your Morning Count with School Breakfast." Ingersoll provides a daily breakfast program available to all students. The cost of a breakfast is 75 cents per student. Students who receive a reduced lunch will pay 35 cents. This amount covers the main breakfast entrée, milk, and juice or fruit. A student can substitute the main entrée for two slices of toast or for cereal and a slice of toast.

STATEWIDE TORNADO DRILL

Severe weather preparedness week is scheduled for March 2-8, 2003. The week is observed to highlight the importance of knowing what steps to take before, during and after severe weather strikes. Ingersoll will be participating in the annual statewide tornado drill schedule for 10 AM, Tuesday, March 4. In addition to this drill, Ingersoll also conducts three fire drills and two bus evacuation drills each year with its students.

APRIL 1 REFERENDUM

Informational pamphlets concerning the upcoming April 1 referendum are available in the Ingersoll office. The pamphlet also provides information for contacting your state legislators, encouraging them to create an equitable funding plan for all Illinois school districts.

Feel free to stop by the office to get one of these informative pamphlets. If anyone is interested in working to move the referendum forward, please contact Pete FranciskKovich, Chairman of the Referendum Committee, at 696-7746 (email-Pmf69@att.net).

PARENT COMMITTEE

Ingersoll has a parent advisory committee that meets once each quarter on a Thursday morning. The committee is open to any parent who wishes to attend. At the meetings, the committee discusses different topics regarding Ingersoll and hears presentations from teachers about a variety of curriculum-related items. The next meeting is scheduled for Thursday, May 1 at 7:30 AM. If you are interested in attending, please call the Ingersoll office to speak with Mrs. Strode so we may add your name to our mailing list.

Figure 12.1

February 2005
A message from Mr. Fulkerson . . .

Last October, many Lincoln parents attended the first Strategic Planning Forum at the high school commons. At the forum parents had an opportunity to participate in discussions detailing plusses and minuses of our school system and the course of direction our district will take in the next five years. Think of this as helping to guide a ship by adjusting the rudder where necessary. The next Strategic Planning Community Forum will be held on March 3rd, from 6:30–8:30 P.M. in the MJSHS Commons. Please mark this on your calendar if you were unable to attend the fall meeting.

Figure 12.2

Increasingly, parents are becoming more involved in the planning and implementation stages of school reform efforts. States involved in new accreditation procedures and reform efforts specify that parents must be represented on the Site Council that is established at all schools. These parents are to serve as a liaison to the community and are also to offer suggestions on what they see needs improving. In addition, all parents are part of the population that is surveyed to determine perceived strengths and weaknesses of a district. Parental input is vital in order for schools to have the support they need for critical issues such as tax initiatives, curriculum reform, redistricting, and consolidation. Empowered parents will make their voices heard; educators who listen make the partnership stronger.

The School Development Program developed by James Comer at the Yale Child Study Center is one excellent model for reform. Since its inception in 1968, the program has worked with more than 1,000 schools, most of which were low-income, high-minority schools. According to Comer (2005), "The framework is based on the theory that student academic performance, behavior, and preparation for school and life can be greatly improved when the adult stakeholders work together in a respectful, collaborative way . . ." (p. 39). In the model the traditional parent association is restructured as the Parent Team, with representatives on the School Planning and Management Team. The Parent Team organizes parent meetings about curriculum, school services, and so forth, and works with teachers to plan back-to-school, holiday, and other special events for families.

In order to get the results schools want, school leaders must work with decision-making groups to ensure that they understand what results are desired (Comer 2005). This understanding must come before decisions are made. In addition, decision makers should be able to articulate how the results will be recognized, documented, and evaluated. Setting some ground rules and expectations for decision-making groups can help alleviate misunderstandings and increase the effectiveness of their work. School personnel understand the chain of command. They know that, for example, even when site-based management exists, the superintendent and ultimately the school board is responsible for ensuring that the decisions made will have a positive outcome. Just as the district superintendent and the school board have a right to accept or reject recommendations from local schools and to overturn decisions made at a classroom or school level, so too the building principal has the right and the responsibility to review carefully each recommendation, accepting only those he or she feels are truly in the best interests of those concerned.

Many educators fear parent involvement in decision making because of experiences they have had with rude—and even hostile—parents who tried to force their opinions and ideas on the school. While parents like these do exist, there are also many thoughtful, cooperative parents who are interested in the well-being of all children in the system. The temptation is to offer committee appointment to only those parents who hold views similar to those held by school personnel. However, this approach often serves to further alienate and anger groups of parents who have different ideas. It is generally better to have those individuals with markedly dissimilar views on the inside working for solutions to problems, rather than to have them on the outside working against solutions. Also, we all know of individuals who are regarded as "difficult to get along with" and "hard to please." Sometimes this characterization is true; however, it is also true that sometimes these individuals are "detail" people. They refuse to "go along"—to offer their support of a solution—until they have exhausted every detail. Often tireless in their efforts and relentless in their role of "devil's advocate," these individuals tend to alienate themselves from the other committee members. Again, while it is very tempting *not* to invite these types of individuals to be members of committees, more harm usually comes when they are refused membership. When they are "on the inside," so to speak, they have a responsibility to support the decisions and recommendations that eventually come from the committee as a whole. This responsibility needs to be made clear to all members of the committee *before* the work is begun. Each member of the committee should have ample opportunity to share his or her own ideas, as well as any supporting evidence. Once this has taken place, the democratic process must proceed with majority opinion ruling. The recommendations that go forward from any committee would, of necessity, be the recommendation from the entire group. For an individual committee member, at this point, to continue to push his or her own convictions would be entirely inappropriate. Such an individual would risk disassociation from the decision-making group.

*I*NVOLVING PARENTS IN SCHOOLWIDE EVALUATION

As consumers of the education system, parents should be involved in evaluation efforts designed to provide constructive criticism for improving the school's programs. While many schools are required to share with parents results of various evaluation instruments and surveys, few districts routinely include parents in the evaluation and accountability process. Each year parents should have an opportunity to respond to surveys in which they are asked to rate the effectiveness of their child's educational experiences. The school as a whole, and specific services and programs provided by the school, should be included. For example, parents should be asked to evaluate specific aspects of the curriculum, as well as any special reading and math programs in which their child participated. Parents of children enrolled in the Western Illinois University, Infant and Preschool Center are asked to evaluate the program annually (see Figures 12.3 and 12.4).

Written surveys can either be sent home with the students or mailed. The survey may also appear in a special edition of the school newsletter. Another option is for the parent-teacher organization to conduct a telephone survey designed to determine parent satisfaction with the school. A combination of methods may be used in an attempt to gather input from as many

May 4, 2004

Dear Parents,

The Western Illinois University Infant and Preschool Center was established in Horrabin Hall with a dual purpose of providing a quality care program for the children of students, faculty, and staff of the University and the community, and for providing important practical experiences with your children for University students.

Evaluation of the center's program is important to see how well the center is meeting the needs of the children, their parents, and the University students. Your input is an important part of this process.

Attached is a form designed to allow you to give us feedback about the quality of services provided.

Please return the survey to the center by Friday, May 7, 2004. There will be a brown envelope by the sign-ins for completed surveys.

Thank you,

Ann Curtis, Director

Andrea Hanna, Assistant Director

Figure 12.3

parents as possible. After the results are compiled, a summary should be presented to parents via the school newsletter or a presentation at a meeting of the parent-teacher organization.

Summary

"Oakwood School . . . *your* public school" and other similar slogans have been adopted by numerous schools across the nation. The intent is to convey to parents and members of the community that the school belongs to them— that they have a responsibility to ensure its success. Yet schools must also realize that ownership and responsibility cannot exist without power. For these individuals to view public education as a shared responsibility, they must be empowered as contributors to decision-making processes. In this chapter we have described a number of strategies for involving parents in decision-making activities. As in any partnership arrangement, with empowerment comes responsibility. Educators, parents, and community members

Parent Evaluation of the WIU Infant and Preschool Center

____Infant/Toddler/Two-Year-Old Room   ____Preschool Room

Please circle the response that most accurately reflects your experiences.

1. My child's teacher knows and cares about my child and responds to her/his individual needs.

<u>Consistently</u>   <u>Sometimes</u>   <u>Rarely</u>   <u>No opinion</u>

2. I feel comfortable and at ease leaving my child here each day.

<u>Consistently</u>   <u>Sometimes</u>   <u>Rarely</u>   <u>No opinion</u>

3. My child's teacher respects me as a parent, supports us as a family, and addresses my concerns respectfully and promptly.

<u>Consistently</u>   <u>Sometimes</u>   <u>Rarely</u>   <u>No opinion</u>

4. I am comfortable with the style and forms of limit setting used by the staff.

<u>Consistently</u>   <u>Sometimes</u>   <u>Rarely</u>   <u>No opinion</u>

5. The communication systems, including newsletters and messages sent home and posted, keep me well informed about what is happening in the program each day and what I need to know to plan.

<u>Consistently</u>   <u>Sometimes</u>   <u>Rarely</u>   <u>No opinion</u>

6. My child's growth and development have been supported and stimulated by her/his participation in the program's daily routines, curriculum, and other experiences.

<u>Consistently</u>   <u>Sometimes</u>   <u>Rarely</u>   <u>No opinion</u>

7. Staff knows what they are doing and are enthusiastic about working here.

<u>Consistently</u>   <u>Sometimes</u>   <u>Rarely</u>   <u>No opinion</u>

8. Daily conversations and parent-teacher conferences sufficiently inform me of my child's progress.

<u>Consistently</u>   <u>Sometimes</u>   <u>Rarely</u>   <u>No opinion</u>

9. In reading the parent handbook, I found the center's policies to be clear and fair.

<u>Consistently</u>   <u>Sometimes</u>   <u>Rarely</u>   <u>No opinion</u>

10. Indoor and/or outdoor spaces are clean, appealing and meet the needs of the children.

<u>Consistently</u>   <u>Sometimes</u>   <u>Rarely</u>   <u>No opinion</u>

21. I have a variety of opportunities and choices about how to participate in the program.

<u>Consistently</u>   <u>Sometimes</u>   <u>Rarely</u>   <u>No opinion</u>

22. Family functions are worthwhile and help me feel more comfortable in the program.

<u>Consistently</u>   <u>Sometimes</u>   <u>Rarely</u>   <u>No opinion</u>

Please take a few minutes to respond to the following items.

1. Are there any ways in which the program and/or staff could better meet your needs?

2. Reflecting upon this past semester, are there any incidents that made you particularly happy or unhappy with the program which you would like us to know about?

3. Are there any other concerns, comments, or suggestions you wish to share at this time?

Thank you for providing us with the information we need to continue to provide high quality child care.

Figure 12.4

must work collaboratively to enrich the educational process by contributing wholeheartedly to efforts aimed at identifying what's working—and what's not—and to taking an active role in seeking solutions that will work for all children.

LOOKING AHEAD . . .

In the final chapter you will find ways to organize a comprehensive program for parent and community involvement. Assessing current efforts, and developing long-range plans with short-term action steps will be examined.

REFERENCES

Comer, J. P. (2005). The rewards of parent participation, *Educational Leadership, 62*(6), 38–42.

Epstein, J. L. 1990. School and family connections: Theory, research, and implications for integrating sociologies of education and family. In D. G. Unger, & M. B. Sussman (Eds.), *Families in Community Settings: Interdisciplinary Perspectives.* New York: Haworth Press.

Building a Comprehensive Plan for Family and Community Involvement

We can say we recognize that all parents are a significant force in their child's education and that we must tap the resources of both home and community. But just saying these things won't make a difference! We must believe them and commit ourselves to the development of a comprehensive plan for family and community involvement.

INTRODUCTION

This book has shared with you a philosophy built on a commitment to forging partnerships with homes and with communities. Research indicating the effects on student achievement and motivation as well as on parent and community support for schools has also been shared, as has a frank discussion of the many barriers to building partnerships with all families. Numerous practical strategies for developing strong partnerships, including the creation of effective school handbooks and newsletters, and strategies for parent conferencing, parent education, volunteerism, community involvement, and public relations, have also been described. In this chapter suggestions for putting all of these components together in an organized, structured fashion atypical of the "piecemeal" approaches that characterize many parent and community involvement efforts will be shared.

PLANNING FOR FAMILY AND COMMUNITY INVOLVEMENT

The key ingredient for overcoming barriers and building strong partnerships with every family is *commitment.* As stated in an earlier chapter, commitment for family and community involvement must be established at the highest administrative level for the greatest benefits to be derived. Simply stated, the district superintendent and the members of the school board need to understand and support schools' efforts for building strong partnerships with families and communities. At the school level a dedicated, knowledgeable principal needs to lead the way by working to build understanding and commitment among all school personnel. Finally, teachers and other school personnel must realize the benefits to be gained through parent and community involvement and must be steadfast in their beliefs that their efforts will make a difference.

The appointment of school-level committees charged with the task of developing comprehensive plans for family and community involvement sends a clear message about the district's commitment. Each school-level committee would be comprised of school personnel, parents, and members of the community who have agreed to provide the necessary leadership for planning the program. This group would assess current strengths and weaknesses in the areas of parent-community involvement, analyze needs and study options, then develop general goals, objectives, and strategies for achievement of these within a realistic time frame. Both long-range and yearly action plans would be constructed. After approval from the faculty-at-large, the members of the planning committee would assist in the implementation and ongoing evaluation of the plan.

Goals and objectives would be derived from surveys conducted with parents, community members, teachers, and students. Information about current efforts, strengths, and perceived needs in home-school communication, parent education, volunteerism, community involvement, and public relations would be gathered. Assessment activities would also include a determination of parents who are *not* currently involved and possible reasons why. In addition, assessing the school's climate—physical characteristics that promote or inhibit parent and community involvement—is recommended. In Figure13.1 is an instrument for use in this assessment process. This tool is comprised of a series of questions designed to help schools identify the strengths and needs of their current practices with respect to parent and community involvement. From these assessment data, a long-range plan to be implemented within the next three to five years could be developed along with short-range yearly action plans. Once these plans are designed, they should be reviewed, accepted, or revised for acceptance by the faculty as a whole.

One school identified as a goal making the physical environment more conducive to family and community involvement. Providing a "You Are Here"

Parental Involvement Survey

Program Component I: Philosophy	Yes	Yes, But Needs Improvement	No	Comments
1. Is there a district/school policy statement about building strong home-school partner-ships?				
2. Are there opportunities for teachers and other staff members to learn ways for promoting parental involvement?				
3. Do teachers and other staff members help parents learn ways they can support their children's learning, including literacy development?				

Program Component II: Outreach/Communication	Yes	Yes, But Needs Improvement	No	Comments
1. Do all families feel welcome in the school environment?				
2. Are special efforts made to reach families from other cultures (e.g., translator, home visits, written materials translated into home language)?				
3. Do teachers make special arrangements to meet with parents whose work schedules prevent their attendance at meetings/conferences held at regularly-scheduled times?				

Figure 13.1

Program Component II: Outreach/Communication	Yes	Yes, But Needs Improvement	No	Comments
4. Is there a school newsletter that could include information for parents about supporting reading and writing development?				
5. Does the school send home a calendar listing dates of parent-teacher conferences, report cards, holidays, and special events?				
6. Do individual classroom teachers send home newsletters containing classroom and curricular information, parent education tips, and ways parents can be involved?				
7. Is an effort made to schedule group conferences when there is more than one teacher?				
8. Is an effort made to provide parents with information about academic subjects and expectations and ways they can support their children's development in these areas?				
9. Is the school persistent in its efforts to communicate with all families, including those "hard-to-reach" families?				

Figure 13.1 (cont.)

Program Component II: Outreach/Communication	Yes	Yes, But Needs Improvement	No	Comments
10. Does the school have a newsletter that is distributed regularly to parents and key members of the community?				
11. Does the school maintain an up-to-date Website with information about its curriculum and programs and do all parents and community members know about the Website?				
12. Are teachers and administrators respectful of diverse family cultures, configurations, and ways of life?				
13. Are there any provisions for home visits, meetings/conferences held outside of the school?				
Program Component III: Parent Education	**Yes**	**Yes, But Needs Improvement**	**No**	**Comments**
1. Does the district/ school have a parent resource library with print and audio-visual materials on a variety of topics of interest to parents (e.g., child/adolescent development, special needs, supporting literacy and math development)?				

Figure 13.1 (cont.)

Program Component III: Parent Education	Yes	Yes, But Needs Improvement	No	Comments
2. Are teachers actively involved in developing ideas for home learning and are these ideas shared with parents through a variety of means (e.g., Website, meetings, workshops, newsletters, and so on)?				
3. Are parents given ample opportunity to suggest topics for workshops, and to request information and resources needed?				

Program Component IV: Collaboration	Yes	Yes, But Needs Improvement	No	Comments
1. Does the school have an "Open Door" policy where parents are welcome any time during the school day?				
2. Does the school project a positive image to visitors and phone callers?				
3. Does the school maintain an up-to-date Website with information about its curriculum and programs and opportunities for involvement from parents and community members?				
4. Does the school permit parents to observe in the classrooms?				

Figure 13.1 (cont.)

Program Component IV: Collaboration	Yes	Yes, But Needs Improvement	No	Comments
5. Does the school gain parental input when developing a new policy/program that affects students and families?				
6. Are parents utilized as resources for the school and its curriculum and programs?				
5. Do teachers' actively encourage parental participation in their child's learning?				
6. Are parents who wish to serve as in-school volunteers utilized effectively and appreciated openly?				
7. Are community members involved as volunteers, advisory board members and resources for the school?				
8. Are community agencies and organizations informed of school curriculum and programs and involved in supporting the schools' academic efforts?				
9. Does the school have a viable public relations plan and use the media appropriately to garner public support for the school and its curriculum and programs?				

Figure 13.1 (cont.)

directory just inside the building, signs directing parents and community members to doors they should enter, the availability of at least one extra adult-sized chair in each classroom, answering phone calls within three rings and in a pleasant and accommodating manner, and greeting visitors immediately in a warm and friendly way were among the specific action steps to be accomplished.

Goals and objectives relating to home-school communication might include revising the parent handbook, developing school or classroom newsletters, and/or implementing new procedures for parent conferencing. Specific action steps and a timeline for accomplishing each would also be designed. For example, the overall goal related to home-school communication might be "to maintain regular contact with each child's family," with one specific objective being "to disseminate a school newsletter." Action steps for achieving this objective might include the purchase of a computer software program for creating newsletters, design of a masthead for the newsletter, translating the newsletter into the major languages spoken at home, methods for delivering the newsletter to various locations within the community, and plans for evaluating the effectiveness of the newsletter.

An action plan for achieving the goal "providing opportunities for parents to learn strategies for being more effective teachers of their children" might include the establishment of a parent resource library with books, brochures, booklets, and videotapes. Offering a series of parent workshops and developing home-learning activities are other activities that could be included.

With respect to volunteerism, the goal might be "establish an ongoing procedure for recruiting, training, and using volunteers." Several objectives, such as "appoint a volunteer liaison from the faculty and secure the services of a community member to serve as the coordinator of volunteers," "survey school and classroom needs," "survey interests and willingness of potential volunteers," and "recruit and train volunteers" could be established to aid in the systematic achievement of this goal. Steps leading to the accomplishment of each objective would be developed. For the objective "recruit and train volunteers," steps such as "write job descriptions for volunteers," "contact representatives of various social, civic, professional, and religious organizations," and "develop a volunteer handbook" may be among those included. Figure 13.2 is a sample plan for recruiting, training, and using volunteers. In addition to activities for achieving this objective, the plan lists the person responsible, date, and how each activity will be evaluated or documented.

Another major goal might be to "increase public awareness of the school and its programs." Objectives relating to this goal could involve frequent dissemination of information related to the school and its programs. "Appointing a school media contact person," "writing biweekly news releases," "dissemination of the school newsletter within the community," and "hosting Open Houses for various community organizations and groups" are samples of action steps designed to accomplish this objective.

Plan to Recruit, Train, and Use Volunteers

Activity	Person Responsible	Date	Evaluation Documentation
1. Community person serves as coordinator of volunteers	Principal	Sep. 2005	Coord. of volunteers named
2. School staff member serves as volunteer liaison.	Principal	Sep. 2005	Liaison named
3. Parents and community persons will be recruited to serve as volunteers.	Coord. of volunteers, liaison	Fall 2005	List of volunteers
a. Delegated recruitment. First Methodist Church takes responsibility for recruiting volunteers for the tutorial program.	Principal, church officials	Fall 2005	
b. Individual recruitment. Past volunteers are called to return, and personal appeals are made to interested individuals.	Liason, coord. of volunteers	Fall 2005	
c. Public recruitment. Letters are sent to parents and community persons.	Liaison, coord. of volunteers	Fall 1996	Copy of letter and mailing list on file.
4. Interview volunteers, decide placement.	Liaisons, coord. of volunteers	Ongoing	Successful volunteers program
5. Plan activities for volunteers.	Liaison, coord. of volunteers	Ongoing	Successful volunteers program

Figure 13.2

Plan to Recruit, Train, and Use Volunteers (con't)

Activity	Person Responsible	Date	Evaluation Documentation
6. Volunteers attend training sessions:	Liaison, coord. of volunteers	Fall 1996	Successful volunteers program
a. Orientation meetings: clerical classroom helpers minicourses			
b. Training sessions: tutors substitutes classroom aides	Liaison Principal, liaison, and teachers	Oct. 1996 Oct. 1996 Ongoing	Successful volunteers program
7. Implement volunteer work:	Coord. of volunteers	Ongoing	Accurate completion of requested successful classroom experiences
a. Clerical help			
b. Classroom aides	Coord. of volunteers, liaison, and teachers	Ongoing	
c. Tutorial program	Liaison, teachers	Ongoing	Improved classroom performance by the students
d. "Friends through Reading"	Resource director, liaison	Ongoing	Participation of community persons and students
e. Substitutes	Coord. of volunteers	Ongoing	Sub. availability Oct. 1996
f. Mini-course series	Coord. of volunteers, Principal	Ongoing	Participation by students and volunteers
8. Appreciation for volunteers:	Liaison, Principal	May 1997	Party held
a. Party for Liaison, tutors, and their students	Liaison	May 1997	
b. Party for other volunteers	Coord. of volunteers	May 1997	Certificate of Appreciation by PTA and school thank-you letters

Figure 13.2 (cont.)

Educators must develop plans to forge strong and lasting relationships with each child's family and with the community-at-large if the benefits inherent in a joint effort are to become a reality. Such plans need to reflect a broad perspective on family and community involvement and should encompass goals, objectives, action steps, and timelines for increasing home-school communication, helping parents become better teachers of their children, encouraging volunteer support of school programs and activities, and increasing public awareness of and involvement in the schools.

SUMMARY

Our schools are among the most central and important institutions in America; yet how often do we, as educators, find ourselves without the active support of not only the parents but also the members of our community? In order for our schools to be really successful, entire school staffs need to demonstrate an active commitment to a partnership philosophy. Research findings to date support a joint effort of parents, teachers, students, and the community to increase the effectiveness of the educational program. In addition, according to the results of the 35th Annual Phi Delta Kappan/Gallup Poll (Rose and Gallup 2003), agreement exists as to the importance of parents and communities: "In identifying factors that are either very important or somewhat important . . . 97 percent point to home-life and up-bringing, 97 percent to the amount of parent involvement, 95 percent to student interest or lack thereof, and 94 percent to community involvement" (p. 43).

At the end of each chapter, you were provided a brief set of questions designed to help you consider your own beliefs with respect to the main points included in that chapter. The answers you gave to those questions should serve as an indication of your philosophy about family and community involvement. Whether or not your school has demonstrated a past commitment to a home-school-community partnership, if you answered "yes" to a majority of the questions, your philosophy is supportive of the involvement of families and community. With the strategies presented in this book, educators who possess such a philosophy can begin to put their beliefs into action. By assessing the school's current efforts in home-school communication, parent education, volunteerism, and public relations, teachers, administrators, and other committed individuals can begin to identify areas deserving of attention. Recognizing that a comprehensive program for parent and community involvement cannot be built all at once, these individuals can lead in the development of a plan for systematically addressing each area of need.

The implementation of a comprehensive plan that incorporates goals and objectives for all major areas of parent and community involvement—communication, education, volunteerism, and public relations—*will* bring your system, your school, and your students much valuable support. Once your school has experienced the active support that is made possible through the creation of strong home-school-community partnerships, you will be forever committed to providing the ongoing support that is necessary for the successful continuation of any worthwhile relationship. After all, what relationship could be more important to our schools and to our students than a healthy, positive relationship with our families and our community?

EFERENCE

Rose, L. C., & Gallup, A. M. (2003). The 35th annual Phi Delta Kappa/Gallup poll of the public's attitudes toward the public schools. *Phi Delta Kappan, 85*(1): 41–56.

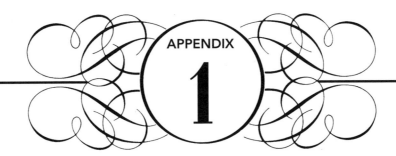

Standard I. Communicating
Communication between home and school is regular, two-way, and meaningful.

Communication is the foundation of a solid partnership. When parents and educators communicate effectively, positive relationships develop, problems are more easily solved, and students make greater progress.

Too often, school or program communication is *one-way* without the chance to exchange ideas and share perceptions. Effective home-school communication is the *two-way* sharing of information vital to student success. Even parent-teacher conferences can be one-way if the goal is merely reporting student progress. A strong parent-teacher partnership requires give-and-take conversation, goal setting for the future, and regular follow-up interactions.

Rating Scale: Check off how your school rates in each area.

Excellent: Activity occurs each year and is consistently implemented throughout the school year.
Good: Activity occurs sometimes during the school year, but is not consistently practiced.
Fair: Activity occurs rarely during the school year.
Poor: Activity does not occur at the school.

Assessment Questions Does the school:	Excellent	Good	Fair	Poor
1. Communicate with parents in a variety of ways (e.g., newsletter, e-mail, home visits, phone calls)?	☐	☐	☐	☐
2. Provide information to parents in a language and format they can understand?	☐	☐	☐	☐
3. Conduct conferences with parents that accommodate needs such as the varied schedules of parents, language translations, and child care?	☐	☐	☐	☐
4. Encourage parents and educators to share information such as student strengths and learning preferences during parent-teacher conferences?	☐	☐	☐	☐
5. Provide clear information regarding school policies and procedures?	☐	☐	☐	☐
6. Discuss student report cards with parents?	☐	☐	☐	☐
7. Disseminate information on topics such as school reforms, policies, discipline procedures, assessment tools, and school goals?	☐	☐	☐	☐
8. Encourage immediate contact between parents and teachers when concerns arise?	☐	☐	☐	☐
9. Distribute student work for parental review on a regular basis?	☐	☐	☐	☐
10. Communicate with parents regarding positive student behavior and achievement, not just regarding misbehavior or failure?	☐	☐	☐	☐
11. Promote informal activities at which parents, staff, the principal, and community members can interact?	☐	☐	☐	☐
12. Provide staff development regarding effective communication techniques and the importance of regular, two-way communication between the school and the family?	☐	☐	☐	☐
13. Use technology (e.g., telephone hotline, translation equipment, e-mail, website) to foster communication with parents?	☐	☐	☐	☐

Reprinted with permission from National PTA, National Standards for Parent/Family Involvement Programs: An Implementation Guide for School Communities (Bloomington, IN: National Educational Service, 2004), 12, 14, 16, 18, 20, 22.

Standard II. Parenting

Parenting skills are promoted and supported.

Parents are a child's life support system. Consequently, the most important support a child can receive comes from the home.

School personnel and program staff support positive parenting by respecting and affirming the strengths and skills needed by parents to fulfill their role. From making sure that students arrive at school rested, nourished, and ready to learn, to setting high learning expectations and nurturing self-esteem, parents sustain their children's learning.

When staff members recognize parent roles and responsibilities, ask what support parents need, and work to find ways to meet those needs, they communicate a clear message to parents: "We value you and need your input" in order to maintain a high-quality program.

Rating Scale: Check off how your school rates in each area.

Excellent: Activity occurs each year and is consistently implemented throughout the school year.
Good: Activity occurs sometimes during the school year, but is not consistently practiced.
Fair: Activity occurs rarely during the school year.
Poor: Activity does not occur at the school.

Assessment Questions Does the school:	Excellent	Good	Fair	Poor
1. Communicate the importance of positive relationships between parents and their children?	☐	☐	☐	☐
2. Link parents to family support services and resources in the community?	☐	☐	☐	☐
3. Share information on parenting issues with all families by including information on the school's website, hotline, and/or newsletter?	☐	☐	☐	☐
4. Establish school policies that recognize and respect families' cultural and religious diversity?	☐	☐	☐	☐
5. Provide an accessible parent/family information and resource center?	☐	☐	☐	☐
6. Work with PTAs, parent educators, or other community groups to host on-site meetings?	☐	☐	☐	☐

Standard III. Student Learning

Parents play an integral role in assisting student learning.

Student learning increases when parents are invited into the process by helping at home. Enlisting parents' involvement provides educators and administrators with a valuable support system—creating a team that is working for each child's success.

The vast majority of parents are willing to assist their students in learning, but many times are not sure what assistance is most helpful and appropriate. Helping parents connect to their children's learning enables parents to communicate in powerful ways that they value what their children achieve. Whether it's working together on a computer, displaying student work at home, or responding to a particular class assignment, parents' actions communicate to their children that education is important.

Rating Scale: Check off how your school rates in each area.

Excellent: Activity occurs each year and is consistently implemented throughout the school year.
Good: Activity occurs sometimes during the school year, but is not consistently practiced.
Fair: Activity occurs rarely during the school year.
Poor: Activity does not occur at the school.

Assessment Questions Does the school:	Excellent	Good	Fair	Poor
1. Provide clear information regarding the expectations for students in each subject at each grade level, as well as information regarding student placement, student services, and optional programs?	☐	☐	☐	☐
2. Regularly assign homework that requires students to discuss and interact with their parents about what they are learning?	☐	☐	☐	☐
3. Assist parents in understanding how students can improve skills, get help when needed, meet class expectations, and perform well on assessments?	☐	☐	☐	☐
4. Involve parents in setting student goals each school year?	☐	☐	☐	☐
5. Involve parents in planning for the transition to middle school, high school, or postsecondary education and careers? (Base your answer on the type of school you are: i.e., elementary, middle/junior high, or high school.)	☐	☐	☐	☐
6. Provide opportunities for staff members to learn about successful approaches to engaging parents in their child's learning?	☐	☐	☐	☐

Standard IV. Volunteering

Parents are welcome in the school, and their support and assistance are sought.

When parents volunteer, both families and schools reap benefits that come in few other ways. Literally millions of dollars of volunteer services are performed by parents and family members each year in the public schools. Studies have concluded that volunteers express greater confidence in the schools where they have opportunities to participate regularly. In addition, assisting in school or program events/activities communicates to a child, "I care about what you do here."

In order for parents to feel appreciated and welcome, volunteer work must be meaningful and valuable to them. Capitalizing on the expertise and skills of parents and family members provides much-needed support to educators and administrators already taxed in their attempts to meet academic goals and student needs.

Although there are many parents for whom volunteering during school hours is not possible, creative solutions like before- or after-school "drop-in" programs or "at-home" support activities provide opportunities for parents to offer their assistance as well.

Rating Scale: Check off how your school rates in each area.

Excellent: Activity occurs each year and is consistently implemented throughout the school year.
Good: Activity occurs sometimes during the school year, but is not consistently practiced.
Fair: Activity occurs rarely during the school year.
Poor: Activity does not occur at the school.

Assessment Questions Does the school:	Excellent	Good	Fair	Poor
1. Ensure that office staff greetings, signage near the entrances, and any other interactions with parents create a climate in which parents feel valued and welcome?	☐	☐	☐	☐
2. Survey parents regarding their interests, talents, and availability to volunteer?	☐	☐	☐	☐
3. Ensure that parents who are unable to volunteer in the school building are given options to help in other ways (e.g., at home or place of employment)?	☐	☐	☐	☐
4. Provide ample training on volunteer procedures and school protocol?	☐	☐	☐	☐
5. Develop a system for contacting parents to volunteer throughout the school year?	☐	☐	☐	☐
6. Show appreciation for parent participation and contributions?	☐	☐	☐	☐
7. Educate and assist teachers to effectively use volunteer resources?	☐	☐	☐	☐
8. Match volunteer activities to volunteer interests and abilities?	☐	☐	☐	☐
9. Track volunteer hours throughout the school year?	☐	☐	☐	☐
10. Include parent involvement activities on the school's report card? (The school's report card is a document on the school's performance, created and mailed by the school or district to all parents.)	☐	☐	☐	☐

Standard V. School Decision Making and Advocacy

Parents are full partners in the decisions that affect children and families.

Studies have shown that schools where parents are involved in decision making and advocacy have higher levels of student achievement and greater public support.

Effective partnerships develop when each partner is respected and empowered to fully participate in the decision-making process. Schools and programs that actively enlist parent participation and input communicate that parents are valued as full partners in the educating of their children.

Parents and educators depend on shared authority in decision-making systems to foster parental trust, public confidence, and mutual support of each other's efforts in helping students succeed. The involvement of parents, as individuals or as representative of others, is crucial in collaborative decision-making processes on issues ranging from curriculum and course selection to discipline policies and overall school reform measures.

Rating Scale: Check off how your school rates in each area.

Excellent: Activity occurs each year and is consistently implemented throughout the school year.
Good: Activity occurs sometimes during the school year, but is not consistently practiced.
Fair: Activity occurs rarely during the school year.
Poor: Activity does not occur at the school.

Assessment Questions Does the school:	Excellent	Good	Fair	Poor
1. Provide workshops for parents that teach them to influence decisions, raise issues or concerns, and resolve problems?	☐	☐	☐	☐
2. Encourage the formation of PTAs or other parent groups that respond to issues of interest to parents?	☐	☐	☐	☐
3. Include and give equal representation to parents on decision-making and advisory committees?	☐	☐	☐	☐
4. Provide parents with current information regarding school policies, practices, and both student and school performance data?	☐	☐	☐	☐
5. Encourage and facilitate active parent participation in the decisions that affect students (e.g., student placement, course selection, and individual education programs [IEPs])?	☐	☐	☐	☐
6. Treat parent concerns with respect and demonstrate genuine interest in developing solutions?	☐	☐	☐	☐
7. Promote parent participation on school district, state, and national committees that focus on education issues?	☐	☐	☐	☐
8. Provide training for staff and parents in how to be collaborative partners and share decision-making in areas such as policy, curriculum, budget, school reform, safety, and personnel issues?	☐	☐	☐	☐
9. Provide parents with an opportunity to participate in professional development activities (e.g., workshops or technology training)?	☐	☐	☐	☐

Standard VI. Collaborating with Community

Community resources are used to strengthen schools, families, and student learning.

As part of the larger community, schools and other programs fulfill important community goals. In like fashion, communities offer a wide array of resources valuable to schools and the families they serve.

When schools and communities work together, both are strengthened in synergistic ways and make gains that outpace what either entity could accomplish on its own:

- Families access community resources more easily;
- Businesses connect education programs with the realities of the workplace;
- Seniors contribute wisdom and gain a greater sense of purpose; and ultimately,
- Students serve and learn beyond their school involvement.

The best partnerships are mutually beneficial and structured to connect individuals, not just institutions or groups. This connection enables the power of community partnerships to be unleashed.

Rating Scale: Check off how your school rates in each area.

Excellent: Activity occurs each year and is consistently implemented throughout the school year.
Good: Activity occurs sometimes during the school year, but is not consistently practiced.
Fair: Activity occurs rarely during the school year.
Poor: Activity does not occur at the school.

Assessment Questions Does the school:	Excellent	Good	Fair	Poor
1. Distribute to staff and parents information on community resources that serve the cultural, recreational, academic, health, social, and other needs of families within the community?	☐	☐	☐	☐
2. Develop partnerships with local business, community organizations, and service groups to advance student learning and assist schools and families?	☐	☐	☐	☐
3. Foster student participation in community service?	☐	☐	☐	☐
4. Involve community members in school volunteer programs?	☐	☐	☐	☐
5. Disseminate information to school community members, including those without school-age children, regarding school programs and performance?	☐	☐	☐	☐
6. Collaborate with community agencies to provide family support services and adult learning opportunities, enabling parents to more fully participate in activities that support education?	☐	☐	☐	☐

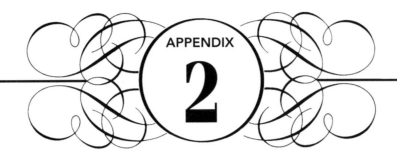

PROGRAM STANDARD 7—FAMILIES
Final Draft Accreditation Performance Criteria
Approved June 15, 2004 by Program Standards/Criteria Commission

Performance Category: **Families**

Program Standard: The program establishes and maintains collaborative relationships with each child's family to foster children's development in all settings. These relationships are sensitive to family composition, language, and culture.

Rationale: Young children's learning and development are integrally connected to their families. Consequently, to support and promote children's optimal learning and development, programs need to recognize the primacy of children's families; establish relationships with families based on mutual trust and respect; support and involve families in their children's educational growth; and invite families to fully participate in the program.

Please note: When a state rule/regulation prohibits the performance expectation outlined in the draft criterion, the state rule/regulation takes precedence. When a state rule/regulation exceeds the performance expectation outlined in the criterion, the state rule/regulation again takes precedence. When state rules or regulations differ in other ways, or mandate a lower threshold of performance, NAEYC's criteria take precedence.

NUMBER	STRAND	FINAL DRAFT CRITERIA
Knowing and Understanding the Program's Families		
7.1	U	As a part of orientation and ongoing staff development, new and existing program staff develop skills and knowledge to work effectively with diverse families.
7.2	U	Program staff use a variety of formal and informal strategies (including conversations) to become acquainted with and learn from families about their family structure; their preferred child-rearing practices; and their socioeconomic, linguistic, racial, religious, and cultural backgrounds.
7.3	U	Program staff actively use information about families to adapt the environment, curriculum, and teaching methods to the families they serve.
7.4	U	To better understand the cultural backgrounds of children, families, and the community, program staff (as a part of program activities or as individuals), participate in community cultural events, concerts, storytelling activities, or other events and performances geared to children and their families.
7.5	U	Program staff provide support and information to family members legally responsible for the care and well-being of a child.
7.6	U	Program staff establish intentional practices designed to foster strong reciprocal relationships with families from the

Draft of Standards 7 and 8 of NAEYC Accreditation Criteria (Families and Community Partnerships). Reprinted with permission.

NUMBER	STRAND	FINAL DRAFT CRITERIA
		first contact and maintain them over time.
7.7	U	Program staff ensure that all families, regardless of family structure; socioeconomic, racial, religious, and cultural backgrounds; gender; abilities; or preferred language are included in all aspects of the program, including volunteer opportunities. These opportunities consider family's interests and skills and the needs of program staff.
7.8	U	Program staff engage with families to learn from their knowledge of their child's interests, approaches to learning, and the child's developmental needs, and to learn about their concerns and goals for their children. This information is incorporated into ongoing classroom planning.
7.9	U	Program staff use a variety of formal and informal methods to communicate with families about the program philosophy and curriculum objectives. They implement a variety of methods, such as new family orientations, small group meetings, individual conversations, and written questionnaires, for getting input from families about curriculum activities throughout the year.
7.10	U	The program works with families on shared child care giving issues, including routine separations, special needs, the food being served and consumed, and daily care issues.
7.11	U	Families may visit any area of the facility at any time during the program's regular hours of operation as specified by the procedures of the facility.
7.12	U	The program facilitates opportunities for families to meet with each other on a formal and informal basis, work together on projects to support the program, and learn from and provide support for each other.
7.13	U	The program's governing or advisory groups include families as members and active participants. Family members are mentored into leadership roles by staff or other families in the program.
7.14	U	Program staff and families work together to plan events. Families' schedules and availability are considered as part of this planning.
Sharing Information Between Staff and Families		
7.15	U	Program staff use a variety of mechanisms, such as family conferences or home visits, to promote dialogue with families. The program staff asks adults to translate or interpret communications as needed.
7.16	P-K	Program staff communicate with families on at least a weekly basis regarding children's activities and

NUMBER	STRAND	FINAL DRAFT CRITERIA
		developmental milestones, shared caregiving issues, and other information that affects the well-being and development of their children. Where in-person communication is not possible, alternative communication practices are in place.
7.17	I-T	Program staff communicate with families on a daily basis regarding children's activities and developmental milestones, shared caregiving issues, and other information that affects the well-being and development of their children. Where in-person communication is not possible, alternative communication practices are in place.
7.18	U	The program compiles and provides information about the program to families in a language the family can understand. This information includes program policies and operating procedures.
7.19	U	Program staff inform families about its systems for formally and/or informally assessing children's progress. This includes the purposes of the assessment, the procedures used for assessment, procedures for gaining family input and information, the timing of assessments, the way assessment results or information will be shared with families, and ways the program will use the information.
7.20	U	When program staff suspect that a child has a developmental delay or other special need, this possibility is communicated to families in a sensitive, supportive, and confidential manner, with documentation and explanation for the concern, suggested next steps, and information about resources for assessment.
Nurturing Families as Advocates for Their Children		
7.21	U	Program staff encourage families to regularly contribute to decisions about their child's goals and plans for activities and services .
7.22	U	Program staff encourage families to raise concerns and work collaboratively with them to find mutually satisfying solutions that staff then incorporate into classroom practice.
7.23	U	Program staff encourage and support families to make the primary decisions about services that their children need, and they encourage families to advocate to obtain needed services.
7.24	U	Program staff use a variety of techniques to negotiate difficulties that arise in their interactions with family members. Program staff make arrangements to use these techniques in a language the family can understand.
7.25	U	Program staff provide families with information about programs and services from other organizations. Staff

NUMBER	STRAND	FINAL DRAFT CRITERIA
		support and encourage families' efforts to negotiate health, mental health, assessment, and educational services for their children.
7.26	U	Program staff use established linkages with other early education programs and local elementary schools to help families prepare for and manage their children's transitions between programs, including special education programs. Staff provide information to families that can assist them in communicating with other programs.
7.27	U	To help families with their transitions to other programs or schools, staff provide basic general information on enrollment procedures and practices, visiting opportunities, and/or program options.
7.28	U	Prior to sharing information with other relevant providers, agencies, or other programs, staff obtain written consent from the family.

PROGRAM STANDARD 8—COMMUNITY PARTNERSHIPS
Final Draft Accreditation Performance Criteria Program Standard
Approved June 15, 2004 by Program Standards/Criteria Commission

Performance Category: **Community Partnerships**

The program establishes relationships with and uses the resources of the children's communities to support the achievement of program goals.

Rationale: As part of the fabric of children's communities, an effective program establishes and maintains reciprocal relationships with agencies and institutions that can support it in achieving its goals for curriculum, health promotion, children's transitions, inclusion, and diversity. By helping to connect families with needed resources, the program furthers children's healthy development and learning.

Please note: When a state rule/regulation prohibits the performance expectation outlined in the draft criterion, the state rule/regulation takes precedence. When a state rule/regulation exceeds the performance expectation outlined in the criterion, the state rule/regulation again takes precedence. When state rules or regulations differ in other ways, or mandate a lower threshold of performance, NAEYC's criteria take precedence.

NUMBER	STRAND	FINAL DRAFT CRITERIA
Linking With the Community		
8.1	U	Program staff maintain a current list of child and family support services available in the co needs they observe among families and based on what families request (e.g., health, mer welfare, parenting programs, early intervention/special education screening and assessme housing and child care subsidies). They share the list with families and assist them in locat resources that support children's and families' well-being and development.
8.2	U	Program staff develop partnerships and professional relationships with agencies, consulta community that further the program's capacity to meet the needs and interests of the chilc
8.3	U	Program staff are familiar with family support services and specialized consultants who ai linguistically appropriate services. They use this knowledge to suggest and guide families
8.4	U	Program staff encourage continuity of services for children by communicating with other a mutually desired outcomes for children and guide collaborative work.
8.5	U	Program staff identify and establish relationships with specialized consultants who can as: participation in the program. This includes support for children with disabilities, behavioral
8.6	U	Program staff advocate for the program and its families by creating awareness of the pro councils, service agencies, and local governmental entities.
8.7	U	Program staff include information gathered from stakeholders in planning for continuous ir involvement in the program, and broadening community support for the program.
Accessing Community Resources		
8.8	U	Program staff use their knowledge of the community and the families it serves as an integ learning experiences.
8.9	U	Program staff connect with and use their community's urban, suburban, rural, and/or triba
8.10	U	Program staff inform families about community events sponsored by local organizations, : storytelling, and theater geared to children.
8.11	U	Program staff invite members of the performing and visual arts community, such as music exhibits, local artists, and community residents, to share their interests and talents with the
8.12	U	The program engages with other community organizations and groups to cosponsor or pa experience of children and families in the program.
Acting as a Citizen in the Neighborhood and the Early Childhood Community		
8.13	U	Program staff are encouraged to participate in local, state, or national early childhood edu attending meetings and conferences. Program staff are also encouraged to participate re public-awareness activities related to early care and education.
8.14	U	The program encourages staff to participate in joint and collaborative training activities or programs and other community service agencies.
8.15	U	The program encourages staff and families to work together to support and participate in projects.

NUMBER	STRAND	FINAL DRAFT CRITERIA
8.16	U	Program leadership builds mutual relationships and communicates regularly with close ne program, seeking out their perspectives, involving them in the program as appropriate, an neighborhood interests and needs.
8.17	U	Program staff are encouraged and given the opportunity to participate in community or sta integration efforts.
8.18	U	Program leadership is knowledgeable about how policy changes at local, state, tribal, or r resources available for children and their families.

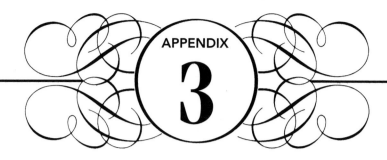

Welcome to Third Grade!

I am looking forward to learning with your child this year. My name is Lynn Traser and this is my 16th year of teaching. I consider myself a patient teacher, and yet have high expectations for all my students. I also insist on a safe learning environment and have a fairly strict discipline plan. Working together, I'm sure this can be a wonderful school year.

Discipline Plan

In an effort to help children learn to make good, responsible choices, and because learning is enhanced in a supportive, orderly, and non-threatening environment, Lincoln School uses a nationally recognized social skills training program called Stop and Think. The plan below is posted in the classroom and outlines my classroom rules and consequences for inappropriate behavior:

Classroom Rules

1. Listen when others are talking.
2. Follow directions.
3. Keep hands, feet, and objects to yourself.
4. Work quietly and do not disturb others.
5. Show respect for school and personal property.
6. Work and play in a safe manner.

A behavior chart with "lights" for each student (and the teacher) is also posted in the classroom, and everyone begins each day on green light. The consequences for inappropriate behavior follow:

Consequences

1. Your green light will be changed to yellow. (This is a warning.)
2. Your yellow light will be changed to blue and you will serve a five- to ten-minute time-out.
3. Your blue light will be changed to red, you will serve at least a 15 minute time-out, and your parents will be notified. The principal may also be involved.

A severe or repeated disruption will be handled on an individual basis.

To encourage students to make good choices I will recognize appropriate behavior with praise, classroom rewards (such as eating lunch together in our classroom while watching a movie), positive notes and phone calls home, and marking "bonus stars" on behavior "lights." When students have accumulated five bonus stars on their green light, they may choose to buy something from my goodie box, which usually contains books, toys, school supplies, and candy.

Snacks and Lunch

There will be a morning snack time every day, but I will not be assigning days on a snack calendar. If your child would like to have a snack, please send something just for your own child. You may send anything you want your child to have.

Your child is welcome to have water at his/her desk throughout the entire school year and not just when it is hot, but please do not send pop or juice. Please make sure the container you send is covered so tragedies due to spills are avoided.

If you need to send lunch money, please put it in an envelope marked with your child's name, 3T (for Traser), and "Lunch Money." The third grade lunch period begins with recess at 11:50 and ends at 12:35.

Adopt-a-Classroom

This wonderful program invites the business world into our classroom and helps students think about careers and see the need for education. Our classroom has been adopted by Macomb Pet Land, and throughout the year different animals will be brought to our classroom. Students may sometimes choose to handle the animals but will never be required to, and will always be supervised.

Take Home Folder

One of the folders you purchased for your child will be used as a "Take Home Folder." It will go back and forth between school and home and be used to send notes, lunch money, homework, and graded work. One pocket is labeled "Leave at Home" and the other "Bring Back to School." Your child will turn this folder in every morning and I will check the "Bring Back to School" pocket. Thank you for checking this folder every evening.

Supplies

It is very important that your child have the tools he/she needs to do a good job. Students feel proud when they can do their best, and having the necessary materials makes that possible. I will send a note home when your child needs additional supplies such as pencils, crayons, or scissors. Thank you very much for providing these supplies for your child.

Things NOT to Bring to School

Please do not let your child bring toys, videos, hand held games, CD players or CDs, stuffed animals, or trading cards of any kind to school. We do not have sharing in 3rd grade, and many problems arise when these items come to school. I will send a note if we are having a special day and something may be brought from home.

Homework

I try to provide enough time for assignments to be completed in school, however, if a student is not able to complete his/her work, they are expected to take the work home, finish it, and bring it back the next day. I will stamp papers that need to be completed at home with a "Homework" stamp.

When your child is absent you can help make sure they don't fall behind by leaving a message requesting their homework, and picking it up from the homework table by the office. Research has shown that attendance has a critical role in academic success. In a study comparing the kindergarten through third grade attendance records for the graduates of three high schools, the results were as follows:

The top 25 graduates averaged 6 absences per year.
The middle 25 graduates averaged 7 absences per year.
The bottom 25 graduates averaged 11 absences per year.
The 25 high school dropouts averaged 13 absences per year.

Grades

The district grading scale is as follows:

92–100% = A (Superior)
82–91%　 = B (Above Average)
72–81%　 = C (Average)
62–71%　 = D (Below Average)
　0–61%　 = F (Failing)

An assignment that receives a D or an F may be corrected and returned in the Take Home Folder the following day. These below average or failing papers will have a stamp on them that says, "Please Correct and Return." Test grades cannot be changed.

Any paper that has a percentage and/or letter grade on it will count toward the student's quarterly grade. If a paper does not have a percentage or letter grade (it may just have a star or some other mark), it will not count toward the student's quarterly grade. A copy of the Mid Quarter Report follows. To help you stay informed about your child's progress, this report will be sent home before each report card, about halfway through each quarter.

SUBJECTS GRADED WITH LETTER GRADES

Reading/Phonics

Your child will be having a wonderful reading experience this year. He/she will read many types of literature from both the third grade reading book and books from our classroom library. Children will receive reading instruction from both a reading specialist and me, and will work in large groups, small groups, with partners, and independently. I will model how to use specific comprehension strategies by reading aloud every day. It is my hope that if your child doesn't already *love* reading, he/she will by the end of third grade.

A major adjustment in third grade is that your child will transition from learning to read, to reading to learn. Recent research confirms what parents and teachers have known all along: the amount of time spent in out-of-school reading makes a tremendous difference on achievement. The **entire year's** *out-of-school* reading for the average child who tested at the 10th percentile (or bottom of the class) amounts to just **two days** reading for the average child at the 90th percentile! You want your child to succeed and so do I. The importance of home reading cannot be overstated.

Your support at home really does matter!

Language Arts/Writing

We will work on many skills this year including: capitalization, punctuation, using prefixes and suffixes, and word usage. Third grade is one of the targeted grades for the Illinois Standards Achievement Test (ISAT), which is given in April. Writing takes on major importance in third grade, so we will be doing a lot of writing including: expository essays, essays in math related to problem solving, and summaries of what we've read in different content areas.

Mathematics

We have a new math series this year, blending traditional and investigative styles. We will work on mastering the math facts in addition, subtraction, multiplication and division, as well as place value, geometry, fractions, algebra, money, time intervals, measurement, and problem solving.

Spelling

As we read selections from our reading book we will work on spelling words that are somewhat related to the stories. A pink paper listing the 15 basic spelling words and the challenge words will be sent home on the first day of each week. Students will be tested over the 15 basic words and may choose to study and take a test over the challenge words. They will earn a bonus star for each challenge word they spell correctly on the final test, but spelling the challenge words correctly or incorrectly will not affect their grade.

A pretest will be given on Mondays and students who spell all 15 basic words correctly (or misspell only one word) will be put on "Spelling Contract." This means that since they have already mastered the spelling words for that week they will be allowed to work on something else while the rest of the class works on spelling. Children on Spelling Contract do not take the final test given on Friday (or the last day of each week), but may choose (like any other student) to try to spell the challenge words for bonus stars.

SUBJECTS GRADED BY PARTICIPATION (EXCELLENT, SATISFACTORY, UNSATISFACTORY)

Science/Social Studies

Our science curriculum includes habitats, plants, and sound. Our social studies curriculum includes social skills training, history, geography, and government. There are other optional units that we will investigate if time permits. A variety of sources will be used in teaching these units including: textbooks, worksheets, guest speakers, field trips, and videos.

Penmanship

We will review the cursive letters taught in 2nd grade by copying from examples, then gradually move to writing cursive independently. Third grade students will be expected to complete most written assignments in cursive by the beginning of the 2nd semester (in January).

Special Classes

Our class will have P.E. on Mondays, Wednesdays, and Fridays, Music on Tuesdays and Thursdays, and Art on Tuesdays. We will check out books from the library every Wednesday at 9:45.

Parking

Parking is difficult at Lincoln School. No cars will be allowed to park in front of the school before 8:00 or after 2:00 so that the buses can load and unload students safely. Parent pickup is from the parking lot south of the building.

Safety and Security

We are dedicated to providing a safe environment for your child. Each staff member wears identification tags, and visitors are required to stop at the office to acquire a visitor tag. This allows us to monitor who is in the building at all times. We have emergency plans in place for fire, tornado, earthquake, bomb threats, and lock down situations.

Questions

I hope you found the information in this packet helpful. You may want to refer to this packet throughout the year, so please keep it in a safe place.

If you have any questions about what is happening in the classroom, or if you need to contact me for any reason, please feel free to do so. You may send a note or call the school office at 833-2095 and I will contact you as soon as possible.

This is going to be a wonderful school year, and I look forward to learning with your child and working with you.

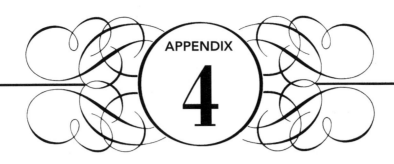

Internet Resources for Parent Involvement and Education

AARP
Grandparent Information Center
601 E Street NW
Washington DC 20049
Voice: 800-424-3410
Fax: 202-434-6470
Contact: Margaret Hollidge, Sr. Program Coordinator
www.aarp.org/grandparents/

Active Parenting Publishers
1955 Vaughnn Rd. NW, Suite 108
Kennesaw, GA 30144-7808
(800) 825-0060 or (800) 235-7755 or (770) 429-0565
Fax: (770) 429-0334
E-mail: cservice@activeparenting.com
www.activeparenting.com

AGS (American Guidance Service)
4201 Woodland Road, P.O. Box 99
Circle Pines, MN 55014-1796
(800) 328-2560 or (651) 287-7220
Fax: (800) 471-8457 or (651) 287-7223
www.agsnet.com
Area work texts geared to helping students with diverse
learning styles and needs.

Avance, Inc.
301 S. Frio Street, Suite 380
San Antonia, TX 78207
(210) 270-4630
Fax: (210) 270-4612
Contact: Gloria G. Rodriguez, Ph.D., President and C.E.O
E-mail: grodriguez_nat@advance.org
www.avance.org

American Library Association (ALA)
www.ala.org/parentspage/
ALA includes websites for children and parents, tips
for parents, and helpful resources.

Appalachia Educational Laboratory (AEL)
1031 Quarrier Street
P.O. Box 1348
Charleston, WV 25325-1348
(304) 347-0400 or (800) 624-9120
Contact: Jane E. Hange, Senior Manager
E-mail: hangej@ael.org
www.ael.org/eric

Becky Bailey, Ph.D.
Loving Guidance & Conscious Discipline
P.O. Box 622407
Oviedo, FL 32762
(800) 842-2846 or (407) 366-0233
Fax: (407) 366-0233
www.beckybailey.com

**Center on School, Family and Community
Partnerships**
Johns Hopkins University
3505 North Charles Street
Baltimore MD 21218
Voice: 410-516-8807
Fax: 410-516-8890
Contact: Joyce Epstein
www.scov.csos.jhu.edu/p2000/center.htm

Center for Successful Fathering, Inc.
13740 Research Blvd., Suite G-4
Austin, TX 78750
(512) 335-8106
Fax: (512) 258-2591
Contact: Dr. Ron Klinger, Director
www.fathering.org

The Center for Nonviolent Communication
2428 Foothill Boulevard, Suite E
La Crescenta, CA 91214 USA
(818) 957-9393
Fax: (818) 957-1424
Contact: Gary Baran, Executive Director
www.cnvc.org/parents.htm

Child Management, Inc.
Children's Hospital of Eastern Ontario
401 Smyth Road
Ottowa, Ontario
K1H 8L1
(613) 737-7600
E-mail: webmaster@cheo.on.ca
www.cheo.on.ca/english/parent.html

Coalition of Community Foundations for Youth
P.O. Box 489
Excelsior Springs, MO 64024-0489
(800) 292-6149
E-mail: ccfy@ccfy.org
Contact: Cindy Ballard, Executive Director
Or Deanna Ouseley, Director of Operations
www.ccfy.org

Committee for Children
568 First Avenue South, Suite 600
Seattle, WA 98104-2804
(800) 634-4449 ext. 6223 or (206) 343-1223
    ext. 6223
Fax: (206) 438-6765
www.cfchildren.org

Communities in Schools (CIS)
277 S. Washington Street, Suite 210
Alexandria, VA 22314
(703) 519-8999 or (800) CIS-4KIDS
Fax: (703) 519-7213
Contact: Neil Shorthouse
E-mail: nshorthouse@cisnet.org
or Linda Harril
E-mail: lhcisnc@aol.com
www.cisnet.org

Compassion Books, Inc.
7036 State Hwy 80 South
Burnsville, NC 28714
(800) 970-4220 or (828) 675-5909
Fax: (800) 970-3350 or (828) 675-9687
E-mail: Heal2grow@aol.com
www.compassionbooks.com

Cultural Diversity and Early Education
National Research Council
Washington, D.C.
www.nap.edu/readingroom/books/earlyed/

Educating Homeless Children
Homeless Education & Neglected/Delinquent
    Programs
Arizona Department of Education
1535 West Jefferson Street, Bin #24
Phoenix, Arizona 85007
(602) 542-4391
Fax: (602) 542-3050
http://coe.west.asu.edu/homeless/index.htm

Family Development Resources, Inc.
1435 Yarmouth Avenue, Suite 102
Boulder Colorado, 80304
(800) 326-2082 or (303) 447-2082
Fax: (303) 449-8788
www.injoyvideos.com

Family Involvement in Children's Education:
    Successful Local Approaches
www.ed.gov/pubs/FamInvolve

Family Literacy Resource Notebook
The Ohio Literacy Resource Center Research I
1100 Summit Street, P.O. Box 5190
Kent State University
Kent, OH 44242-0001
(800) 765-2897
http://literacy.kent.edu/Oasis/famlinotebook/index.html

Family Support America
20 N. Wacker Drive, Suite 1100
Chicago, IL 60606
(312) 338-1522
Contact: Virginia Mason, Executive Director
www.familysupportamerica.org/content/home.htm

Harvard Family Research Project and the Family Involvement Network of Educators
Harvard Graduate School of Education
3 Garden Street
Cambridge, MA 02138
(617) 495-9108
Fax: (617) 495-8594
E-mail: hfrp@gse.harvard.edu
Contact: Stacey Miller, Publications/Communication Manager (617) 495-9108
E-mail: stacey_miller@harvard.edu
www.gse.harvard.edu/hfrp/projects/fine.html

Institute for Urban and Minority Education (IUME)
Box 75
Teachers College, Columbia University
New York, NY 10027-6696
(212) 678-3780
Fax: (212) 678-4137
E-mail: ef29@columbia.edu
http://iume.tc.columbia.edu

Kids Can Learn
Family Learning Association
www.kidscanlearn.com

McREL Educator Resources
The Early Childhood Digest
www.mcrel.org/lesson-plans/

MiddleWeb: Exploring Middle School Reform
Resources for parents and communities working with young adolescents
E-mail: Norton@middleweb.com
www.middleweb.com/mw/resources/MWRpublic.html

National Association for the Education of Young Children (NAEYC)
1509 16th Street, NW
Washington, DC 20036-1426
(202) 232-8777 or (800) 424-1426
Contact: Pat Saphr, Information Services Director
E-mail: pubaff@naeyc.org
www.naeyc.org

National Association of Partners in Education (NAPE)
901 N. Pitt Street, Suite 320
Alexandria, VA 22314
(703) 836-4880
Fax: (703) 836-6941
E-mail: NAPEhq@NAPEhg.org
http://napehq.org

National Center for Children in Poverty
215 W 125th Street, 3rd Floor
New York, NY 10027
(646) 284-9600
Fax: (646) 284-9623
E-mail: info@nccp.org
www.nccp.org

National Center for Fathering
P.O. Box 413888
Kansas City, MO 64141
(800) 593-DADS
Fax: (913) 384-4665
Contact: Ken Canfield, President
www.fathers.com

National Center on Fathers and Families
University of Pennsylvania
3700 Walnut Street, Box 58
Philadelphia, PA 19104-6216
(215) 573-5500
E-mail: mailbox@ncoff.gse.upenn.edu
Contact: Vivian Gadsden, Director

National Center for Strategic Nonprofit Planning and Community Leadership
2000 L Street, N.W., Suite 815
Washington, DC 20036
(888) 528-NPCL
Fax: (202) 822-5699
E-mail: info@npcl.org
Contact: Jeffrey Johnson, President and CEO
www.ncpl.org

National Clearinghouse on Families & Youth
(301) 496-5133
Contacts: Dr. Duane Alexander, Director
www.nichd.nih.gov

National Coalition for Parent Involvement in Education
3929 Old Lee Highway, Suite 91-A
Fairfax, VA 22030-2401
(703) 359-8973
Fax: (703) 359-0972
Contact: Sue Ferguson, Chair
E-mail: ferguson@ncea.com
www.ncpie.org

National Education Association
www.nea.org

National Fatherhood Initiative
101 Lake Forest Boulevard, Suite 360
Gaithersburg, MD 20877
(301) 948-0599
Fax: (301) 948-4325
E-mail: nfil995@aol.com
Contact: Wade Horn, President
www.fatherhood.org

The National Institute of Literacy
1775 I Street, NW, Suite 730
Washington, DC 20006-2401
(202) 233-2025
Fax: (202) 233-2050
www.nifl.gov

National Latino Fatherhood and Family Institute
5233 East Beverly Boulevard
Los Angeles, CA 90022
(323) 728-7770
Fax: (323) 728-8666
Contact: Jerry Tello, Director
www.nlffi.org

National Network of Partnership Schools (NNPS)
John Hopkins University
3003 N. Charles Street, Suite 200
Baltimore, MD 21218
(410) 516-8800
Fax: (410) 516-8890
Contact: Beth S Simon, Dissemination Director
E-mail: nnps@csos.jhu.edu
www.csos.jhu.edu/p2000

National Parenting Association
444 Park Ave so., Suite 602
New York, NY 10016
(212) 362-7575
Fax: (212) 679-3127
Contact: Ruth A Wooden, President
www.parentsunite.org/CFparentsunite/index2.cfm

National Parent Information Network
ERIC (Educational Resources Information Center)
http://npin.org/

National Parent Teacher Association (PTA)
330 N. Wabash Street, Suite 2100
Chicago, IL 60611-3630
(312) 670-6782 or (800) 307-4PTA (4782)
Fax: (312) 670-6783
Contact: Patricia Yoxall, Public Relations Director
www.pta.org

Northwest Regional Laboratory School-Family-Community Partnership Team
101 SW Main Street, Suite 500
Portland, OR 97204
(503) 275-9487
Fax: (503) 275-9152
E-mail: partnerships@nwrel.org
Contact: Steffen Saifer, Team Lead
E-mail: saifers@nwrel.org
www.nwrel.org/index.html

Oregon Department of Education
255 Capitol Street NE
Salem, OR 97310-0203
(503) 378-3569
www.ode.state.or.us/

Parent and Family Resources on the Web, 1999
www.lacnyc.org/welcome.htm

Parents as Teachers National Center
10176 Corporate Square Drive, Suite 230
St. Louis, MO 63132
(314) 432-4330
Fax: (314) 432-8963
E-mail: patnc@patnc.org
www.patnc.org

Parent Involvement: Literature Review and Database of Promising Practices
www.ncrel.org/sdrs/pidata/pi0over.htm

Project Success
North Central Regional Educational Laboratory
1120 E. Diehl Road, Suite 200
Naperville, IL 60563-1486
(630) 649-6500
Fax: (630) 649-6706
Contact: Greg Hall
E-mail: ghall@ncrel.org
www.ncrel.org/projectsucess/

Reach Out and Read
Boston Medical Center
One Boston Medical Center Place
South Block High Rise, 5th Floor
Boston, MA 02118
(617) 414-5701
Contact: Matt Veno, Executive Director
www.reachoutandread.org

Read Across America
www.nea.org/readacross/

Redleaf Press
10 Yorkton Court
St. Paul, MN 55117-1065
(800) 423-8309
Fax: (800) 641-0115
www.redleafpress.org

Resource Center for Fathers and Families
Human Services Bldg, Suite 305
1201 89th Ave. NE
Blaine, MN 55434
(763) 783-4938
Fax: (763) 783-4900
Contact: Arnie Engelby, Director
www.resourcesforfathers.org

Robert R. McCormick Tribune Foundation
435 N. Michigan, Suite 770
Chicago, IL 60611
(312) 222-3512
Fax: (312) 222-3523
E-mail: rrmtf@tribune.com
www.rrmtf.org

Scholastic Inc., Early Childhood Division
557 Broadway
New York, NY 10003
(800) 724-6527
*www.scholastic.com/products/product_info/early_
    childhood.htm*

School Development Program (SDP)
Comer School Development Program
55 College Street
New Haven, CT 06510
(203) 737-1020
Fax: (203) 737-1023
http://info.med.yale.edu/comer.

Stop and Think
49 Woodberry Road
Little Rock, AR 72212
(501) 312-1484
Fax: (501) 312-1493
Contact: Howard M Knoff, Director
E-mail: knoffprojectachieve@earthlink.net
www.stopandthinksocialskills.com

U.S. Department of Education
400 Maryland Avenue, SW
Washington, DC 20202
(800) 872-5327
Fax: (202) 401-0689
www.ed.gov/index.jhtml

Wisconsin Department of Public Instruction
P.O. Box 7841
Madison, WI 53101-7841
(608) 266-9356
Contact: Jane Grinde
www.dpi.state.wi.us/dpi/dlcl/bbfcsp/fcsphome.html

**Zero to Three: National Center for Infants,
    Toddlers and Families**
Matthew E. Melmed, Executive Director
734 15th Street, NW, Suite 1000
Washington, DC 20005
(202) 638-1144
Fax: (202) 638-0851
Contact: Matthew E. Melmed, Executive Director
www.zerotothree.org

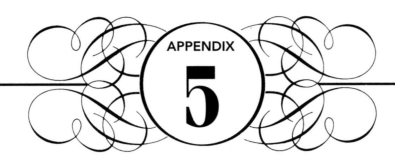

Suggested Books and Print Resources for a Parent Library

Child Development

Alexander, D. W. (1999). *Children Changed by Trauma: A Healing Guide.* Oakland, CA: New Harbinger Publications.

Berger, E. (1999). *Raising Children with Character: Parents, Trust, and the Development of Personal Integrity.* Northvale, NJ: Jason Aronson.

Clark, R. (2004). *The Essential 55 Workbook: Everything You Need to Help Your Child Succeed in School.* New York, NY: Hyperion.

Denham, S. (1998). *Emotional Development in Young Children.* New York, NY: The Guilford Press.

Galbraith, J., & Espeland, P. (Ed.). (2000). *You Know Your Child Is Gifted When . . . : A Beginner's Guide to Life on the Bright Side.* Minneapolis, MN: Free Spirit Publishing.

Gottman, J., & De Claire, J. (1997). *The Heart of Parenting: Raising an Emotionally Intelligent Child.* New York, NY: Simon & Schuster.

Greenspan, S. (2003). *The Secure Child: Helping Our Children Feel Safe and Confident in a Changing World.* New York, NY: Da Capo Press.

Laforge, A. (1999). *What Really Happens in School: A Guide to Your Child's Emotional, Social. . . .* New York, NY: Hyperion.

Mack, A. (1990). *Dry All Night: The Picture Book Technique That Stops Bedwetting.* New York, NY: Little, Brown.

Lamb, M. (2003). *The Role of the Father in Child Development.* Hoboken, NJ: Wiley.

McDevitt, T. M. (2002). *Child Development and Education.* Upper Saddle River, NJ: Merrill/Prentice Hall.

Murphy, A. (1998). *The Parents Answer Book: Everything You Need to Know About Your Child's Physical, Emotional, and Cognitive Development, Health, and Safety.* New York, NY: Golden Books Family Entertainment.

Pruitt, D. (1998). *Your Child: What Every Parent Needs to Know About Childhood Development from Birth to Preadolescence.* New York, NY: HarperCollins Publishers.

Rosemond, J. (1990). *Ending the Homework Hassle.* Kansas City, MO: Andrews McMeel Publishing.

Schaefer, C. E., & DiGeronimo, T. F. (2000). *Ages and Stages: A Parent's Guide to Normal Childhood Development.* Hoboken, NJ: Wiley.

Sclafani, J. D. (2004). *The Educated Parent: Recent Trends in Raising Children.* Westport, CN: Praeger Publishers.

Webb, J. T., & Meckstroth, E. A. (1989). *Guiding the Gifted Child: A Practical Source for Parents and Teachers.* Scottsdale, AZ: Great Potential Press.

Behavior/Discipline

Briesmeister, J. M., & Schaefer, C. E. (1997). *Handbook of Parent Training: Parents as Co-Therapists for Children's Behavior Problems*. Hoboken, NJ: Wiley.

Chidekel, D. (2002). *Parents in Charge: Setting Healthy, Loving Boundaries for You and Your Child*. New York, NY: Simon & Schuster.

Edwards, C. D. (1999). *How to Handle a Hard-to-Handle Kid: A Parents' Guide to Understanding and Changing Problem Behaviors*. Minneapolis, MN: Free Spirit Pub.

Forehand, R., & Long, N. (2002). *Parenting the Strong-Willed Child, Revised and Updated Edition: The Clinically Proven Five-Week Program for Parents of Two- to Six-Year-Olds*. New York, NY: McGraw-Hill.

Greene, R. W. (2001). *The Explosive Child: A New Approach for Understanding and Parenting Easily Frustrated, Chronically Inflexible Children*. New York, NY: Quill.

Hunter, M., & Carlson, P. V. (1994). *Improving Your Child's Behavior*. Thousand Oaks, CA: Corwin Press.

Kelly, K. (2003). *The Baffled Parent's Guide to Stopping Bad Behavior*. New York, NY: McGraw-Hill.

Mendizza, M., & Pearce, J. C. (2004). *Magical Parent, Magical Child: The Art of Joyful Parenting*. Berkeley, CA: North Atlantic Books.

Paul, H. A. (2000). *Is My Child OK?: When Behavior is a Problem, When It's Not, and When to Seek Help*. New York, NY: Dell.

Samalin, N., & Jablow, M. M. (1998). *Loving Your Child Is Not Enough: Positive Discipline That Works*. United Kingdom: Penguin Books.

Wenning, K. (1999). *Winning Cooperation From Your Child: A Comprehensive Method To Stop Defiant and Aggressive Behavior in Children*. Northvale, NJ: Jason Aronson.

Children with Disabilities

Baker, B. L., Brightman, A. J., Blacher, J. B., & Heifetz, L. J. (2003). *Steps to Independence: Teaching Everyday Skills to Children with Special Needs*. Baltimore, MD: Brookes Publishing Company.

Brutten, M., Richardson, S. O., & Mangel, C. (1979). *Something's Wrong With My Child: A Parent's Book About Children With Learning Disabilities*. San Diego, CA: Harcourt.

Durand, V. M. (1997). *Sleep Better!: A Guide to Improving Sleep for Children With Special Needs*. Baltimore, MD: Brookes Publishing Company.

Falvey, M. A. (2005). *Believing in My Child with Special Needs!: Helping Children Achieve Their Potential in School*. Baltimore, MD: Brookes Publishing Company.

Fialka, J., & Mikus, K. C. (2000). *Do You Hear What I Hear? Parents and Professionals Working Together for Children with Special Needs*. Ann Arbor, MI: First Page Publications.

Flanagan, D. P., Ortiz, S. O., Alfonso, V. C., & Mascolo, J. T. (2001). *The Achievement Test Desk Reference: Comprehensive Assessment and Learning Disabilities*. Needham Heights, MA: Allyn & Bacon.

Klein, S., & Kemp, J. (2004). *Reflections from a Different Journey: What Adults with Disabilities Wish All Parents Knew*. New York, NY: McGraw-Hill.

Morris, L. R., & Schulz, L. (1989). *Creative Play Activities for Children With Disabilities: A Resource Book for Teachers and Parents* (2nd ed.). Champaign, IL: Human Kinetics Publishers.

Nasef, R. A. (2001). *Special Children, Challenged Parents: The Struggles and Rewards of Raising a Child with a Disability*. London, United Kingdom: Jessica Kingsley Publishers.

Painting, D. H. (1983). *Helping Children with Specific Learning Disabilities: A Practical Guide for Parents and Teachers*. Upper Saddle River, NJ: Prentice Hall Trade.

Slayton, J. (1982). *Taking on the World: Empowering Strategies for Parents of Children with Disabilities*. San Diego, CA: Harcourt.

Smith, R. (Ed.). (1993). *Children With Mental Retardation: A Parent's Guide*. Bethesda, MD: Woodbine House.

Venkatesan, S. (2004). *Children with Developmental Disabilities: A Training Guide for Parents, Teachers and Caregivers*. Thousand Oaks, CA: SAGE Publications.

Nutrition

Baker, S., & Henry, R. (1987). *Parents' Guide to Nutrition: Healthy Eating from Birth Through Adolescence.* Boulder, CO: Perseus Books.

Collins, L. C. (1999). *Caring for Your Child with Severe Food Allergies: Emotional Support and Practical Advice from a Parent Who's Been There.* Hoboken, NJ: Wiley.

Duyff, R. L. (2002). *American Dietetic Association Complete Food and Nutrition Guide* (2nd ed.). Hoboken, NJ: Wiley.

Evers, C. L. (2003). *How to Teach Nutrition to Kids.* Portland, OR: 24 Carrot Press.

Fish, H. T., Fish, R. B., & Golding, L. A. (1989). *Starting Out Well: A Parents' Approach to Physical Activity and Nutrition.* Champaign, IL: Human Kinetics Publishers.

Jaqua, I. (1982). *Nutrition for the Whole Family: A Guide to Better Health for Parents, Teachers, and Children.* Upper Saddle River, NJ: Prentice-Hall.

Jennings, D. S. (1995). *Play Hard, Eat Right: A Parent's Guide to Sports Nutrition for Children.* Hoboken, NJ: Wiley.

Marotz, L., Cross, M. Z., Rush, J. M., & Gaylord, T. (2000). *Health, Safety, and Nutrition for the Young Child.* Albany, NY: Thomson Delmar Learning.

McWilliams, M. (1986). *Parent's Nutrition Book.* New York, NY: Wiley & Sons Inc.

Mindell, E. (1992). *Parents' Nutrition Bible: A Guide to Raising Healthy Children.* Carlsbad, CA: Hay House.

Nissenberg, S. K., & Pearl, B. N. (2002). *Eating Right from 8 to 18: Nutrition Solutions for Parents.* Hoboken, NJ: Wiley.

Winick, M. (1982). *Growing Up Healthy: A Parent's Guide to Good Nutrition.* New York, NY: William Morrow & Co.

Math

Benjamin, A., & Shermer, M. B. (1999). *Teach Your Child Math: Making Math Fun for the Both of You* (3rd ed.). New York, NY: McGraw-Hill.

Immergut, B. (2001). *How to Help Your Child Excel in Math.* Albany, NY: Thomson Delmar Learning.

Kenschaft, P. C. (1997). *Math Power: How to Help Your Child Love Math, Even If You Don't.* Boston, MA: Addison-Wesley Publishing Company.

Latterell, C. M. (2004). *Math Wars: A Guide for Parents and Teachers.* Westport, CT: Praeger Publishers.

Lee, M. (2001). *40 Fabulous Math Mysteries Kids Can't Resist.* New York, NY: Scholastic Professional Books.

Mokros, J. (1996). *Beyond Facts & Flashcards: Exploring Math with Your Kids.* Portsmouth, NH: Heinemann.

Nordstrom, P. D. (1994). *Solve Your Children's Math Problems: Quick and Easy Lessons for Parents.* New York, NY: Simon & Schuster, INC.

Ohanesian, D. C., & Connolly J. (2000). *Macaroni Math.* New York, NY: McGraw-Hill.

Polonsky, L., Freedman, D., Lesher, S., & Morrison, K. (1995). *Math for the Very Young: A Handbook of Activities for Parents.* Hoboken, NJ: Wiley.

Tang, G., & Paprocki, G. (2003). *Math-Terpieces: The Art of Problem Solving.* New York, NY: Scholastic.

Yeatts, L. K. (2000). *Cereal Math.* New York, NY: Scholastic.

Reading

Bishop, A., Yopp, R. H., & Yopp, H. K. (1999). *Ready for Reading: A Handbook for Parents of Preschoolers.* Needham Heights, MA: Allyn & Bacon.

Bouchard, D., & Sutton, W. (2001). *The Gift of Reading: A Guide for Educators and Parents.* Victoria, Canada: Orca Book Publishers.

Burns, M. S., Snow, C. E., Griffin, P., & Alberts, B. (Eds.) (1999). *Starting Out Right: A Guide to Promoting Children's Reading Success.* Washington, DC: National Academy Press.

Christie, K. (1999). *A Guide to Teaching Beginning Reading for Teachers and Parents.* Westminster, CA: Teacher Created Materials.

Curtis, B. (1998). *Ready, Set, Read!: A Start-To-Finish Reading Program Any Parent Can Use.* Nashville, TN: Broadman & Holman Pub.

Hall, R. V., Delquadri, J. C., & Duvall, S. F. (1996). *Parents as Reading Tutors.* Longmont, CO: Sopris West.

Hall, S. J., & Moats, L. C. (2002). *Parenting a Struggling Reader.* New York, NY: Random House.

Hall, S. J., & Moats, L. C. (1998). *Straight Talk About Reading: How Parents Can Make a Difference During the Early Years.* New York, NY: McGraw-Hill.

Larrick, N. (1983). *A Parent's Guide to Children's Reading.* Louisville, KY: Westminster John Knox Press.

Leonhardt, M. (1993). *Parents Who Love Reading, Kids Who Don't: How It Happens and What You Can Do About It.* New York, NY: Crown.

Michel, P. A., & Ancillotti, M. (1993). *Child's View of Reading: The Understanding for Teachers and Parents.* Needham Heights, MA: Allyn & Bacon.

Oelwein, P. L. (1995). *Teaching Reading to Children with Down Syndrome: A Guide for Parents and Teachers.* Bethesda, MD: Woodbine House.

Rath, L. K., & Kennedy, L. (2004). *The Between the Lions Book for Parents: Everything You Need to Know to Help Your Child Learn to Read.* New York, NY: HarperCollins Publishers.

Wise, J., & Buffington, S. (2004). *The Ordinary Parent's Guide to Teaching Reading.* New York, NY: Norton, W.W. & Company, Inc.

Zimmerman, S., & Hutchins, C. (2003). *7 Keys to Comprehension: How to Help Your Kids Read It and Get It!* New York, NY: Crown Publishing Group.

Writing

Czerniewska, P. (1992). *Learning About Writing: The Early Years.* Malden, MA: Blackwell Pub.

Dierking, C. C., & Anderson-McElveen S. (1998). *Teaching Writing Skills With Children's Literature.* Gainesville, FL: Maupin House Publishing, Inc.

Hill, M. W. (1989). *Home: Where Reading and Writing Begin.* Portsmouth, NH: Heinemann.

Kaye, P. (1995). *Game for Writing: Playful Ways to Help Your Child Learn to Write.* New York, NY: Farrar, Straus and Giroux.

Martin, J. H., & Friedberg, A. (1989). *Writing to Read: A Parent's Guide to the New, Early Learning Program for Young Children.* New York, NY: Warner Books.

Metropolitan Tronto School Board (Ed.) (2004). *Home Working: 101 Everyday Activities for Reading and Writing.* Markham, Canada: Pembroke Pub Ltd.

Moore, J. E. (1999). *Writing Poetry With Children.* Monterey, CA: Evan-Moore Educational Publishers.

Reason, R., & Boote, R. (1994). *Helping Children With Reading and Spelling: A Special Needs Manual.* New York, NY: Routledge.

Rose, M. (2002). *15 Easy Lessons That Build Basic Writing Skills in Grades K-2.* New York, NY: Scholastic Professional Books.

Taylor, D. (1998). *Family Literacy: Young Children Learning to Read and Write.* Glendview, IL: Good Year Books.

Wiener, H. S. (1995). *Any Child Can Write.* New York, NY: Oxford University Press.

Science/Social Studies

Benson, P. L. (1997). *All Kids Are Our Kids: What Communities Must Do to Raise Caring and Responsible Children and Adolescents.* San Francisco, CA: Jossey-Bass.

Chicola, N. A., & English, E. B. (2002). *Creating Caring Communities with Books Kids Love.* Golden, CO: Fulcrum Publishing.

Fredricks, A. (2005). *Science Fair Handbook: The Complete Guide For Teachers and Parents.* Glendview, IL: Good Year Books.

Guinn, A. M. (2004). *Evolution and Creationism in the Public Schools: A Handbook for Educators, Parents, and Community Leaders.* Jefferson, NC: McFarland & Company.

Levenson, E. (1994). *Teaching Children About Life and Earth Science: Ideas and Activities Every Teacher and Parent Can Use.* New York, NY: McGraw-Hill.

Simmons, K. (2003). *Bags, Boxes, Buttons, and Beyond with the Bag Ladies: A Resource Book of Science and Social Studies Projects for K-6 Teachers, Parents, and Students.* Gainesville, FL: Maupin House Publishing, Inc.

Skolnick, J. (1997). *How to Encourage Girls in Math & Science.* White Plains, NY: Dale Seymour Publications.

Turner, T. N. (2003). *Essentials of Elementary Social Studies.* Needham Heights, MA: Allyn & Bacon.

White, N., & Weinberg, F. (2002). *Get Ready! For Social Studies: Geography.* New York, NY: McGraw-Hill.

*B*ROCHURES & BOOKLETS

International Reading Association
800 Barksdale Road
P.O. Box 8139
Newark, DE 19714-8139
800-336-7323
http://www.reading.org

Beginning Literacy and Your Child: A Guide to Helping Your Baby or Preschooler Become a Reader
Books Are Cool!: Keeping Your Middle School Student Reading
Help Your Child Learn English As a Second Language
I Can Read and Write!: How to Encourage Your School-Age Child's Literacy Development
Parents, Teens, and Reading: A Winning Combination
Your Child's Vision Is Important
Your Gifted Child and Reading: How to Identify and Support Advanced Literacy

National Association for the Education of Young Children
1509 16th St. N.W.
Washington DC 20036
(800) 424-2460
http://www.naeyc.org

A Caring Place for Your Toddler
A Caring Place for Your Infant
A Good Preschool for Your Child (also available in Spanish)
A Good Kindergarten for Your Child (also available in Spanish)
A Good Primary School for Your Child
Choosing a Good Early Childhood Program: Questions and Answers
Love and Learn: Positive Guidance for Young Children
Raising a Reader, Raising a Writer
Helping Children Learn Self-Control
Toys: Tools for Learning (Also available in Spanish)
Play is FUNdamental
Ready to Go: What Parents Should Know about School Readiness

National PTA
541 N. Fairbanks Court
Chicago, IL 60611-3396
(800) 307-4782
www.pta.org

Helping Your Child Succeed:
> *Dressing for Success*
> *Can I Really Make a Difference?*
> *How Do I Help My Child Succeed?*
> *What Happens If I Get Involved?*
> *10 Ways To Help Your Child Succeed*
> *100 Ways For Parents to Be More Involved in Their Child's Education*

Network for Instructional TV, Inc.
11490 Commerce Park Drive
Reston, VA 20191
Available at:
http://www.teachersandfamilies.com

Developmental Screening
Play-Key to Learning
Your Child and No Child Left Behind
Everything That's Important You Learned in Kindergarten
Tutoring-A Guide for Parents
Kindergarten: Full Day or Half Day?
Understanding Standardized Test Scores
School Bus Basics
Understanding "No Child Left Behind"
and more . . .

U.S. Department of Education
400 Maryland Avenue, SW
Washington, DC 20202
Available at: *www.ed.gov/parents/landing.html*

Helping Your Child Learn History
Helping Your Child Learn Science
Helping Your Child Learn Mathematics
Helping Your Child Become a Reader
Toolkit: Providing Extra Academic Help
Office of innovation and Improvement
Tutors for Kids
and more . . .

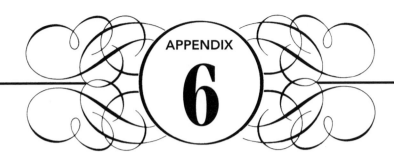

APPENDIX
6

DVD's and Videotapes for Parent Education

Active Parenting Publishers
1955 Vaughn Rd. NW, Suite 108
Kennesaw, GA 30144-7808
(800) 825-0060

Active Parenting Now!
　　Parenting in the 21st Century
　　Active Communication
　　Effective Discipline
　　Sidestepping the Power Struggle:
　　Building Character, Courage and Self-Esteem in Your Child
　　The Magic of Family Meetings
Active Parenting of Teens
　　What's Your Parenting Style?
　　Your Child's Success Cycle
　　Sidestepping the Power Struggle
　　Effective Discipline
　　Active Communication
　　The Magic of Family Meetings
1,2,3,4 Parents!
　　What You Need to Know about Your 1- 4-Year-Old: Discipline and Beyond
　　Building Better Behavior
Parents On Board!
　　Preparing your child to succeed in school
　　Encouraging positive behavior
　　Reinforcing your child's academic skills

AGS Publishing
4201 Woodland Road
Circle Pines, MN 55014-1796
(800)328.2560

STEP Programs
    STEP Early Childhood
    STEP Spanish
    STEP Teen

Baby Bumblebee, Inc
P.O. Box 1117
Crystal Beach, FL 34681
(888) 984-5500
www.babybumblebee.com

Alphabet Phonics & Fun (2003)
Opposites & More (2003)
Crazy for Colors (2002)
All About Me (2005)
Motorized Madness (2005)
Action Words! 1-3 (2004)
Bee Smart Baby Vocabulary Builder (2004)
Numeracy & Sequencing (2004)
BumbleBee's 123 Set (2005)

Consumervision, Inc.
66 Newton Lane, Suite 3
East Hampton, NY 11937
(631)-329-4680
www.consumervisiononline.com

Touchpoints Box Set (2002)
    Vol. 1 Pregnancy, Birth & The First Weeks of Life
    Vol. 2 First Month Through the First Year
    Vol. 3 One Year Through Toddlerhood
Ten Things Every Child Needs (1999)
I Can Go Potty! (2003)
Giggle Together! (2004)
Talking Hands (2001)

Council for Exceptional Children
1110 North Glebe Road
Arlington VA 22201
800-224-6830
www.cec.sped.org

Successfully Parenting Your Baby with Special Needs (1999)

Edvantage Media, Inc.
12 Forrest Avenue
Fair Haven, NJ 07704
(800) 375-5100
www.edvantagemedia.com

Successfully Parenting Your Baby with Special Needs- Early Intervention Ages Birth to Three (1999)
The Three R's for Special Education. Rights, Resources, and Results! (1995)
Autism and the New Law (2000)
A New IDEA for Special Education. Understanding the System and the New Law (2000)

GO Media
6245 North 24th Parkway, Suite 112
Phoenix, AZ 85016
(800) 755-7867
www.gomediaco.com

How to Be a Better Parent (1994)
Handling Sibling Rivalry, Anger, and Temper Tantrums (2000)
Ages and Stages: Knowing What to Expect and When (2000)
Preschooler Discipline- Making It a Positive Experience (2000)
Working Parents and Your Preschooler (2000)
Preparing Your Preschooler for Success in School (2000)
Be a Better Parent in 30 Minutes (1998)
Healthy Children for Life, Love, and Laughter (2001)
Defending Yourself: Bullying, Teasing, and Put-Downs (2002)
Abused Kids: See It! Stop It! (2002)

International Reading Association
800 Barksdale Road
P.O. Box 8139
Newark, DE 19714-8139
(800) 336-7323
www.reading.org

Paired Reading: Positive Reading Practice (2003)
Read to Me (1991)

Meridian Education Corporation
2572 Brunswick Pike
Lawrenceville, NJ 08648
(800) 727-5507
www.meridianeducation.com

The Five Essentials of Successful Parents
    Love and Stability (2003)
    Time Together (2003)
    Inspire and Challenge (2003)
    Positive Discipline (2003)
    Safety and Health (2003)

Aspects of Child Development, Ages 4-11
    Constructing the Self (2003)
    The Learning Process (2003)
    Helping Them Flourish (2003)
The Essentials of Discipline
    Toddler Trouble! (2004)
    Our Child Is Out of Control (2004)
Single Parenting
    Life with Dad (2002)
Turning Points: Steps to Success for Single Parents (2001)

National PTA
541 N. Fairbanks Court
Chicago, IL 60611-3396
(800) 307-4782
www.pta.org

Taking Charge of Your TV (1997)
The Family Nest (El Nido de la Familia)

Paraclete Press, Inc.
P.O. 1568
Orleans, MA 02653
(800) 451-5006
www.paracletepress.com

Raising Children of Divorce: Practical Help for Parents (2004)
Shattered Dreams: Healing after Divorce (2002)
When Tempers Flare (2004)
Calming the Tempest: Helping the Explosive Child (2004)
Stop Bullying! Stand Up for Yourself and Others (2004)
A Cry For Help and Warning Signs—Video Set (2004)
Hungry Hearts: Recognizing and Preventing Eating Disorders
Bumps in the Road, What Kids Wish Their Parents Knew (1995)

Reading Is Fundamental (RIF)
1825 Connecticut Avenue NW
Suite 400
Washington DC 20009
877-RIF-READ
www.rif.org

Becoming a Family of Readers

Small Fry Productions
1200 Alpha Drive, Suite B
Alpharetta, GA 30004
(800) 521-5311
www.small-fry.com

Baby's First Impressions: Shapes (2004)
Baby's First Impressions: Numbers (2004)
Baby's First Impressions: Sounds (2004)
Baby's First Impressions: Letters (2004)
Baby's First Impressions: Head to Toe (2004)
Baby's First Impressions: Seasons (2004)
Opposites (1997)
Shapes & Colors (2002)
Animals (2002)
ABC's (2002)
123's (2002)

Tapeworm Video Distributors, Inc.
27833 Ave Hopkins, Unit 6
Valencia, CA 91355
(661) 257-4820
www.tapeworm.com

How to Behave So Your Children Will, Too! (2000)
The Parents Connected Guide to Family Activities Online (2001)
The Parents Connected Guide to Online Safety (2001)
Helping Your Child Learn Potty Training (1997)
Parenting Puzzle (1998)
Parenting Series: Flexible Work Options (1998)
Your Baby Can Read: Review (2001)
Gifts of Fathering (1995)
ABC's of Teaching the ABC's (1994)
Helping Your Child Succeed in School (1998)

About the Author

Dr. Kathy Barclay is a professor of reading/language arts and early childhood at Western Illinois University in Macomb, Illinois and former chair of the Department of Curriculum and Instruction. She served as external co-chair of the Illinois Right to Read Initiative and as a member of the Reading First Steering Committee for the Illinois State Board of Education and project director for the Illinois Center for Achieving Reading Excellence, a grant-funded project at WIU. She has worked with the Center for Best Practices in Early Childhood as the co-director for Project ELIPSS: Emergent Literacy Instructional Program and Support Services, a grant funded by the U.S. Health and Human Services, The Head Start Bureau. An invited speaker at national and state early childhood and literacy conferences, Dr. Barclay has authored numerous articles on literacy strategies for educators and families, and is author of a regular column on emergent literacy for *Children and Families,* the journal of the National Head Start Association. Dr. Barclay is Editor of the *Illinois Reading Council Journal* and serves on the Publications Committee for the International Reading Association.

Index